NUPTIAL BLESSING

NUPTIAL BLESSING

A Study of Christian Marriage Rites

KENNETH STEVENSON

New York
OXFORD UNIVERSITY PRESS
1983

First published in Great Britain 1982
for the Alcuin Club by SPCK

First published in the United States 1983
by Oxford University Press, Inc.

Library of Congress Cataloging in Publication Data

Stevenson, Kenneth (Kenneth W.)
Nuptial blessing.

Bibliography: p.
Includes index.
1. Marriage service—Liturgy. I. Title.
BV199.M3S73 1983   265'.5   82-22525
ISBN 0-19-520418-2
ISBN 0-19-520419-0 (pbk.)

The illustrations in this book are by the Reverend Dr. Eric Stevenson ARIBA

Printed in the United States of America

Preface

'Why not write a history of marriage liturgy from Isaac and Rebecca onwards?' So wrote Geoffrey Cuming to me, sparking off an idea which has resulted in the pages that follow. It seemed appropriate to write such a book, particularly as marriage is the subject of much scrutiny and interest, as well as the fact that there has not yet been a specifically liturgical study in the English language.

At the outset I made certain limits: it is a *liturgical* study, so that matters of Canon Law and social history, whilst being of intrinsic interest, have been deliberately relegated to second place, otherwise the book would become too unwieldy. The book has been divided into five parts, each with its own particular approach. In Chapter 1, Background, we trace the institution of marriage within a biblical perspective, and attempt to paint a picture of marriage liturgy from the few materials available; I am convinced that the Jewish origins of the liturgy are of the utmost significance, and that the common assumption that there was no early Christian marriage rite is false. In Chapter 2, Efflorescence, we deal with the classical texts of the Christian West, first the Sacramentaries and then the multifarious rites of Spain, England, and elsewhere, always adapting their own traditions to developing needs. Chapter 3, The East, takes us to a different milieu, where we travel lavishly through the world of Chrysostom's successors, and the more overtly Semitic Syriac Christians, who never lost a sense of wonder, joy, and celebration in marriage. Then, in Chapter 4, Reformulations, we see the effect of the Reformation, in these islands against the theological background of Luther and Calvin, and I have argued for a more Reformed theology of the marriage service on the part of Cranmer than has hitherto been fashionable. Trent takes the Middle Ages to a logical conclusion and deprives the liturgy of much of its vitality, leaving us to wait for the fifth, and final part, 'Foreground', when the various Churches of the West are able to revise their liturgies, learn

v

from each other, and begin to realize that marriage as an institution needs not just definition but *celebration* in an age where Christian values cannot be assumed but must be lived.

The study is limited—it has not been possible to open all the libraries of Europe, to probe for the details behind later medieval Italy, or Protestant Holland—and I hope the reader will forgive the concentration on the British Isles that is both necessary and appropriate here. As I have written these passages, I have done so from the point of view of the nuptial blessing-prayer as the liturgical expression of what marriage can be when brought before God and offered to him. I have adopted this perspective because I thought it was time that the Christian West tipped the scales in the direction of marriage euchology, instead of an almost exclusive concentration on the promise to marry, which, important as it came to be, cannot tell the whole story, as the rich variety of marriage prayers described and quoted in these pages will (I hope) demonstrate. As a parish priest for some years, I always took the view, when helping couples through their marriage service, that the rite consists supremely and solely of the offering to God of a resolve, in order to ask for his blessing and strength.

Many people deserve my thanks for their encouragement and assistance in the preparation of this book. Father Pierre-Marie Gy, O.P., of the Paris Liturgical Institute, for launching me into unknown waters and providing constant guidance; Father Achille Triacca, SDB, of the Anselmo Institute in Rome, for trying to widen my insular attitudes; The Rev David Tripp, of Hounslow, who steered me through the Reformers and his own Methodist tradition; The Rev Bryan Spinks, of Cambridge, for help with the Christian East; and my father, The Rev Dr Eric Stevenson, for clarifying Scandinavian Lutheranism, a joint heritage. I must also place on record my gratitude to several Libraries, including the John Rylands University Library of Manchester, and the Library of New College, Edinburgh. And Mrs Jenny Haymes has brought her Baptist piety—and efficiency—to the task of producing a clean typescript for the printers. In Manchester I must also thank friends and colleagues in the Faculty of Theology, and some distinguished medievalists; as well as my fellow-chaplains, who have graciously borne with me, especially in the final stages. But by far the biggest debt is owed to Sarah, my wife, who has given me that measure of encouragement and patience which has been wonderful whilst writing on marriage liturgy. To her this volume is dedicated.

Kenneth Stevenson

Feast of the Transfiguration, 1981
Manchester

It is a pleasure to see a liturgical study published in the United States so soon after its first appearance in the United Kingdom, particularly as the marriage rites of the various North American Churches have made (and continue to make) significant contributions to the story. I have taken the opportunity of including a small list of additions and corrections which are included in an Appendix (p. 259).

What makes this edition all the more welcome is that I have been appointed to a Visiting Professorship in the Department of Theology at the University of Notre Dame, Indiana, for the spring semester, 1983. This means that at the time of writing this Preface, I have in prospect a whole number of experiences, from delivering a course of lectures based on this book for an M.A. graduate class, to my first encounter with the rigour (and vigour) of North American liturgiology.

K.S.

All Saints' Day
Manchester 1982

Acknowledgements

The prayer beginning 'We praise you, Father' (p. 248–9) is from the Marriage Service in *The Alternative Service Book 1980*, and is reproduced by permission.

The extract from *The Rite of Marriage* (p. 248) is reproduced by permission of C. Goodliffe Neale, England.

The extract from *The Saint Andrew Daily Missal* (p. 245–6) is reproduced by permission of Editions Desclée-De Brouwer, Belgium.

The Jewish Seven Benedictions (p. 245) from *The Authorised Daily Prayerbook* (ed. J. Hertz) are reproduced by permission of the Bloch Publishing Company, USA.

Contents

1 *Background*

1   Biblical and Jewish Models

The Bible does not give us a single and developed view of
marriage, less still one of marriage practice. Indeed one can
almost say that the Old Testament betrays from its pages the
same struggle of subsequent centuries—to work out a viable
procedure, based on a conviction that marriage is an
institution that is 'under God', and to do this against secular
and pagan pressures. It is only in Talmudic practice that we get
a set pattern, which changes little as time goes on. The New
Testament offers us even less at first sight, but the total picture
is less unclear than it seems.

a. The Old Testament

Ancient Near Eastern mythology tells us a good deal of how
the people of that area understood marriage and sexuality. The
Ugaritic god El was creator of creatures, and creator of the sky
and the earth, and he is portrayed in one story as producing
two sons by two spouses; he is essentially a god of fertility.[1]
Another Ugaritic myth tells of a divine marriage, an 'archetype'
as some would describe it, in which Nikkal marries the
Moon-god.[2] In the Epic of Gilgamesh, we come across the
theme of sexual drive between Ishtar (corresponding to Venus)
and Tammouz, god of vegetation.[3]

These three themes of fertility, marriage, and passion are
adapted in the Old Testament, where marriage is gradually
subsumed into the God–Israel relationship. If God made and
loves Israel, then this must have consequences for how Israel
carries on its existence, which includes how Israelites marry.
The two creation myths in Genesis show this clearly. The J
narrative (Gen. 2.18–25) makes man and woman equal (even
though man is created first), and the notion of man and woman
being one flesh makes its first appearance: 'Now this, at
last—bone from my bones, flesh from my flesh!' Thus sexual
union is given a new meaning, for it is taken to refer to the
single relationship of marriage, one man and one woman,
which is all the more surprising since it was written when
polygamy was allowed (see below on Abraham).

The other creation myth—the P narrative (Gen. 1.26–
9)—supposes the same monogamy ('male and female he

3

created them'), and there is Rabbinic evidence for interpreting 'man in our image and likeness' as man *and* woman, not just man.[4] However, there is a development: God makes them, and then *blesses* them, and tells them to 'be fruitful and increase ...' Augustine makes much of this close juxtaposition of blessing and fruitfulness; and it is more than likely that this blessing echoes a liturgical blessing, which at the time of the P writer would include at least a reference to creation and fruitfulness. So what in both accounts distinguishes Adam and Eve from ancient Near Eastern mythology is that God creates, and that the human marriage-relationship grows out of what God has made, a human prototype, not a divine archetype.[5]

We must next look at the 'ideal couples' in the patriarchal tradition, not just because they are interesting in themselves, and reappear constantly through the Middle Ages in liturgical prayers, but because they reflect different social customs. Abraham and Sarah cannot produce offspring, and so Abraham at her suggestion has intercourse with a slave-girl (Gen. 16.1ff); but Sarah does conceive (Gen. 21.1ff). Infertility is thus seen as a reproach, a withholding of divine blessing. Isaac and Rebecca give us a different scene: Isaac must marry from the patriarchal family (Gen. 24.3–4), and the marriage is subject to negotiation with Rebecca's family and a betrothal. When she leaves home, she is given a blessing from her family, which asks for her to bear children (Gen. 24.60). She subsequently meets Isaac, but veils herself before being seen by him. He takes her into his tent, and they live together. Jacob similarly must marry within the family (Gen. 28.1–2), although he can have slave-girls also (Gen. 30.3–12), but we see yet again the connection between marriage and fertility, in such a way that infertility loses for a wife her husband's love (Leah, at Gen. 29.31). Husbands also have to work in order to gain for themselves wives, as with Jacob and Rachel (Gen. 29.20). The wedding takes on a formal tone with a seven-day feast (Gen. 29.22), and we come across it again, as in the case of Samson (Judg. 14.10–18). When we turn to the prophets, some further developments are discernible. Hosea is naturally the writer to work out more fully than any other the imagery of the marriage of God and Israel, and although we have to wait until Malachi (2.14) before marriage is actually described as a covenant, such imagery is under the surface in Hosea. Whereas hitherto we have been aware of the importance attached to *fertility*, the application of the God–Israel, man–wife comparison is more concerned with *fidelity* (Hos. 4.2; 6.6). Both these themes, however, are united in the Song of the Vineyard in Isaiah (5.1–7), and the same interrelation is to be found in Jeremiah (2.29–35, and, powerfully, at 31.31–4). Ezekiel takes the marriage comparison one stage further in two allegories— salvation history as a love-drama (16) and as bigamy (23). It is hard to know whether these virtues were incorporated into liturgical prayer at the time.

More liturgical evidence can be gleaned from chance references. The bride wears gorgeous clothes and girdle in her procession (Isa. 49.18 and Jer. 2.12); and Second-Isaiah refers to the bridal pair wearing crowns (Isa. 61.10). Similar accoutrements occur in the Song of Sol. (3.11), which as a book seems to come from some kind of para-liturgical tradition,[6] the shouts of joy and jubilation during the bridal procession to which Jeremiah refers several times (Jer. 7.34; 16.9; 25.10; 33.11). In spite of the difficulties concerning the origin of the Song of Songs, it is a remarkable example of the sacralization of sexuality which only Judaism could produce, combining tenderness and profundity in a unique manner. 'Wear me as a seal upon your heart' (8.6) sums up a great deal of what the prophets say in their protests against infidelity.

The Old Testament gives us a varied picture, but hardly a consistently worked out scheme. At root, however, is the conviction that marriage is divinely inspired. The only liturgical ingredients which are hinted at are the agreement to marry at betrothal; a bride-price; some sort of blessing; a veil for the bride, or else crowns for both; a procession; a lengthy feast; and the consummation of the marriage. Ps. 45 illustrates some of these features, and Ps. 127 reinforces the fertility theme as well as fidelity. What we have is a series of liturgical forms which arise out of ordinary life.

b. *Later Judaism*

Tobit is a charming example of later Jewish literature. No one is sure as to its date, or place of origin, and there are many textual difficulties. Otto Eissfeldt regards it as coming from the 'eastern diaspora' in the second century BC, though Palestine is not ruled out.[7] What concerns us here is the marriage between Tobias and Sarah, in chapters 7 and 8. First, Tobias asks

5

Raguel for Sarah's hand, which he is pleased to give: 'From now on, you belong to her and she to you; she is yours for ever from this day. The Lord of heaven prosper you both this night, my son, and grant you mercy and peace' (7.12). The Vulgate text puts this in slightly more formal terms, which reappear in the *Liber Ordinum*, the Pontifical of Roda, and the Sacramentary of Vich in the eleventh century, so it is worth quoting in full: 'May the God of Abraham, the God of Isaac, and the God of Jacob be with you, and may he himself join you together, and fill you with his blessing.'[8] This is quite a new feature. Apart from the (traditional) association with the three Patriarchs, God actually *joins* the couple in his blessing on them.

The marriage contract is then written down by Raguel and the feast begins. The couple spend the night together in a specially prepared room. Before they sleep, Tobias prays with her as follows:

> We praise thee, O God of our fathers, we praise thy name for ever and ever. Let the heavens and all thy creation praise thee for ever. Thou madest Adam, and Eve his wife to be his helper and support; and those two were the parents of the human race. This was thy word: 'It is not good for the man to be alone; let us make him a helper like him.' I now take this my beloved to wife, not out of lust but in true marriage. Grant that she and I may find mercy and grow old together.

This is in effect a *yadah*-prayer, beginning with praise for creation leading into supplication for the marriage, and the motive is made clear: not for lust but for 'true marriage'. Yet another blessing is said on the morning after the night before, but it only occurs in the Vulgate text. Raguel blesses his daughter 'through' Tobias: 'may blessing be said over your wife, and over your parents; and may you see your children, and your children's children to the third and fourth generation; and may your seed be blessed by the God of Israel, who reigns for ever and ever' (Vulgate, 8.10–12). This prayer becomes used in more than one way in the medieval West.[9]

It is worth noting the tendency in the Vulgate text to add liturgical material, but even in the original text the marriage here is formalized, takes on a procedure, and is punctuated by blessings, the longest of which is said by the husband before the union is consummated. Elsewhere in the book Raphael and other protecting angels make their appearance, and although not in set prayers here, they occur later on in the Middle Ages at a time when short blessing-prayers were developing between the marriage and the nuptial mass.[10]

The second area of later Judaism is more difficult to date precisely, the 'Talmudic', which comes from the third century AD, although it reflects earlier practice.[11] Marriage divides into two parts, the betrothal and the marriage itself. In the Mishnah girls dance on the Day of Atonement in order to entice young men to ask them to be betrothed to them. Betrothal can take place either by money, or by contract (the commonest), or by cohabitation (shunned), and there is a short *berakah* to be pronounced over each in order to ratify the betrothal, which often lasted twelve months. The marriage proper (*nissu'in*) took place (according to the Mishnah) on Wednesdays for maidens and Fridays for widows. This restriction obviously shows a desire to avoid traditional Jewish fast-days, even if it ironically coincides with later Christian ones; the traditional fast-days were done away with by the Talmud and only survived in some circles in the Middle Ages, though Eastern European Jews revived the procedure in the nineteenth century.

The couple have fasted all day, and confessed their sins, as on the Day of Atonement. Both bride and bridegroom wear crowns of myrtle and the bride (if a virgin) wears a long veil (*hinnumah*), as she processes with her companions to the house of the bridegroom for the evening feast. Her procession is accompanied by music and dancing, the precise forms of which were subject to debate from time to time. She is led to the threshold where the contract (*kethuba*) is written down. There were set forms of *kethuba*, and without it the marriage could not proceed.[12] After the meal the bridegroom himself pronounced the *sheva berakoth*, the Seven Blessings (see Appendix 1). Their date is not known, but both Hertz and Epstein are convinced that they are at least Talmudic, and Epstein notes that they appear to be well-established in time of Rabbi Judah, which may mean that they were known by Jews at the time of the New Testament. Epstein is captivated by them: 'the loftiness of tone and the beauty of style of these benedictions are unsurpassed. The blend of biblical strength and midrashic sweetness seems to point to an early date'.[13]

What do we find in these blessings? After the opening vine-blessing, there are blessings for creation, the creation of mankind, and God's purpose; supplication for Zion, the barren one; supplication for the couple, with reference to the Garden of Eden; blessing for the joy of the couple; and a long blessing and supplication for the qualities of married life, with reference to the marriage feast. The progression of ideas is, in fact, very similar to the long blessing pronounced by Tobit with Sarah on their own. The main differences are the absence in Tobit of the vine-blessing at the beginning, and the reference to barren Zion (which would have been added after AD 70). The allusions to 'joy and gladness' and 'mirth and exultation, pleasure and delight' echo similar references in Jeremiah.

This scheme of Jewish marriage takes us one step further from what we have seen in Tobit, though there is enough in common in both for the parentage of Tobit (however indirect) to be obvious. Four subsequent developments took place in the post-Talmudic era. First, the blessing at the end of the feast was taken over by the rabbis, and, indeed, one Rabbinical source affirms that 'from the manner in which a man recites the benedictions (including the Seven), we can discern whether he is a boor or a scholar'.[14] Secondly, instead of taking place at the groom's home, the contract and blessings came to be carried out under a *huppah*, or canopy, symbolizing the groom's home. The canopy was supported on four poles, and bears clear comparison with the canopy used in later medieval Western Christian rites. [15] Thirdly, during the Middle Ages, the rites of betrothal and marriage were gradually brought together. Finally, again during the Middle Ages, and probably under Christian influence, a ring was given (or else a coin) during the recital of a special formula.

The importance of the Seven Blessings must not be overlooked. Liturgiologists once thought Jewish prayers were solidly fixed by the time of Christ and were not subject to any changes, but the extensive work of Joseph Heinemann (among others) has shown that although the *structures* of the various Jewish prayer formulae were set at an early stage, the *content* could, and did, vary.[16] If he is right, then there would have been an agreed structure by the time of the Talmud for the Seven Blessings, but the details would vary from place to place and from one tradition to another. It is only in the fourth and fifth blessings that he demonstrates the truth of this theory, but we can assume that it applies to the rest of the sequence.[17]

Another important feature of the Jewish rite concerns what we may describe as 'sacralizing the secular'. From what little we can see of the emergence of the Jewish liturgy of marriage we can discern a desire to adapt to changing circumstances. The ideal and its teaching are implicit from an early stage, in the tenth century BC, with the J writer. The prophets sharpen this teaching, and allude to para-liturgical practices (the procession, the crowns), which have obviously come about as popular customs rather than as sacred liturgical forms. By the time of Tobit we can see formality, even in the intimacy of a domestic marriage with few others involved, and no betrothal; and the Talmudic and post-Talmudic evidence points to a formal rite, eventually taken over by the rabbis, but leaving intact the ancient Seven Blessings. It is neither necessary nor accurate to assume that the development before the time of the Talmudic texts was simply a move from informality to formality; indeed the matter of domestic blessings is clearly laid open by our treatment of Genesis and by the hints of divine blessings which we have seen elsewhere in the Old Testament. However, I would suggest that even as far back as the J writer, and certainly at the time of the P writer, there was a marriage rite which contained both the main elements which we have seen so far: agreement to marry and blessing; and that such a blessing or blessings would have referred to creation, fidelity, and procreation, as we see in the classical form of the later Seven Blessings.

c. The New Testament

The New Testament gives us even less than the Old, which is hardly surprising. Set against the Old Testament background, we can assume that the first Christians regarded marriage as part of their life of faith; any desire for celibacy, however, can be paralleled by practice at Qumran.[18] Turning to the New Testament, we can broadly divide material into two categories: texts concerned with teaching about Jesus, and texts concerned with marriage discipline.[19]

The Gospel writers and Paul extend the Jewish imagery of God–Israel to Jesus–Christians, and that is why Jesus is referred to as the bridegroom (Matt. 9.15 = Mark 2.19 = Luke 5.34). In the parable of the wise and foolish virgins, the bridesmaids wait at the groom's house, in order to accompany him on his way to the bride's house, so that they can walk together back to the groom's house for the wedding feast, and it all happens in the evening; all this is in line with what we have seen already of late Jewish practice (Matt. 25.1–13). Many have been the ways in which this parable has been interpreted; perhaps the most accurate is also the most straightforward; the point of the story is to show that the Church must be ready for Jesus when he comes. Liturgically, the details of the story add little to what we know of Jewish marriage customs, except that the bridesmaids walk both ways, they do not merely walk back with the bride.

Of considerable importance is the miracle at Cana in Galilee (John 2.1–11), a favourite lection in many later liturgical books.[20] Jesus attends a wedding as a guest; in other words, marriage is an important institution which Jesus 'hallows'. But how does he 'hallow' it? When the wine runs out, he provides more from the water in the pots used by the guests to wash themselves at the beginning and the end of the meal. But there appears to be a subtle twist which has liturgical (and other!) consequences: before the end of the meal, the new wine is miraculously produced by the guest. It would have been at the end of the meal that the bridegroom whose wedding Jesus was attending as a guest pronounced the Seven Blessings, or something like them. Jesus' blessing precedes, and is of much greater significance. As in the parable of the wise and foolish virgins, conventional Jewish liturgy is used as the background for propounding the teaching of the Christian faith. Leaving aside the exegetical problems, Jesus' miracle takes on a meaning which refers specifically to marriage, and can only be understood fully in its liturgical setting.

This 'bridegroom teaching' is echoed by Paul: 'I betrothed you to Christ, thinking to present you as a chaste virgin to her true and only husband' (2 Cor. 11.2). The wedding has not yet happened because it will come at the end of time. As an anticipation, however, Christians are *betrothed* to Jesus, and must remain virgin-pure, firm in the faith (cf. Joseph and Mary). To his mixed congregation at Corinth, such a distinction between betrothal and marriage would be immediately understandable, since the two stages in matrimony were practised among Hellenistic Greeks in a similar way to Jews themselves. The imagery is taken further by the author of Ephesians (whether Paul or not makes no difference to our discussion) in a well-known and lengthy passage (Eph. 5.22–33). The purpose of the author is 'to promote the highest view of marriage as a loving relationship, using the analogy of Christ and the Church', in the words of Barnabas Lindars.[21] If Paul gives a negative impression in his views on marriage elsewhere (see below), here we have the working out of the Christ–Church image in a way that appears to be lush by comparison.

Wives must be obedient, but this obedience is seen in relation to the obedience all Christians owe to Christ himself. The husband is the head, so is Jesus the head of the Church. Wives must obey husbands as Christians obey Christ, a stronger accent on obedience than anything we have seen in the Old Testament. The analogy is taken further to explain Christ's sacrificial death, a figurative 'washing' which probably echoes the ceremonial washing of the bride before the betrothal rite; moreover, the distinction drawn between redemption and consummation (verses 26, 27) may correspond to betrothal and marriage. So the loving care which Christ lavishes on the Church is to be the model for husbands to love their wives. Then comes the 'one-flesh' image, taking up Gen. 2.24; man and wife are one flesh, and it is the intention of God to unite all things in Christ (cf. 1.9–10). What is the author's intention in this passage? Clearly it is to deepen the Christian understanding of marriage, building on Jewish foundations. The old customs are in the background, as is the important theological insight of the J writer, that husband and wife become one flesh; and by amplifying the 'bridegroom theology' he not only spiritualizes the marriage relationship further, but adds another dimension to his hearers' understanding of the meaning and purpose of Christ's death. Perhaps most important of all is the author's insistence that the husband should *love* his wife, rather than regard her as a possession, or a means of sexual fulfilment, and no more. Nonetheless, egalitarian-minded critics do not entirely like this passage, nor have successive drafters of liturgical texts, for in the West it is only in the Gregorian Sacramentary nuptial blessing (and, by derivation, the English Prayer Book) that this analogy is to be found, other rites preferring different ideas and images for their prayers.[22] Twentieth-century compositions tend to avoid it.

The bridegroom image appears again at the end of the Revelation of John (19.6ff) in a liturgical framework, but we are given no hints of marriage liturgy, except that the bride is ready and is robed in a dress of 'fine linen, clean and shining', and that the wedding supper corresponds with the Jewish marriage feast in the evening.

Those passages which deal with marriage discipline give little help. Jesus' commendation of celibacy (Matt. 19 10–12) is not meant to undermine marriage, and doubtless reflects Essene (and other) ideas about the unmarried state, but earlier on in that Gospel, in the Sermon on the Mount, Jesus accuses those who have adulterous thoughts of having committed adultery already (Matt. 5.28), thus emphasizing the view that purity of heart is the foundation of Christian living. Jesus' teaching on divorce, though the subject of a great deal of discussion, is firm in exalting monogamous marriage as belonging to the demands of the end-time (Matt. 19.9 = Mark 10.10–12).[23] His teaching about marriage after the death of a partner is grounded not in a condemnation of remarriage, but because he wishes to contrast the resurrection state from the earthly (Matt. 22.23–33 = Mark 12.18–27 = Luke 20.27–40).

Paul's teaching adds little to this. In 1 Cor. 7, he insists on monogamy and commends celibacy (2.7–9), but he does the latter because the Corinthians condemn it themselves. The so-called 'Pauline privilege' (12–16) brings Paul to the point where he has to differentiate between the Christian view of marriage as it is developing, and other views. A non-Christian wife who wants to divorce should be prevailed upon not to. Widows may marry again (39–40), though he obviously prefers that they should remain as widows.

The Pastoral Epistles do not give much information; all that we find are directions about Christian living which require that church-officers should be monogamous and faithful and run good homes. If the passages concerned (1 Tim. 3.4f, 12f; 5.4, 10; Titus 1.6; 2.3–5) are taken with Ignatius' Letter to Polycarp (5.2), which says that the bishop should be concerned with marriages in his flock, then we see a picture emerging of the Christian community settling down to an ordered existence.

d. How did early Christians marry?

This question is impossible to answer with certainty, because firm evidence is lacking, and in any case the New Testament covers a period of time and a geography that is too varied for a single procedure to be discernible, or indeed workable. But hints are nonetheless there. The gospels base some teaching on Jewish practice, and the Pauline Epistles develop this further. From these hints, it is possible to suggest that before and after the expulsion of Christians from the synagogue, marriages were celebrated in the Jewish manner, with betrothal, followed at some point by a formal agreement, and the marriage. The marriage centred round a feast, to which the bride processed in a special robe with her attendants and probably wearing a veil (or else a crown, also worn by the groom). What liturgical form sealed the union is unknown, but it is unlikely that Jewish influence was absent, particularly if we take seriously recent research into this subject, and accept the general conclusion that early Christian prayer was based, in part, on Jewish models.[24] If the eucharistic prayer is derived from the *birkat ha-mazon*, then the nuptial blessing which we shall see emerging in the next two chapters must have been derived from the kind of blessings which appear in Tobit and are being established in the Talmud in the form of the Seven Blessings. Such an argument can only be hypothetical, but, taking the New Testament texts together, they suggest a blessing after the meal. Who said it and what it contained must be shrouded in mystery until new evidence comes to light, but I would argue for a christianized form of the Seven Blessings, recited by the bridegroom or some local minister.[25]

2   Literary Evidence: the First Three Centuries

The first three centuries yield us very little direct evidence of any marriage rite. It is a formative era in the development of Christianity, and in the authors we shall now look at, all we have to go by is what they say about marriage, its rationale and practice, and from that we may be able to build up some sort of picture of how marriage was celebrated in one or two places, but that is all.

The earliest non-biblical remark about marriage is also the most oft-quoted, and it comes from Ignatius of Antioch, (c. 35–c. 107) in his letter to Polycarp (5.2):

> It is right for men and women who marry to contract their union with the advice of their bishop, so that their marriage is made in the Lord, and not for the sake of passion.[1]

What does he mean? Ignatius may be reflecting the kind of prescriptions in the Pastoral Epistles about church order, and since we know that he had strong views about episcopacy such remarks as these should not surprise us. Until recently, the passage has been interpreted at its face value—marriages between Christians should be celebrated by the bishop, and this would be done in accordance with a definite procedure, because there already was such a thing as *Christian* marriage, as opposed to *pagan* marriage. Ritzer tends to minimize some evidence, and he does so with Ignatius, to the extent that he suggests Ignatius is exceptional among early Christian writers (which he may be over episcopacy), and all he means is that the bishop should be *pastorally* involved in the marriage, but there is no reason to suggest that he conducted a *marriage service* for Christian couples.[2] He could be right, and if he is, then Christian couples at the turn of the second century in Antioch may simply have asked for their local bishop's permission, as representing the Church as a whole, and celebrated their marriage at home, in the manner we suggested in the previous chapter, perhaps with a christianized form of the Jewish Talmudic rite, with the groom pronouncing the blessing. If Ritzer is wrong, then the bishop may have gone to the home for the marriage ceremony. Even if Ignatius is prescribing an exceptional procedure, which would reflect his tightening grip upon the flock, what he writes about to Polycarp proves that at least one Christian congregation thought it wise to make marriage sufficiently important as to involve the bishop, and this marks an important step.

Athenagoras of Athens (second century) gives us a little more, but not much. In his *Legatio*, he writes as follows:

> Since we hope for eternal life, we despise the things of this life, including even the pleasures of the soul. Thus each of us thinks of his wife, whom he married according to the laws that we have laid down, with a view to nothing more than procreation.[3]

It is clear that Athenagoras knows of a definite procedure regarding marriage, and that he is referring to a recognized form, involving some sort of liturgy. Whether or not that liturgy mentioned the reason for marriage which he gives (procreation—a theme which comes up again, particularly in Augustine[4]) is not clear, but it seems highly likely. Schoedel points out that this doctrine about marriage is originally Stoic, and is 'a corollary of Stoic opposition to the arch-vice, "pleasure" '.[5] Leslie Barnard goes even further: 'Athenagoras' view of marriage would have commended itself to the Roman emperor [Marcus Aurelius]'.[6] Justin Martyr holds a similar view. In another passage Athenagoras mentions that Christians 'marry like everyone',[7] and in making such a remark, he is probably trying to show that Christians are normal people, with respectable views on the value of human life, which seems to be his purpose in the passage quoted from the *Legatio*. Similarly Stoic views, taken a bit further, seem to reappear in Dionysius of Corinth (*c.* 170) in a letter to Pinytus of Cnossus, in which he recommends the Cretan bishop 'not to inflict on the young a weight too heavy for them in regard to continence, but to take account of the weakness of the great number of them', and to let them marry.[8] Christian asceticism has already taken its hold on church authorities.

Clement of Alexandria (*c.* 150–*c.* 215) was the first Christian theologian to consider marriage and family life in any length.[9] His definition of marriage is much the same as Athenagoras: 'marriage is the first union of a man and a woman for the procreation of legitimate children'.[10] Apart from stressing monogamy and legitimacy (which the earlier writers would have praised anyway), this is a repeat of what we have seen already. Later on in the second *Stromateis* Clement goes further, and recommends marriage 'for the sake of the fatherland',[11] an interesting piece of incipient (and proleptic) Erastianism; and while he realizes that marriage is in part a remedy against human weakness, it is still a dignified relationship, blessed by God; he invokes Gen. 1.28 to support this, and even alludes to Eph. 5.22–33 when he says that 'as the Law is holy, so is marriage. This is why the Apostle compares this mystery with Christ and the Church'.[12] Marriage is indissoluble, and 'each of us is free to betroth himself lawfully to the woman he wants', which presumably reflects the two distinct stages in Greek law at the time, of *engusis* ('coming-together') and *ekdosis* ('giving-away').[13]

Unfortunately perhaps, Broudéhoux follows Ritzer in his interpretation of possible references to marriage liturgy.[14] In one place Clement pours scorn on bridal wigs, and insists that it is the real hair of the girl, and not the wig, that gets blessed by the priest's hands. It is hard to see how such a passage can fail to describe a priestly blessing at marriage; and if Clement *does* mean such a rite, then we have, at last, our first concrete evidence of Christian development of the Jewish practice. What was the rite, and what effect it was supposed to have, other than blessing the union, is unknown. Again in the fourth *Stromateis* he waxes Pauline, in his delightful style: 'marriage is surely sanctified which is done according to the Logos, if the union is submitted to God and is directed with a sincere heart, in the fullness of faith, the heart purified of all conscious taint, the body washed in pure water, guarding the promising of hope . . .'.[15] Here he is really talking about baptism, though the marital allusion, even if it is pagan (the nuptial bath), is surely implied.

Tertullian (*c.* 160–*c.* 225) has much to say on marriage, and it is full of the theological rigorism which eventually took him over to Montanism. In his *De Pudicitia*, he makes much of Paul's teaching on marriage, in order to controvert those with sensualist views, and Le Saint is right in concluding that Tertullian's basic view of marriage stems from his interpretation of 1 Cor. 7.9 ('It is better to marry than to burn'): 'marriage is not an absolute good but is called good only in comparison with something that is very bad.'[16] In the *De Oratione* he discusses the place of women; virgins should always be veiled, 'for they have married Christ'. Virgins are betrothed to be married by a kiss and by the giving of the right hand, and should be veiled from that day onwards;[17] here is evidence for the Christian use of the pagan Roman betrothal and marriage according to the law. But he attacks the (Roman) pagan use of garland-crowns at marriage in the *De Corona*, which he regards as an idolatrous practice, since the bride should be veiled,[18] and he even refers to the *lex velaminis*,[19] twice alluding to the presence of angels at marriage;[20] Rebecca's sanctity as well as her use of the veil are called in for support.[21] In marriage, man and wife become one flesh,[22] and the blessing of marriage is fertility.[23] He also refers twice to the use of the ring at betrothal.[24]

In two passages, however, Tertullian extends himself in some detail over marriage procedure, and the fact that their interpretation is in dispute makes it doubly appropriate that they should be quoted in full. The first is from the *De Monogamia*:

So then, you propose to marry in the Lord, as the law and the Apostle require—supposing that you bother about this at all. But

16

how will you dare request the kind of marriage which is not permitted to the ministers from whom you ask it, the bishop who is a monogamist, the presbyters and deacons who are bound by the same solemn obligation, the widows whose way of life you repudiate in your own person? Our adversaries, it is plain, will give husbands and wives in marriage indiscriminately, as they dole out pieces of bread, for thus they understand the text: 'Give to everyone that asketh of you'. They will celebrate your nuptials in a virgin church, the one spouse of the one Christ. You will be praying for both your husbands, the new and the old alike.[25]

The second is the oft-quoted passage from his *Ad Uxorem*, which we shall quote together with the important sequel:

How shall we ever be able adequately to describe the happiness of that marriage which the Church arranges, the Sacrifice strengthens, upon which the blessing sets a seal, at which angels are present as witnesses, and to which the Father gives his consent? For not even on earth do children marry properly and legally without their father' permission.

How beautiful, then, the marriage of two Christians, two who are one in hope, one in desire, one in the way of life they follow, one in the religion they practice. They are as brother and sister, both servants of the same Master. Nothing divides them, either in flesh or in spirit. They are, in very truth, 'two in one flesh'; and where there is but one flesh there so also but one spirit. They pray together, they worship together, they fast together; instructing one another, encouraging one another, strengthening one another. Side by side they visit God's church and partake of God's Banquet; side by side they face difficulties and persecution, share their consolations . . . . They need not be furtive about making the Sign of the Cross, nor timorous in greeting the brethren, nor silent in asking a blessing of God . . . .[26]

Both these passages have traditionally been taken at their face value, especially the second, so that they are seen to give evidence of marriage in church, by the bishop, with the rest of the community present; and the rite consists of a nuptial blessing, either with a nuptial Eucharist, or else followed at some stage by a Eucharist at which the couple are present.

Ritzer takes two decisive steps in the opposite direction in his treatment of these passages. He dates them both to *after* Tertullian's secession to Montanism, which leads him to conclude that Tertullian is only describing the élitist procedure of Montanists, not the ordinary practice of common-or-garden catholic Christians. He also minimizes the liturgical references, in the same way as he deals with Ignatius.[27] He may be allowed his point over Montanism; it is important to set all documents, liturgical and non-liturgical, in their proper context, and we must guard against concluding that what X does in B at a certain date is automatically what Z does in D at a similar time. But even so, it is hard to share his scepticism, which has been uncritically followed by other writers.[28] Henri Crouzel, a recognized authority on church life in the early centuries, has written on these two passages, and finds otherwise.[29]

The first passage presses for marriage to be celebrated in church, with the whole assembly of officials (and the faithful, presumably) present. Marriage must take place only once, and the rite includes prayer for the husband (!), as well as, we may conjecture, for the wife. Crouzel is ready to allow that this is rigorism, but in the *De Pudicitia* (written when Tertullian was still Catholic) he condemns secret marriages, and insists on the rite taking place in church.[30] The second passage is a catena of technical language which, as commentators (including Le Saint)[31] point out, is meant to show that for each of the stages in the pagan Roman marriage procedure, there is a corresponding Christian one. The Church 'arranges': *conciliat* echoes the *conciliator*, a relative or close friend who brought about or arranged the marriage. The sacrifice 'strengthens': *confirmat oblatio* echoes the sacrifice offered by the bride and groom on the morning of the wedding at a local altar. The 'blessing sets a seal': *obsignat benedictio* echoes the seal placed on the marriage contract in the pagan Roman rite. 'At which angels are present as witnesses': *angeli renuntiant* echoes the presence of the household gods; and *pater rato habet* ('to which the Father gives his consent') echoes the consent given by the father of the bride. So far so good. It is a carefully worked out passage, which would appeal to the North African, with his strong sense of Christianity upstaging unsatisfactory pagan activities. But on what grounds can these references be toned down out of all specific significance? It is indeed difficult to follow Ritzer in interpreting *conciliat* and *benedictio* in a deliberately non-liturgical sense, though he has a point in cautioning against assuming a nuptial Eucharist. Crouzel is, in our opinion, correct in rehabilitating the traditional view, that the words not only echo pagan practice but also refer to a specifically Christian marriage liturgy; and even if his prescriptions may reproduce his own Montanist church order, there is at least a case for suggesting that many Catholics did the same. In any case, the second part of the passage perhaps provides the key; marriage is set in the context of worship and life, and I would myself see indirect liturgical allusions to nuptial Eucharist and blessing, with the couple side by side, in such references as 'God's Banquet' and 'a blessing of God'. The rhetorical style of 'one in hope . . . desire . . . way of life' may even be quotations from a marriage homily (or perhaps a marriage prayer) used by Tertullian. Thus, for all the qualifications needed to set these texts in a wider perspective, we still have evidence of North African practice regarding Christian marriage at the turn of the third century.[32] Betrothal precedes marriage, and it consists of a kiss and joining of hands, and the giving of a ring, after which the bride is veiled. No indication is given of the length of time before the wedding, which has to take place in church, in the presence of all and sundry. The rite may involve a special Eucharist, otherwise a Eucharist follows, either immediately or on another day. The nuptial blessing is given by one of the clergy, and it probably included allusions to angelic protection, procreation of children, and the common hope, desire, and way of life of the bridal pair.

The Apocryphal *Acts of Thomas*, a Gnostic document of the late second to mid-third century, emanating from Edessa, contains an account of a marriage at which the apostle is present, and a blessing is prised from him. The blessing follows: a long series of invocations to the Most High and to Christ, only at the end actually referring to 'this young couple'.[33] Ritzer makes much of it, and concludes that 'a bishop or a priest of the second or third century could well have blessed a young couple with this formula'.[34] But there are problems. The precise origin of the various sections of the Acts is not completely settled. No one doubts that it is Gnostic, and originally Syriac. The *Sitz im Leben* is a missionary church and a domestic wedding, at which it looks as if the blessing would have been pronounced by one of the family (the father?), had not the apostle come along by chance. Furthermore, the blessing itself follows no pattern, and rambles along, not even mentioning marriage until the end; it looks like an 'all-purpose' prayer, composed by someone who was devout and long-winded. There can be little doubt that it was used in something of the form and setting of the *Acts*, but more work needs to be done by Syriac scholars on the evolution of early Syriac euchology before we can come to any firm conclusions about the provenance of this blessing among clergy in the second and third centuries.

For the rest of the ante-Nicene literary evidence there is little that is new. Hippolytus (c. 170–c. 236), the hotheaded source of much twentieth-century liturgy, cannot help us out over matters marital; he was enough of a snob to attack Pope Callistus for allowing upper-crust Christians to marry freedmen and slaves.[35] Theophilus of Antioch (late second century) condemns those who break their chastity either in act or thought.[36] Minucius Felix (second/third century, Africa), following in the wake of Tertullian, will have nothing to do with floral garlands, especially when the pagan Caecilius tries to give them a good rationale.[37] Cyprian of Carthage (d. 258) speaks of clergy as 'curators' of the people, and although not specifying marriage as something requiring clerical presence, seems to imply it;[38] he shuns mixed marriages, and forbids Christians to take part in riotous pagan marriage feasts, which presumably means that Christians were present and joined in.[39]

So much for the first three centuries. The evidence is inconclusive from a liturgical point of view. But we do get some kind of picture, and we can disern a gradual shift from a domestic rite, which was led either by a member of the family or a local cleric, to a church wedding, presided over by a bishop or presbyter. We may conjecture that the domestic rite involved some sort of nuptial blessing, and followed (after some unspecified space of time) the betrothal, with the joining of hands, and common undertaking to get married; the girl either took the veil at this point, or, if the betrothal immediately preceded the marriage, took it there and then. We may have hints of what the nuptial rite contained from Tertullian's language, but this can in no sense be regarded as normative, still less the blessing in the *Acts of Thomas*. Since both the Graeco-Roman and Jewish practices involved betrothal and marriage, it would have been no difficult thing to adapt them to Christian rites, but it is hard to say *when* the rite becomes specifically Christian, and how far local communities distinguished a Christian marriage from a non-Christian one in the earlier part of our period. I would suggest that there *was* such a distinction early on, together with a recognized liturgical rite, at least for marriage itself, consisting of implicit consent, and a blessing, even though such an idea has been called into question.[40] But it is essentially a rite emerging out of a common life, and not one that conveys sacramental 'effect'. Tertullian's discourse to his wife expresses this in tender and faithful terms, and captures something of the natural and supernatural aspects of experienced Christian wedlock. And why the blessing? Because Roman Law dictated that consent made marriage, and for the early Christians this was right, but insufficient.

3   Literary Evidence; the Fourth to the Sixth Centuries

Since the fourth century brought great changes in Christian liturgy, it marks a sensible stage at which to draw a line of division between an era of origins and an era of development. But we have no texts; we still have to make do with echoes and allusions (though these get stronger); and it would be a false assumption to say that because all the other main rites (Eucharist, Initiation, Ordination) grew in different ways along certain lines that the same is necessarily true of marriage rites. For reasons of convenience, we shall separate East from West, and deal with each main author according to his area. The Eastern Fathers are noted for a very positive view of marriage and take further the glorious dictum of Methodius of Olympus' (d. c. 311) that in marriage 'the Creator is still fashioning men'.[1]

a. The East

i. Cappadocia and environs

The Cappadocian Fathers help us. Basil of Caesarea (c. 330–79) makes several important allusions to marriage procedure, and also formulates some significant rules. In the great treatise On the Holy Spirit he refers to those who are joined together,[2] and in the Hexaemeron he discusses Eph. 5.25, in which he describes marriage as 'the bond of nature, the yoke (made) by the blessing, the uniting of those who are separate'.[3] Such a description can only mean that the institution of marriage is focused and completed in a liturgical rite, at the heart of which is a priestly blessing. It is in his Canonical writings to Amphilochus, bishop of Iconium, that he deals with marriage discipline. Those who marry for the third or further time are not to be thrown out of church, but are to do penance (Canon 4); and from Canon 22 it is plain that Basil knew of the two-stage process of betrothal and marriage, though it does not seem as if betrothal is legally binding; in Canon 26 he declares that 'marriage is not fornication, nor is fornication the beginning of marriage'. It is in Canon 27 that he is most explicit. He condemns private marriages performed by priests, emphasizing that this is a cheapening of the blessing, which he defines as 'the imparting of consecration'; he goes on to say that to have a marriage in church is the way of making Christ present at the wedding, an allusion to Cana in Galilee.[4] Three times in this Canon he uses the word *eulogia* as a noun or verb; it is obvious what he sees as the climax of the marriage rite, which he is anxious not to let be subject to abuse, but to keep in church, at all costs, since offending clergy are to be disciplined.

Gregory of Nazianzus (329–89) is as informative, but in a more homely manner. In a baptismal homily he likens the Church to the bride in marriage, and refers to a crown (*stephanos*) on the bride's head,[5] something which he would not have done unless it was common practice, and an important piece of evidence, since Basil does not allude to the crown at all. In his letters he is more explicit about marriage. In writing to Procopius, he counsels against rowdy wedding feasts[6] but in three other letters he makes direct liturgical allusions. To Eusebius he mentions the bridal bed, decorated with flowers, and offers his own *epithalamion*, by which he presumably means a marriage prayer in hymnic form[7] and quotes Psalm 127 ('The Lord bless you from Zion'); and immediately goes on to suggest themes for this *epithalamion*, that the Lord 'fit the yoke' on the couple, so that they should be 'stronger'; the father (of the bride?) crowns them, as is prayed in the rite, and he repeats the connection between the crowns and the prayers.[8] Here is substantial material indeed! Although it is not clear if the service takes places at home or in church, the liturgy involves the crowning of the couple by the father of the bride, at the point when a special liturgical prayer is recited by the priest, which either quotes Ps. 127, or that psalm is used immediately before the prayer, which in any case prays for the future life of the couple, and for divine grace and help.

In a letter to one Theodosius or Theodorus, Gregory insists that the 'yoke' comes through the liturgical prayer, as the action of God fitting the couple together, thus re-echoing what he writes to Eusebius.[9] When he writes to Diocles, he apologizes for not being able to come to the wedding of his daughter in the polite and tender terms which one would expect of a popular bishop. He waxes rhetorical, and insists that Christ will ·be there nonetheless, as he was at Cana, when he turned the water into wine, and there will also be present 'bishops and laughter, prayers and applause, psalmody and stringed music', a delightful juxtaposition of allusion to liturgical rite and domestic rejoicing.[10] All this supports what he says to Eusebius, and none of it contradicts. But we are still unsure if the rite takes place in church, or home, or both; I suspect that there was a service in church, and prayers at home round the bed after the main feast. The crowning of bride and groom is supported by references in two other contemporaries, the other Cappadocian, Gregory of Nyssa (c. 330–c. 395), and also Evagrius of Pontus (346–99).[11]

ii. Syria and Palestine

John Chrysostom (c. 347–407) lets us know even more. In a homily on St Matthew's Gospel, he says that in marriage the two become one flesh, and in another Matthew homily, whose authorship is contested, he insists that it is the consent and not the cohabitation which makes marriage.[12] He speaks generally of marriage in several places, and understands the relationship between the man and wife in Pauline terms, the man being the head. He also inveighs against over-riotous feasts such as were known among pagans, and urges people not to over-do the dressing-up on these occasions, since the bride's real decorations are those virtues which have made her marriageable.[13] But even though he disapproves of domestic orgies, he does say in two places that it is normal for the feasting to go on for seven days, as in Judaism.[14] In another disputed work he compares the marriage at Cana with a normal wedding: Christ is present, through the priest; the virtues of Rebecca and Isaac, Rachel and Jacob are sung; the couple agree to be married; there is a feast at home.[15] It is, however, in a homily on the First Letter to Timothy[16] that he defends the practice of the crowning, as the crowns are 'symbols of victory' over passion and the couple proceed with this victory to their marriage bed. He seems to imply that the crowns used at weddings are not just any crowns, but special ones, reserved for liturgical use. Perhaps the crowning ceremony was disapproved of by some at the time. Elsewhere Chrysostom also refers to the giving of *arrhas* (= pledge) before the marriage, which seems to be a ring, placed on the finger, and later in the same piece we come across the special bridal robe.[17] The most important passage, however, comes from one of his homilies on the book of Genesis.[18] Marriages are conducted by the priests, who 'through prayers and blessings bind (them) together in the same will and the same home', in order that the groom's love may increase, and the 'shame' (*sophrosune*) of the girl may be stretched; he alludes to the 'works of virtue' in the home, banishing the schemes of the devil, a pleasurable life together, under the protection of God. It is clear what the great preacher describes: a service conducted by the priest (bishop), which consists of prayers and blessings, which contain certain themes, about their life together in the future, under God. He sees a great deal of importance in the rite; it is possible that the 'prayers and blessings' may be diaconal biddings and priestly blessing-prayers;[19] and it is also possible that the prayers do refer explicitly to the love of the groom, the 'shame' of the bride, works of virtue at home, the banishing of the devil, a pleasurable life in the future, and all under the grace of God; it could well be that he is quoting the liturgy.

Ephraem the Syrian (306–73) says little about marriage, but seems to imply that there was a procedure, and he alludes to crowning, as well as hand-laying.[20] Cyril of Jerusalem (*c.* 315–86) refers to the white garment, and uses the awesome phrase, 'marriage of solemnity', presumably in the need to defend the relationship against those who would trivialize it.[21] Jerome (*c.* 342–420) attains the height of presbyteral bigotry in warning priests to keep well away from marriage feasts.[22] None of this adds much to our story.

iii. Egypt

Cyril of Alexandria (d. 444) likewise alludes to there being a liturgical form,[23] but it is in the *Lausiac History* (*c.* 419–20) of Palladius (*c.* 365–425) that we get the fullest account of an Egyptian marriage, in what he writes about Amoun of Nitria:

Since he was not able to withstand his uncle's pressure, it seemed best to him to be crowned, and to take his place in the bridal chamber, and go through with the whole marriage. After they had all put the couple on the couch in the bridal chamber and departed, Amoun got up and closed the door. Then sitting down, he called his saintly companion to him and said to her: 'Come here, my lady, and I will explain this matter to you. The marriage which we have just gone through is not efficacious. We will do well if henceforth each of us sleeps alone so that we may please God by keeping our virginity intact.[24]

It is, indeed, an hilarious scene. Poor old Amoun is bullied into marriage, and the rite is commonly understood at the time of Palladius as 'crowning', as the later Byzantine and other Eastern rites describe it. The gathering escorts the couple to the bridal chamber, and leaves them alone. But because there was not the *will* to marry (and, presumably, this will was not explicit in the liturgy in any case), the marriage is described as 'not efficacious'. It could be that Palladius is using the liturgical terminology of his native Asia Minor, though unlikely; the circumstances he describes are, surely, faithful to Egyptian practice at the time.

The only other reliable Egyptian evidence is from Timotheus of Alexandria, (d. 477), the Monophysite Patriarch, who may have known domestic nuptial Eucharists in his time,[25] but that is all.

So much for the East. We cannot, obviously, put all the evidence together, in order to make up a kind of all-purpose Eastern marriage liturgy pastiche, cooked from Cappadocian meat, mixed well with Syrian herbs, served with Egyptian sauce. But the beginnings of a liturgical rite do emerge. Betrothal is known and practised, even with the ring. The marriage ceremony is presided over by the priest, and involves psalmody, crowning of both the bridal pair by near-relatives, with the recitation of solemn priestly blessings; the feast follows at home, and the couple are taken to the chamber afterwards, with or without prayer. The crowning is sufficiently important for the entire rite to be referred to as 'crowning', which distinguishes it from how Western writers understand it.

The Eastern Councils do not yield much more, except that they reflect obvious abuses. Thus, Ancyra (314) lays down that those who are betrothed must be returned to their spouses, even if they are taken off by others. Neo-Caesarea (314–25) insists that clergy must keep away from the feast of marriage when one of the partners is marrying for the second time; the priest's presence is taken to imply 'assent' by the Church. The Council of Laodicea (end of fourth century) makes several regulations: Canon 1 allows those who have married for the second time 'lawfully . . . and not clandestinely' to be received back into communion after a short time; Canon 31 insists that Christians should only marry other Christians, and not heretics; Canon 52 forbids weddings in Lent; Canon 53 forbids Christians to dance at wedding feasts, 'but modestly sup and dine as becomes Christians' (a nice contradiction of Chrysostom!); and Canon 54 takes this one stage further by laying down that clerics must not 'witness the shows at weddings, but before the players enter they must rise up and depart'.[26] All this evidence points to a tension between Church and home, and increasing concern over who marries whom, and under what circumstances.

b. The West

i. Italy

The first piece of strong evidence for the nuptial blessing as a definite liturgical form comes in the mysterious author, Ambrosiaster, who probably lived in Rome during the time of Damasus I (366–84); he contrasts the blessing with Jewish practice, closely links it with Genesis 1.28, and restricts it to first marriages.[27] Certainly his two latter insights are reflected by later Western practice. Then Pope Siricius I (384–99), finding a letter from Himerius, bishop of Tarragona, which had been unanswered by his illustrious predecessor, lays down the firm procedure that the bride is to be veiled, and that this veiling is to be associated closely with the blessing given by the priest, which, moreover, is not to be given to those outside the Church, as this would be sacrilegious.[28] But Siricius is known to have been a romanizer in matters liturgical; we cannot be sure if his advice was followed.

Ambrose of Milan (339–97) has much to say about marriage, mainly in relation to women, although he seldom seems to refer to the liturgy. A frequent theme in his writings about marriage is the virtue of *pudor*; another favourite theme is the production of children.[29] But by far the commonest way of speaking about marriage is the image of the *vinculum* ('link') or *jugum* ('yoke') as a description of the union of man and woman.[30] In the *Hexaemeron* he seems to echo Basil of Caesarea, when he refers to the 'link between separate persons', and he goes on to speak of the 'oath of love' and the 'necks joined together by the same yoke of blessing of each',[31] which describes the nuptial blessing. In one place he has recourse to the Greek *harmosai* in order to define the bringing together of man and woman;[32] and we also encounter the phrase *pactio conjugalis*,[33] which describes agreement to marry; in several places he alludes to a rite of betrothal, prior to marriage, which is binding and is symbolized in a kiss.[34] Most important, however, are his references to the nuptial veiling, of which there are a few. Virgins must wear the veil, following the example of Rebecca, who then removed her veil after being married. Women who are going to marry must similarly wear a veil.[35] In a letter to Vigilius, recently made a bishop, Ambrose writes of the 'priestly veil', and links it with the blessing, and he goes on to the *fidei concordia*, which the blessing may contain and even be said to impart.[36] He seems to be aware of betrothal and marriage as two distinct stages, for he discusses *conjugium* as being the result of *desponsata* ('betrothed') and *tradita* ('given away') when speaking of a woman marrying.[37] In a key passage he says that 'although first marriages are made by God, second marriages are still permitted. The first marriages are celebrated under the blessing of God'; this presumably means that the nuptial blessing is what constitutes the liturgical rite of marriage, and that this blessing is withheld from people marrying a second time.[38] He mentions psalmody somewhat vaguely in connection with wedding ritual.[39]

Pope Innocent I (d. 417) in a canonical letter to Victricius of Rouen (sometimes ascribed to Decentius of Gubbio) decrees that when it comes to the form of blessing used at weddings, care is to be taken that it is according to long tradition in the Church,[40] which gives us evidence of the fact that there were already 'norms' for nuptial blessing; this supports much of what we have said hitherto on this question. The decrees which are attributed to Innocent and are also found in the *Statuta Ecclesiae Antiquae* describe the blessing of both of the bridal pair, and the presence of parents or 'paranymphs', who offer them for blessing.[41] This may be reflected in some of the prayers in the later Sacramentaries, where the eucharistic gifts are offered by the wedding-party, for the bridal couple.

Of particular charm is a part of an *epithalamium* (following in a tradition going right back to Catullus, and earlier) composed by Paulinus of Nola (353/4–431), in which he describes the wedding of Julian, son of the bishop of Benevento, to the daughter of the bishop of Capua.[42] Of course, such a wedding cannot be said to typify late fourth-century practice, as anyone who has taken part in a wedding involving two clerical families will know well. In the relevant section of this *Carmen* 25 we come across enough to conclude that we are in church, the bishop blesses with his hand, bestowing the grace of Christ, with angelic help, giving justice and peace; and, in a recognized manner, he places a veil over the shoulders of *both* the man and the woman, and blesses them, and so Christ gives them reverent hearts through the chaste hands of the bishop. Thus, the nuptial blessing is given by a bishop, with a veil, and there hints of what that blessing might contain.

Returning to the north of Italy, we find in the writings of Gaudentius of Brescia (fourth–fifth century) the first attempt to compare the Christian marriage procedure with the Jewish. He not only sees a domestic Jewish wedding in the famous account of Jesus at Cana, but also knows that Jews had begun to bring in rabbis to preside at the wedding feast, instead of using the 'master of the feast', who would have been a member of the family. On Christian marriage, however, he says little, except that it is instituted and blessed by God, and he uses Gen. 1.28 as his evidence.[43]

Gregory the Great (c. 540–604) preaches an austere understanding of marriage, and insists, like other earlier writers, that marriage is 'for the purpose of procreation', and here he is probably quoting *tabulae matrimoniales* which he knew.[44]

ii. Gaul

Sidonius Apollinaris (c. 423–80) was bishop of Clermont Ferrand, and had a racy style of Latin in a time of great turgidity. In an epistle written about 471, he describes an unsuitable marriage, which involves the presence of the bishop, and also *tabulae matrimoniales* (the agreement to get married) which are to be read out.[45] Nothing about the service can be gleaned from his story, but here is firm evidence that in Gaul in the fifth century, the marriage takes place under episcopal care, and with a signed document. We shall hear more of these *tabulae* when discussing Augustine.

Caesarius of Arles (*c.* 470–542) is a little more informative. In one sermon he refers to the Roman custom of the bride refraining from asking for the nuptial blessing if she is not a virgin, as if commending the practice to his own people. In another he describes the *tabulae matrimoniales* as giving the reason for marriage, *liberorum procreandorum causa* ('for the procreation of children'). And he goes on to say that penitents are not worthy of receiving the nuptial blessing, which is (here) for both the bride and the groom.[46]

Cyprian of Toulon (d. 549), in his Life of Caesarius of Arles, describes the custom of telling couples to abstain from sexual relations for three nights after the wedding, in order to give reverence to the (nuptial) blessing.[47] This clerical custom increases in the Middle Ages, though whether or not it was observed by the couples is impossible to tell.

iii. North Africa

Augustine is a giant in the development of Western theology, and although what he has to say about marriage is considerable, little of it is drastically new as far as marriage procedure is concerned. It has been fashionable to draw attention to the negative side of Augustine concerning sexuality and marriage, but Pedro Langa is probably right in emphasizing the positive aspects.[48] Because there is much repetition in the many references, we shall deal with them by theme and subject. He insists that the bishop must be involved in arrangements concerning marriage.[49]

First of all, marriage is not merely a *vinculum* ('link, joining'), but also a *sacramentum*,[50] a solemn obligation; here he is probably consciously developing the thought of Ambrose, his great mentor in earlier years. He also makes a great deal of marital virtues, such as sincerity, reliability, peacefulness, chastity, fruitfulness, as well as others.[51] But there is one triad of reasons for marriage which occurs many times in his writings: *fides, proles, sacramentum*, that is, 'fidelity, offspring, solemn obligation'.[52] Because of the frequency of this triad, it is very tempting to suggest that he is quoting the liturgy, or at least a liturgical homily, and I suspect that these three aspects of marriage came across clearly in a wedding service conducted by the great North African bishop. But we cannot tell for certain.

Secondly, he mentions repeatedly the *tabulae matrimoniales*, which the bishop writes down and reads out,[53] and each time they are mentioned, out comes the formula, 'for the procreation of children'.[54] In all the references there is no variation whatever, and we may conclude that he is referring to a well-established tradition in his church, and one which in his sermons he could easily take for granted that his congregation would know.

Thirdly, he refers again and again to Gen. 1.28, and connects closely the blessing of God on Adam and Eve (the 'first parents') in their marriage with the command to 'increase and multiply'.[55] It occurs so frequently that again it is tempting to conclude that the nuptial blessing which he normally pronounced used this juxtaposition, perhaps near the beginning, like prayers of the Visigothic tradition in later centuries.[56] On one occasion he even says that 'fruitfulness pertains to the blessing of married women'; but his view on sexuality is Pauline; 'it is better to marry than to burn'. Such references as these and his allusions to marital virtues suggest that the nuptial blessing which he knew was *bridal*, like the prayers of the Roman Sacramentaries; Augustine thinks marriage is about women changing their state and fulfilling their function, to put it somewhat crudely.[57]

Finally, he refers to the bridal veil, but only on one occasion, and this, coupled with a chance reference to the entry (into church?) of the wedding-party ('paranymphs' and all), adds up to a little bit more.[58] He mentions Tertullian,[59] too, and certainly the vigour with which he insists on the need for marriage to be conducted properly reflects an influence from his North African predecessor, even if only indirectly. Possidius, in his Life of Augustine, mentions the *tabulae matrimoniales* and Augustine's insistence that rowdy parties were forbidden; he described the great man as intervening between quarelling couples![60]

Augustine's influence is visible on the thinking of Fulgentius of Ruspe (462–527), who regards marriage as the work of God, and Augustine's three reasons for marriage may be echoed in a passage from the Third Letter of Fulgentius to Proba, in which he says that the Lord joins a married couple in a 'link' by *faith*, favours them with the gift of a *blessing*, and multiplies them with the increase of *children*; it is from God that come *fidelity* between partners, *love* for each other, and *fruitfulness*.[61]

Although there is more material from Western authors, we do not get as clear a picture from them of the marriage rites, but we can conclude that betrothal was known and practised; that the custom of having *tabulae matrimoniales* agreed and written by the officiating cleric was widespread; that the bridal veil was usual, probably connected with an understanding of marriage which sees the woman's change of state as of fundamental importance[62] (and thus radically different from Eastern writers); and that the marriage rite contained a blessing, probably according to set forms, which might vary from one tradition to another, but which in Augustine's Africa no doubt quoted Gen. 1.28. The Roman blessing of the bride, duly veiled, is a superb example of the christianizing of a pagan custom, the old *flammeum*.[63] However, we do not know if the service was connected with a Eucharist, even though the priestly role is being emphasized by many of the writers. Conciliar documents of the time deal mainly with matters of discipline. Elvira (Spain, *c.* 306) tightens up on those who marry pagans, as does the First Council of Arles (314). There is a tendency to insist that clerics get married in church, from which we may assume that 'ordinary' laypersons in some cases did not bother, or else perhaps had a domestic ceremony, connected with a feast. The Second Council of Milevis (416) gives directions about liturgical procedure in general, and identifies prayer-forms at the laying-on of hands as one of those liturgical functions which must be according to official versions; this probably included the nuptial blessing.[64]

Literary evidence can only take the researcher part of the way, and the picture, though foggy, can still be made surefootedly. Conciliar evidence also indicates a growing reluctance to marry in Advent and Lent. Archaeological evidence, however, corroborates much of what we have said already, for it suggests the use of the veil in the West, crowning in the East, the joining of hands, and the use of the ring, at a betrothal, in the context of specifically Christian worship.[65] On the crown and the veil East and West already begin to diverge. It is on the foundations of these writings and customs and thinking that are built the classical forms of marriage service of the East and West which later chapters will examine in more detail. Sometimes a later rite reflects something that we have already seen described explicitly, or just hinted at; but often the passage of time and the inevitable development of the liturgy are the only explanations.

2 Efflorescence: The Medieval West

1 The Roman Sacramentaries

We now move to an era which has proper liturgical books. Nonetheless there are textual problems, particularly in the first so-called Sacramentary, which was once attributed to Leo the Great, but is now agreed to be neither Leonine, nor a Sacramentary, but a *libellus missarum* of Verona which shows signs of Roman origin.[1]

a. The Leonianum: Verona 85

During the month of September there appears the title *incipit velatio nuptialis* ('nuptial veiling'),[2] and no less than six prayers. The first two and the fourth make up a recognizable mass-set. The first is a collect, which makes no reference to marriage, but asks for God's blessing on what is being done; it comes from a Leonine *libellus*, and could have been written for any mass at which something special was going to be done. The second prayer is recognizably a *secreta*, and asks that the eucharistic gifts presented by a woman[3] be received *pro sacra lege coniugii* ('for the holy law of marriage'), a strong expression, which assumes the binding and established nature of matrimony. The fourth prayer is about the couple as joined together by God, and we can assume that it served as an introductory prayer to the long blessing, which follows it, and which refers to marriage as instituted by God for the propagation of children. Between the second and the third comes a special *hanc igitur*, to be inserted at the appropriate point during the canon. Like the long nuptial blessing, this prayer is exclusively bridal. The Eucharist is offered *pro famula tua illa*; just as she has reached the right age for marriage, so she must now be joined to her husband with God's blessing, and grow old with him.

Although the long blessing, *pater mundi conditor* ('Father, maker of the world'), comes at the end, some commentators assume that it was actually recited earlier in the mass, between the canon and the communion, as directed for the corresponding blessing in the Gelasian and Gregorian Sacramentaries.[4] The manuscript variants in this prayer are numerous, and at certain points the meaning is not entirely clear. This might suggest that it was an *ad hoc* composition, an assumption reinforced by the fact that the Gelasian tradition 'corrects' it at several points, and the Gregorian has another prayer altogether, but with markedly similar themes. The sequence of ideas is nonetheless logical: creation, the creation of Adam, the creation of woman from his rib, propagation of the human race; woman as the weaker sex, joined to the stronger, children to come, without dying early; prayer that she may be a good wife and keep 'the eternal laws' (*aeterna iura*) and that the marriage is not just for children but for keeping faith. There is an Augustinian tang to these prayers. At this point the editions give the impression that another section of the prayer is beginning, and it certainly reads as if it should end now; but it goes on, with a catalogue of Old Testament characters, preceded by a clause strongly reminiscent of Paulinus of Nola's *carmen*, 'faithful and chaste may she marry in Christ' (*fidelis et casta nubat in Christo*), and imitate holy women: she is to be lovable as Rachel, wise as Rebecca, longliving and faithful as Sarah; she is to remain faithful and fruitful, and after death have a share in the heavenly kingdom. In this final section there is one classic petition: *sit verecundia gravis pudore venerabilis, doctrinis caelestibus erudita.*[5]

What are we to make of this?

i. Both the *hanc igitur* and this blessing are for the bride only, the bridegroom being mentioned by implication. In liturgical writing this is the first time that we have come across such a notion so far, and it is of paramount importance as we set out to cover the Middle Ages. It is a feature only known in original compositions in the Sacramentaries, all other nuptial blessing-prayers in the West being for both the man and the woman; the only evidence in the East for bridal blessing is in a rite which has counterbalancing bridegroom blessings as well! As was noted in the previous chapter, this may be a local Roman archaism, a survival from the pagan wedding rites as described, for example, in the poems of Catullus, and adapted by the time of Siricius[6]—not that there is anything pagan or unchristian in the text of prayer. Indeed, it is a masterpiece of biblical allusion.

ii. The biblical material consists mainly of creation motifs, support for the idea that women are the weaker sex, and some well-known Old Testament women as exemplifying specific virtues. It is significant that none of the prayers mentions the presence of Jesus at the wedding in Cana, or the passage in Ephesians about Jesus as the bridegroom of the Church.

iii. If there is a link between the long blessing-prayer and the Jewish Seven Blessings, it is in the sequence of ideas, rather than in a specific liturgical form. There is no initial blessing of God (*berakah*), but this element is not found in the eucharistic prayers of the time of Verona 85 either. And another development from Jewish origins, already seen hinted at in previous writers, is the transference from a domestic wedding feast with blessing at the end, to the eucharistic feast in church.

iv. In the long blessing-prayer in particular, a theology is propounded which shows many of the features which we have seen in the Bible, and, more especially, in the writings of the Fathers. God instituted matrimony, and it is not only for children, but also for the exercise of fidelity, love, mutual support, and that untranslatable of Latin virtues, *pudor*; and although the rite contains no vows (betrothal probably made up for this), the binding nature of the commitment to marriage is implicit in the texts of the prayers.

But one final point. Why and when *velatio nuptialis*? The text gives no indication of anything other than the prayers themselves. Thus we do not know what readings were used, or chants. From the hints we have gleaned from previous writers, and from later evidence, it *may* have been during the long prayer that the veil was extended over both the man and the woman; the main evidence for such an action is from Paulinus of Nola, who describes a wedding in which both the bridal pair are blessed and veiled, whereas the rite which we have here is a blessing of the bride only. Another possibility is that the veiling is of the bride only; such an interpretation would reflect the implication of the title of the service, *incipit velatio nuptialis*. Yet another interpretation (and to this writer the most probable) is that the bride arrived in church already veiled, and remained so throughout, for, unlike other later prayers (e.g., Spanish),[7] there is no mention whatever of veiling in the *texts* of the prayers, which in itself is significant, for it gives the impression that the veiling is a long-standing tradition which the rite is not specifically concerned with.

b. The Gelasian Sacramentary: Vat. Reg. 316 and its derivatives

The Gelasian Sacramentary in its oldest version dates from the beginning of the eighth century, and—according to Chavasse—was written down by the Benedictines of Chelles in North

France, but based on a Roman ancestor, and represents the first romanization of the Gallican rites in the era before Charlemagne.[8] The marriage rite which it contains is at root a Roman rite, which has much in common with the Leonine, but also has certain Gallican features.

Book III, chapter 52 is headed, *incipit actio nuptialis*, a significant difference from *velatio*.[9] As in the Gelasian books, two formulae for the collect appear. The first is the prayer which the Leonine places just before the long blessing, which fits better here, since it means that the mass actually starts on a marital note. The second is the post-communion from the Leonine, which prays for the couple to live long together, and it follows naturally from the previous prayer, which is about having children. Female chauvinism, however, enters at the *secreta* (a new composition) which refers to the gifts of 'your female servants here' (*famularum tuarum illarum*), a possible reference to the 'paranymphs' producing the eucharistic gifts on this occasion (cf. Leonine at this point); and it goes on to pray for the bride in terms similar to the Leonine *hanc igitur*; she has reached the age for marriage—may she be filled with divine grace. A proper preface appears for the first time, an objective composition which describes marriage as a 'yoke of concord' and an 'indissoluble chain of peace'; offspring are for the increase of membership of the Church.[10] The *hanc igitur* is much the same as the Leonine.

After the canon and the Lord's Prayer, 'you bless her in these words', as the direction goes. A new preparatory prayer comes now, which Ritzer suggests (against Chavasse) is a Gallican composition, a suggestion he bases on its *cursus*.[11] All it does is to point further to the long blessing (which follows) as for the bride only. The long blessing consists of a revised version of the Leonine *pater mundi conditor*, and after it is the direction 'Peace be with you, and so you communicate them; then after they have communicated, you say over them blessings in these words'. The first of these is the first Latin blessing-prayer for both man and wife that we have encountered so far, which from its *cursus* looks more Gallican than the preparatory prayer mentioned above.[12] Divine blessing is connected with the production of children, and freedom from the snares of the enemy. The second prayer is the same as the collect in the Leonine.

The Gelasian sequence is followed carefully in all its derivatives,[13] which is proof that the Roman structure of the marriage rite penetrated into Gaul through the eighth century, replacing whatever the Gallican rites did in marriage, a matter which we shall discuss in the following chapter. Clearly, the compiler of the Gelasian book relied in some measure on the Leonine, some of whose prayers are taken over and rearranged. The principle new features are as follows:

i. the *secreta* as well as the *hanc igitur* invoke God's blessing on the bride only, and in the former some presentation of the gifts by the paranymphs may be the reason behind the phraseology of the prayer.

ii. The main nuptial blessing is unequivocally placed between the canon and the communion, and the language of the preparatory prayer heightens the bridal nature of this blessing.

iii. As if to compensate for bridal prayers, an additional prayer is given at the end of the rite, referring explicitly throughout to both the bride and the groom.

iv. Finally, the position of the long blessing. In the Leonine it is unclear whether the blessing was given at the end, as the manuscript suggests, or before the communion, as in the other Sacramentaries. Now there is no doubt whatever, but *why here?* Some have suggested that it is an example of Gallican influence on the Roman rite, for in the Gallican books an episcopal blessing before communion was a distinctive feature, which had probably developed under Eastern influence.[14] To support this theory, Moeller singles out two Spanish prayers (discussed in a later chapter) as indicating a primitive Franco-Spanish tradition of a nuptial blessing before communion. We have argued elsewhere that these prayers in fact indicate the reverse; they bless the bride only, unlike all other marriage prayers of Frankish and Spanish traditions, and show signs of structural and linguistic dependence on a Roman original.[15]

More likely is the explanation that connects nuptial blessing at Rome with those other special blessings that take place between the canon and communion, discernible in the *Apostolic Tradition* of Hippolytus, and known through the Middle Ages in the West. To count the nuptial blessing in this category would be to hold the conviction that certain blessings need to be closely associated with the eucharistic action. Jungmann discusses this question with many examples.[16] Our theory of Jewish influence would support this suggestion indirectly, for it amounts to a desire to keep the meal-blessings together.

Before leaving the Gelasian Sacramentary, it is worth drawing attention to one other special form which we encounter here for the first time, the *hanc igitur* for use at anniversaries. Referring to both bride and bridegroom throughout (as the offerers), it asks for continued blessing on the couple, and at the end for children; the concluding phrase echoes the 'Raguel' prayer in Tobit,[17] and we shall come across it again. Apart from the eighth-century Gelasians, the only time these prayers, and, in particular, the long blessing, occur again is in the tenth-century Fulda Sacramentary, a composite work which will be discussed later on.[18]

c. The Gregorian Sacramentary

We now come to the liturgical Rolls-Royce of the Middle Ages, and we are on much surer ground about dates and origins, for the marriage rite alters little from the earliest until the later manuscripts. It is clear that the Leonine is in the background, as with the Gelasian rite: both the Gelasian and the Gregorian are in different ways dependent on the Leonine.[19]

The title varies in the manuscripts, the original giving *oratio ad sponsas velandas* (prayer for veiling wives), but there is a noticeable shift in later versions, not just after Alcuin (or Benedict of Aniane, if Deshusses is correct), to replace *velandas* with *benedicendas*,[20] which may be a Gelasian touch. The service begins with the old Leonine collect in its original position, and continues with the Leonine *secreta* (called *super oblata* in most texts). After it, the Gelasian preface appears, and a *hanc igitur* based on the *secreta* of the Gelasian rite, but exclusively bridal.[21]

Things change at this point. 'Before the Peace of the Lord is said, he says (this) prayer', a new introductory prayer for the nuptial blessing, modelled on the one which comes in the Leonine. The nuptial blessing (*deus qui potestate virtutis*) is the climax of the whole rite, and is obviously a reworking of the Leonine, with similar themes, but significant new features; a much smoother composition altogether, it is actually called *benedictio*. The sequence of ideas is as follows: creation of the world from nothing, creation of man, creation of woman as help to man, with reference to the saying of Jesus that marriages should not be broken; then comes a new passage, with a theme which we have not seen so far in liturgical prayers: a reference to the Ephesians analogy of Christ as the bridegroom of the Church; and this leads into the idea of man and wife as companions in spite of original sin and the flood. All this has been in the '*deus qui*' category, and the blessing now starts in earnest. 'Look favourably on your servant here', it continues, and ideas similar to those expressed in the Leonine follow, including that she should marry faithful and chaste in Christ, and exemplify the virtues of the holy women of the Old Testament. The final section reproduces much of the Leonine but it is recast, referring to the gift of children (complete with the 'Raguel' blessing about 'seeing children's children') and ends on the theme of old age (arriving at the eternal kingdom comes *before* the production of children, an illogical sequence not found in the Leonine prayer!) The full text is given in Appendix I.

Deshusses gives a full list of the textual variants in his critical edition. One feature in these is clearly discernible at the end and is significant—a variant that does not exactly alter the *sense* of the prayer so much as change its *direction*. For in the manuscript tradition there is a tendency to pluralize the final verbs, either all three ('arriving at the eternal kingdom', 'seeing children and children's children', and 'arriving at old age') or just the last two. The earliest text which does this is Cambrai 164 (159), which Lietzmann dates 812 in his edition,[22] and which Deshusses identifies as an early copy of the version sent by the Pope to Charlemagne, but with 'compléments intéressants' added.[23] The next appearances are in the family of texts which Deshusses terms 'Hadrianum authentique corrigé', but, significantly, none are to be found in the more numerous groups of manuscripts described as 'Grégorien d'Aniane' and 'Grégorien d'Aniane corrigé'.[24] In those which opt for a plural verb, the last two become *videant* and *perveniant*, and in those few which pluralize all three, the antepenultimate is another *perveniant*. It is interesting to note the drift in the later texts back to the more authentic singular reading.[25]

Why pluralize the ending? Two reasons can be offered. One, to bring the blessing into line with other prayers, for example the *hanc igitur*, which prays for the bride, and for the bridegroom by implication only. At first sight, this appears a likely theory, but it breaks down when the *hanc igitur* is examined further, for the bridegroom is hardly present; indeed, one might almost say, he is in the wings! Another reason which can be offered is connected with the manuscript tradition. When the Gregorian prayer came into use in Charlemagne's empire, it went against local traditions, which knew of nothing akin to the Roman practice of blessing the bride only, and in order to soften the thrust of the prayer (like the Gelasian addition of a blessing for both at the end of mass), the ending started being pluralized. It is not an unimportant point by any means, since it reflects the way in which one tradition is brought into conflict with another. The two Spanish blessings mentioned earlier have an identical structure to the Gregorian nuptial blessing with the plural ending; it obviously inspired local compositions along Roman lines. The tenth/eleventh-century Sacramentaries of Roda and Vich, which are Catalonian amalgams of Visigothic and Roman elements, probably written to convince the pope that the Mozarabic rite was not so terrible after all, contain the Gregorian blessing with the plural ending.[26] Later in this chapter we shall see how the Gregorian rite fares as the Middle Ages develop, but at this stage we simply note the unresolved debate about what sort of blessing the bride gets.

d. The spread of the Gregorian Sacramentary

Given its high pedigree and the imperial legislation which accompanied it on its way, it is hardly surprising that the Gregorian Sacramentary should spread all over Frankish territory, as the manuscripts show from their date and place of origin, although local independence persisted for some time.[27] Whatever preceded it in the way of local marriage rites (and this is a matter which is not entirely clear), its nuptial mass took over or else was added to, in order to incorporate existing traditions. The major exception is the eleventh-century Köln 141 MS, in which the precatory section of the nuptial blessing is rewritten, in order to refer to both the bride and the groom; the adaptation is so pointed that the man comes before the woman in the text.[28] This experiment is not repeated, so far as we know, until the post-Vatican II reforms.

Of particular importance to England is the Durham Collectar, an Anglo-Saxon ritual, which has been variously dated in the ninth and tenth centuries.[29] The precise dating does not affect our discussion here, but what we find in the rite *ad sponsas benedicendas* is the Gregorian form, complete with collect, *super oblata, hanc igitur*, the classic blessing *deus qui potestate virtutis* (with its introductory prayer), and the post-communion prayer. Into the order are inserted two readings (1 Cor. 6.15–20; Matt. 22.2–14), and the nuptial blessing is the old version, with singular ending. Of great interest is what comes at the end. A blessing in the thoroughly medieval form (*benedicat vos* . . .), followed by another short one. Then comes a blessing of the bedchamber followed by other blessings, which include the ring, and the bed itself.

We shall discuss in a later chapter the origin and importance of these prayers and rites. For the present we simply note of the Durham Collectar that it illustrates the way in which the Gregorian mass and an earlier domestic marriage rite are combined.[30] Whether the blessing of both at the end of mass is a prayer that was written to form a bridge between the new mass form and the older domestic rite is also unclear. But the service as it stands is already made up of different elements, and that is a critical step for any rite to make.

e. Readings

Apart from the Durham Collectar, nothing has been said so far about the choice of readings at a nuptial mass. The Würzburg Lectionary takes us back to the era before the known texts of the Gregorian Sacramentary, according to Morin,[31] as far back as the end of the sixth century. The readings indicate Roman usage, and for the service described as *ad sponsas velandas* (the earlier Gregorian nomenclature), we find a choice of epistle, either 1 Cor. 6.15–20, or 7.32–5. The former warns us to shun fornication, and the latter is an implicit commendation of the celibate life—hardly the sort of readings to go down well with a young couple! The first reading persists in lectionaries throughout the period before, during, and immediately after the Gregorian Sacramentary.[32] An interesting exception is the so-called Pontifical of Poitiers, a tenth-century book,[33] which gives Isa. 61.10–11 as the first reading, a daring and beautiful idea, which is not repeated in the Middle Ages, and which was probably chosen because it refers to wedding-garlands and bridal robes. The most significant absence is Eph. 5.22–33, the Christ-bridegroom image. (Ritzer could only find this once, and much later, in the twelfth-century Troyes Missal.[34])

Greater variety is seen in the choice of gospel-readings. The earliest one for the marriage rite is an Anglo-Saxon Evangeliary, written about 700, but showing signs of Italian influence. For *in velanda* (note the brevity of the title) the wedding in Cana is given, John 2.1–11. In Frere's exhaustive study of the gospel readings, John 3.27–9 occurs for *ad velandam maritatam*, referring to Christ as the bridegroom, but the later books tend to give Matt. 19.1–6 as the gospel, with its description of a man leaving his family and staying by the same wife. An Italian lectionary dating from the end of the eighth century directs the parable of the wedding feast (Matt. 22.2–14).[35]

f. Nicholas I's reply to the Bulgarians, 13 November 866

How can we see the Gregorian rite actually happening at a wedding? The text simply gives the prayers, and we are left to guess the accompanying procedures. Fortunately we have a corroborative text in the form of the 'reply' which Pope Nicholas I gave to the Bulgarians when they enquired about joining communion with Rome in 866. Naturally that part of the reply which relates to the marriage rite, like much of the rest of what he has to say, is framed in such a way as would make sense to people accustomed to the ninth-century Byzantine rite:[36] Nicholas is anxious to explain differences.

The Pope's words yield a great deal of background material. A betrothal ceremony is described, in which the pair agree to pledge themselves to be married some time in the future (*futurarum sunt nuptiarum promissa foedera*), and this is symbolized by the giving of a ring and a gift, according to an established custom. All this takes place some time before the wedding, and it bears out the procedure which we observed in an earlier chapter, that the betrothal and marriage rites were separate.

When he goes on to talk about the marriage itself, the ground is familiar. They both come to church *cum oblationibus quas offerre debent deo* ('with gifts which they must offer to God'). They receive the blessing and veiling of the priest, which Nicholas compares with the blessing God gave to Adam and Eve before he told them to 'be fruitful and increase'; and he compares this blessing also with what Tobias prayed, in company with his wife, before they slept together. (The veil is not to be taken when people marry for the second time.) After the wedding, the couple wear crowns on their heads outside the church, but the crowns are special ones, reserved for use at weddings only. Pope Nicholas describes this procedure as the *iura nuptiarum* and the *pacta coniugiorum sollemnia*, strong language, reminiscent of some of the prayers in the Sacramentaries.

The betrothal ceremony (with which the Bulgarians would have been familiar) is a separate affair, and no mention is made of whether it happens in church or not, but it involves consent, and the giving of gifts, and it is (as in Israel of old) binding. The marriage service is clearly a mass, and involves the *couple* offering the gifts, which seems somewhat strange, since the Gregorian and Gelasian books have *secreta* and *hanc igitur* formulae which refer to the bride, but not the groom. The blessing and veiling is also meant to be for both the bridal pair, which also seems strange, unless Nicholas is giving a kind of shorthand, in order to convince the Bulgarians (who would have known no blessings of bride only).

g. *The Marriage of Judith, the daughter of Charles the Bald, and King Edilwulf of Essex—856*

Hincmar of Reims was already involved in 860 in the unhappy affair of King Lothar II, who wanted to divorce his wife. Hincmar involved Nicholas I in the fight that followed. But four years earlier he recorded the rite used at the marriage of another royal, King Edilwulf of Essex to the daughter of Charles the Bald.[37] In this service the ring-blessing and giving precedes a series of blessings, one of which seems to be an adaptation of the Gelasian preparatory prayer; the ring-giving and the giving of the bride to the groom are both pronounced by the priest (in this case, doubtless Hincmar himself). No clue is given as to *where* the rite took place in relation to the mass, but it would seem that these ceremonies were performed at the end of the nuptial mass itself. The rite here cannot be said to be typical of Frankish practice, but it does give us evidence of what may have been an older rite, domestic in character, and involving not only the ring, but also (as here) other precious gifts.

h. *Conclusion*

The Roman Sacramentaries give part of the foundation of the marriage rites of the medieval West. Behind them can be discerned, as recent studies have suggested, a considerable tradition of extemporizing prayers on set themes for certain occasions alongside an established custom of writing such compositions down.[38] Only in the long nuptial blessing do we see an item of liturgical genre distinctive about the nuptial mass in the Roman rite, and, for all the differences between these prayers as they appear in the Leonine/Gelasian tradition on the one hand, and the Gregorian on the other, they have the same structure, the only major difference being the inclusion in the Gregorian of the Ephesians analogy of the bridegroom Christ. If the assumptions are correct about the evolution of the Sacramentaries from *libelli missarum*, and these, in turn, from a previous tradition of extemporizing, then we can identify the nuptial blessing as one ingredient which was as much subject to this evolution as all the other prayers.

The set themes would have been as follows: creation, creation of man, creation of woman, with reference to the blessing of God and the command to multiply the human race; prayer for the bride (and, outside the Roman tradition, the bridegroom also), and for the future married life, for marital virtues of fidelity and love, for grace to follow the examples of the esteemed characters of the Old Testament, for the gift of children and children's children, and for life in eternity.[39]

Also discernible behind the Sacramentaries is a conflict between the Roman tradition of blessing the bride only, and the rest of Europe, which, in the Spanish and Frankish traditions, knew only blessings of the bride and bridegroom. In the Gelasian Sacramentary we can see this in the added blessing at the end of the mass, and, perhaps, in the *secreta*, which is deliberately bride-centred in order to rationalize the exclusively bridal *hanc igitur* and nuptial blessing. In the Gregorian Sacramentary this conflict is gleaned from the important manuscript variants at the end of the blessing. Moreover in a Frankish royal wedding, we find important evidence for the use of the ring, ritually expressed, at a service that seems to be at the end of a mass, but nonetheless contains Gelasian influence. In an important article the Dutch scholar De Jong[40] argued some years ago for the authenticity of the bridal nuptial blessing, linking it closely with the Ephesians analogy (even though this does not appear in the Leonine prayer). He attempted to show that the earlier Roman tradition blessed both the bridal pair, but that in the period giving rise to the Sacramentaries a bridal blessing developed, arising out of the lower status given to woman in the ancient world, and also in order to identify the bride with the Church, taking up the imagery of Ephesians. One of De Jong's intentions was to save the bridal blessing from possible suppression in the wake of liturgical reform at the Second Vatican Council, and his article was (in part) successful.[41]

There is, however, no concrete evidence for De Jong's theory, and, in any case, Metz's[42] thorough study of the rite of consecration of virgins has demonstrated that the blessing of virgins with the veil during a special mass arose from the corresponding blessing of the bride which we see in the Sacramentaries, and not *vice versa*, which would further support the notion that the bridal blessing is a very old Roman tradition. The question really centres round the *use* of the Ephesians passage, and I would venture to suggest that it was inserted as a relatively new idea by the author of the Gregorian prayer (it is not a favourite image of marriage among the Fathers) in order to explain an already-existing and long-standing custom at Rome which went right back to pagan times. The fact that the modern mind finds it hard to understand should not blind us from its real origins, which in any case persist in popular religion to this very day, for we still speak of the wedding as 'the bride's day'!

So, from the Sacramentaries we see a developed rite, and a developed theology expressed in that rite, drawing on both biblical and non-biblical concepts. In the Leonine the rite has a distinct shape, which the Gelasian and Gregorian books elaborate and adapt, the latter in the great masterpiece, the long blessing, *deus qui potestate virtutis*, which give to Western Europe a liturgical expression of marriage at once fine and one-sided. This one-sidedness meets with Spanish and Frankish adaptation by the insertion of a new prayer altogether in Gelasian books, and the plural ending in some Gregorian books. But neither of these adaptations succeeds entirely. The Middle Ages are already on their way, and we have entered an era of accumulation rather than originality.

2 Visigothic Creativity

How the ancient Visigothic Kingdom ordered its liturgical life has long been a matter of fascination among liturgists, but, frustratingly enough, we do not have any firm marriage rite texts before the turn of the eleventh century. However, we can attempt some sort of reconstruction with the aid of certain tools. First of all, Férotin's[1] vast study of the *Liber Ordinum* (hereafter referred to as *LO*) of Silos in Old Castile contains two related marriage rites, an examination of which (with the aid of Visigothic material) can probe behind these formulae to something resembling indigenous liturgy as far back as the fifth century, a daring but rewarding adventure.

Since his time a number of important studies have been made, of the Daily Office,[2] the rites of Initiation,[3] and the Eucharist,[4] all of which point to certain Visigothic features, which are most obvious for being manifestly *un*-Roman. These include a tendency to elaborate liturgical traditions taken over from elsewhere, as instanced by Brou in the psalm-collects.[5] Then there are the editions of the tenth/eleventh-century Roda and Vich books, mixing the Roman Gregorian rite with other elements which are to be found in the *LO*.[6] Of great importance to the discussion also is the account of marriage procedure given by Isidore of Seville, which has not been given sufficient attention by scholars hitherto.[7] Finally, and perhaps most important of all, the influence of Visigothic euchology and liturgical customs in marriage rites is abundantly plain in the later medieval books of Southern France, as well as in the eccentric tenth-century Fulda Sacramentary; and the influence is wider still, if the spread of individual prayers to other local rites is also taken into account.

a. The Liber Ordinum

Nothing could be more different from the Roman Sacramentary tradition, for what Ritzer says of the *Liber Ordinum* is indeed true, 'The Mozarabic rite shows a particularly rich development of the marriage service'.[8] The two rites which it contains (A and B in Férotin's terminology) both date from the eleventh century. A was written down by a priest, called John, in 1039; closely related to it is B, which was finished on 18 May 1052, and presented to Pope Alexander II in 1065 when papal legates were on their way to suppress the old Visigothic liturgy. It was written by a priest called Bartholomew, on the orders of the abbot of the monastery of St Prudentius at Laturce, in the province of Legrono; the manuscript shows signs of a few corrections by a later hand, but none which add or subtract in any way from the marriage rite.[9]

B begins with an order for blessing the bedchamber, quite different from what we saw in the Durham Collectar,[10] which comes *after* the mass, and whose prayer forms are briefer. The opening directions in B describe a service taking place late in the afternoon before the wedding, with sprinkling of salt in the bedchamber itself, or throughout the house. The opening prayer asks for God's blessing on the dwelling of the couple. There follows a longer and unmistakably Visigothic blessing, with 'Amens' interposed after each clause, asking for *i.* sanctification of the marriage-union, expulsion of all evil spirits with the help of angels, *ii.* honesty of living, *iii.* fine ideals not 'shipwrecked' by wrong desire, and *iv.* that their *'pudicitiae honestas'* may be rewarded by sharing in the eternal kingdom. The manuscript breaks off at this point; there were probably other prayers to conclude this domestic part of the rite.

This blessing is quite different from the prayers we have seen so far. For a start, linguistically it uses a new format, with the imperative *'benedicito'* at the beginning. Unlike the Gregorian nuptial blessing, this prayer is clearly broken up into short sections—the *Amens* do not seem to be a recent addition; and it also is concerned with the couple and the wedding feast, as well as the bedchamber. The build-up of opening verse and prayer suggest that it might have been used as a separate rite without the mass etc., which follows the next day; given the peculiar characteristics of this prayer, this might place it considerably earlier in the Visigothic tradition than the eleventh century. But it could also have been specially composed to dampen down the high spirits of the wedding feast, a sort of liturgical kill-joy.[11] After the break in the manuscript we find ourselves, according to Férotin, at Vespers, which ends with a verse, and a blessing, asking God to receive the vows (*vota*), which presumably refers to the intention to be joined together. A new office comes next, entitled *ordo arrarum*, the 'order of pledges'.[12] Evidence suggests that the giving of a wedding-token went quite far back in Spain, but in the opening sentence of this rite, it is clearly a second-best to the giving of *two* rings (N.B. the first appearance). The prayer which immediately follows, however, refers explicitly to the tokens, and invokes the example of the marriage of Isaac and Rebecca in this practice, and seeks God's blessing on the union to be made. Again the prayer goes back earlier than the date of the manuscript, most probably to the time when tokens were used exclusively, and rings were occasionally, if ever, given.[13] Another short prayer comes now, asking that the pledges may be accepted by God, but 'A' has another prayer, and, like the bedchamber blessing, it is broken up into short sections, and punctuated by Amens; it begins with the imperative formula *benedic, domine*, and asks for blessing on the tokens, mentioning Abraham and Sarah, Isaac and Rebecca, and Jacob and Rachel; and it uses horticultural imagery: 'may they flourish like the rose planted in Jericho'. They then give rings to each other.

The 'Order for blessing those who are newly married' appears next in the manuscript, which in both texts seem to come just before communion.[14] The girl's family (or her supporters) give her by the hand to the priest (A just says that 'they' approach the priest), and both the bride and bride-groom are veiled with a pall, the woman completely, the man just over his shoulders. In each rite three prayers follow, the first a bidding, unmistakably referring to both throughout. This is by the eleventh century an old prayer, for it appears in the (domestic) rite of the ninth-century Bobbio Missal.[15] The first blessing now comes: marriage for the propagation of children, creation of woman from man, man and woman one flesh in marriage; and then the blessing-clauses, each punc-tuated by *Amen*, asking for love, mutual support, fidelity, material blessings, and children, love for others, long life, eternal desires, see children's children, and the eternal king-dom. This is the longest prayer in the tradition so far, and, we may surmise, regarded as *the* blessing. But the two manu-scripts take different tacks at this stage. B continues with a 'blessing of the girl only', a prayer about the veiling, which tries to work out specifically female symbolism from it, '*pudor*' and chastity and obedience, as well as the procreation of children. It appears to be a later composition than the other prayers, and written in order to make sense of the veiling, perhaps under direct or indirect Roman influence.[16] Another blessing speaks of virtues of friendship with others as well as parenthood, and the priest then hands the girl over to the man, telling them to abstain from sexual intercourse, because they are about to communicate; after communion, the deacon gives the dismissal, and another short blessing is given, but not specifically marital in its content.

Instead of the 'blessing of the girl only', A has the longest blessing of any Western rite,[17] a remarkable *catena* of biblical and non-biblical material, more 'worked out' on paper than extemporized by a gifted celebrant. The sequence of ideas is familiar: creation of man in the image of God (with quote about it not being good to be alone); blessing on both (with quote about man leaving family to set up home of his own), as on Abraham . . . . as well as Zachariah and Elisabeth; that they may be brought together in all that they do; and continue to be aware of God's power, and thereby remain good to each other and not fall into evil. The prayer lacks smoothness, and on closer inspection reveals the following features: the initial section, with its laboured biblical allusions does not fit well with the central section about marital unity in life (where the *Amens* are frequent); and the final section seems to be a separate composition, beginning *respice* (look down), as in the Gregorian nuptial blessing. The author appears to be drawing on at least two separate sources. The Lord's Prayer follows, together with its embolism, the communion antiphon, communion of the couple, and a short blessing (similar to the one in B given *before* communion), and the same short blessing which appears at the end of B. But now comes the real novelty: the priest hands the girl over to the man and after pronouncing the invocation of the Trinity, he recites the Vulgate version of the 'Raguel' prayer over Tobias and Sarah,[18] joining the couple together. The service moves to a swift conclusion with the priest advising the couple to come again to communion, and a short dismissal.

What have we here? Two rites which have much in common, but which diverge significantly in the latter part of the wedding mass. Both place the main nuptial blessing before the communion, with B adding a blessing of the bride only, while A employs a much longer and involved blessing of both. After communion the couple are joined together by the priest, but in A the priest has a specific prayer, taken word-for-word from the mouth of Raguel, thus assuming for the Christian family the paternal role. It is a neat use of a biblical text to give liturgical expression to an emerging tradition.

What lies behind the rites? It is impossible to say with certainty. The blessing of the chamber at the beginning of B (A lacks this entirely) is in all probability an old domestic rite, originally used on its own, to which the mass was added for those who wanted to come to church: it is inconceivable that the couple were intended to live together before marriage.[19] The 'order of pledges' betrays an earlier custom by its very title, and by the content of the main prayer (surely the tokens antedate the ring?); but here is yet another remarkable Visigothic development, for we have *two* rings. In the mass the main blessing comes *before* communion, as at Rome. Whether or not this was the original practice when a mass was celebrated at marriage, it is hard to tell, but it probably was, in view of the Spanish-Frankish custom of having special blessings before communion, though these were originally episcopal.[20] Signs of varied composition are discernible at this point, however, for in B there is a self-consciously bridal blessing, the only one in the entire Visigothic repertoire,[21] and the corresponding prayer in A is a strange mixture of material, biblical and Visigothic (the central section, with the 'Amens'), and a Roman-sounding conclusion.[22] It could be that *LO* is reflecting a certain ordered eclecticism at this point; and I suggest that Roman influence is at work, however indirectly.

Another point worth noting is the way in which B spreads the marriage rites over four stages—blessing of the chamber, Vespers,[23] giving of tokens, and the mass. Whether or not the last three followed in close or distant succession would obviously depend on circumstances, but it would appear from the manuscripts that the giving of tokens by this time took place immediately before the mass; but it does seem clear that originally the giving of tokens was part of a separate rite, corresponding to the betrothal described by Nicholas I in his reply to the Bulgarians, and, indeed, alluded to much earlier in known Christian practice.[24]

Why do B and A diverge? Again, this is impossible to say. The two most important points of difference (the blessing of the girl in B, and the presence of the 'Raguel' prayer in A) suggest that A is the more developed, even though it is the earlier; in any case the fact that A is only earlier by a matter of thirteen years need not matter. This would make the blessing of the girl a later addition, not in any sense a long-established custom. The most important features of these rites are the way in which popular customs are incorporated into the liturgy, in the office for the blessing of tokens; the equality of the sexes of the rites as a whole, with blessings of both the man and woman, and the giving of two rings; and the creative use of a native Latin euchology. The Visigothic marriage rites must have been well in advance of Roman ones in their time.

b. Isidore of Seville, c. 560–636

Isidore became Archbishop of Seville in succession to his brother in 600, a post of considerable prestige in the Spanish Church, and one from which he wrote a number of important works, including the *De ecclesiasticis officiis*, which sets out the way in which the Spanish Church was organized and how it worshipped. In a section dealing with marriage[25] he begins with a rationale for the nuptial blessing by the priest, in which he quotes the Genesis narrative, that God made man in his image, blessed the couple, and told them to be fruitful.[26] This took place in paradise, so the blessing happens in church. Weddings should be carried out properly and monogamously. Wives are veiled when they are married, as a sign of submissiveness, and the example of Rebecca is called in as support.[27] The blessing by the priest is indissoluble. The garland (*vitta*) worn by the couple is white and purple, the former symbolizing purity, the latter the blood of future generations; but the couple should abstain from relations unless they want children. A ring is given by the groom to the bride, as a token of faith, and it is placed on the fourth finger, because (according to an ancient tradition) the vein of this finger goes to the heart. The *dotales tabulae* are then mentioned, which begin the reason for marriage, namely the creation of children.

A number of points can be raised from this passage. In common with Augustine (and others) Isidore links creation with blessing in Genesis, and abstaining because sexual relations should only take place for children with Paul's warning in 1 Cor. 7; and, like Augustine, the marriage contract is an essential part of marriage.[28] Then, marriages should take place in church, and before a priest, whose blessing cannot be 'undone'. This is probably more than just a statement, but an actual defence, aimed at those who would contract marriages privately, or who just live together. Moreover, brides are veiled, and this veiling is linked with the priestly blessing. Finally, folklore is incorporated into the rite, in the quaint rationalization given to the garlands.[29] Thus Isidore corroborates some of the practice we have seen in the *LO*, though there is much that is missing. Some time between the seventh and eleventh centuries *two* rings came to be given, and the rite developed into its more extended form. Nothing in what he says seems to imply a special blessing of the bride, and he may link the giving of the ring with the settling of the marriage contract (the *tabulae*), but this is not clear.

c. *The Pontifical of Roda and the Sacramentary of Vich*

The Pontifical of Roda and the Sacramentary of Vich[30] are two important Catalonian rites, dating from the turn of the eleventh and the first half of the eleventh centuries, respectively. Each comes from the province of Tarragona, in Eastern Spain; Vich is the diocesan seat, and Roda's rite is a pontifical one, though it has been subsequently adapted for the use of presbyters. Both contain marriage rites which are a kind of halfway house between *LO* and the Gregorian Sacramentary; whereas Roman influence *may* lie behind some parts of *LO*, Roda and Vich show unmistakable signs of the incorporation of Roman material. But they still spread the various services over three rites (Vespers has disappeared), consisting of the blessing of the tokens, the blessing of the chamber, and the nuptial mass itself. They each do it in approximately the same manner, but there are slight differences in the order of prayers in the mass.

In the blessing of tokens the opening prayer from *LO* reappears, which is followed by a new prayer, which has nothing to do with marriage-tokens, but simply asks for God's favour on the couple; a clumsy composition, we do not come across it again. The third prayer comes from *LO* A, with the lavish image of the rose in Jericho, but Olivar notes wryly that it has been romanized, because the intercalated 'Amens' have gone in the editorial process.[31] The blessing of the bed-chamber is the same as *LO* B, with the three prayers in their sequence, but Vich omits the third and longest prayer, which we suggested before was an ancient Visigothic composition.

In the mass, Roman structure and influence is obvious. The Gregorian prayers, collect, etc., appear, together with the proper preface and *hanc igitur*. Before the Pax, the same procedure is adopted as *LO*: the wedding-party comes forward, and the bride's hand is given to the priest, and the veil is spread over bride and groom (shoulders only for the groom). From this point until after the communion the orders in Roda and Vich diverge, but the material is substantially the same. Several of the long blessings in *LO* are placed around the Gregorian nuptial blessing and its introductory prayer, and in both we come across the use of the preface-form ('Lift up your hearts')[32] for the first time, a custom that we shall encounter again as the Middle Ages progress; the plural-ending version is used in each case. Then Roda and Vich also include a special blessing from *LO* for the girl only, when she marries a widower, thus adapting its use; but there are significant textual changes, in a definitely Roman direction, for the Visigothic Amens disappear in both versions, and the ending is singularized (in *LO* it was plural). We have argued a case for concluding that the prayer was originally written under Roman influence.[33] Just before the Pax Roda inserts a prayer which one of the manuscripts suggests was originally used only by bishops, a pontifical prayer with Byzantine echoes which still has the old Visigothic 'Amens';[34] we have included this prayer in Appendix I, in the collection of nuptial blessing-prayers, since it seems to characterize the vivacity, biblical allusion, and pastoral thrust of the ancient Spanish euchological tradition. At the Pax the priest hands the girl over to the man, using the 'Raguel' prayer from *LO*, but omitting the reference to God 'joining' the couple. Why? Perhaps because the 'joining' was supposed to have taken place already, and the use of such a prayer, albeit biblical in source, was taken to imply priestly powers which the churches of Catalonia did not accept; whatever the reason, the 'excision' seems deliberate. The couple are warned to abstain from sexual relations for three nights, out of reverence.

The main difference between Roda and Vich is that the former places a series of three blessing-prayers right at the end of the mass, whereas the latter puts them between the main nuptial blessing and the communion. The first is the main blessing from *LO*, but without the tell-tale Visigothic Amens; the second is a short one, from *LO* again; the third is new, and reappears in England later: 'God of Abraham, Isaac, Jacob . . . sow the seed of eternal life in their hearts . . . .'[35] (A later hand in Vich puts this after communion, thus bringing it into line with Roda.)

Roda and Vich show the way in which the Roman rite could remain intact, as long as foreign elements were added without actually dislodging anything Gregorian. It must be confessed that pre-communion and post-communion blessings make up an unbearable clutter, but this observation may simply reflect the outlook of another era altogether; nonetheless, the compilers of these two rites, working along such similar paths, do betray a desire to have the best of both worlds, to bless both the man and the wife, before communion, but also to bless the bride only; and in so doing, they show their anxiety by the new use of the *LO* bridal blessing now reserved for when the bride marries a widower. The addition of the preface-formula to the Gregorian nuptial blessing (a liturgical convention becoming popular in other solemn blessings at this time) is their last resort to give the Gregorian prayer that prominence which it seems to deserve.

By way of postscript to these wonderful works of art, it is significant that the only prayers in *LO* B and Vich which do not occur elsewhere again are two independent compositions which each make mention of the liturgical veil.[36] In other words, the editors wanted to give liturgical expression to a folk-custom; the Sacramentary traditions of Rome had never sought to do this.

d. *The Bobbio Missal*

The Bobbio Missal is a ninth-century mass-book of Irish–Spanish origins, probably written for the use of travelling monks, and is part of the great Irish monastic missionary movement during the Dark Ages. The 'blessing of the bedchamber over those being married',[37] as the rite is called, is another domestic rite, reflecting the liturgical practice of a missionary church, antedating any popular tradition of a nuptial mass. There are three prayers.

The first is a bidding, the same one as appears before the main blessing prior to communion in *LO*, Roda, and Vich. The second is one of the blessings used in *LO* for the blessing of a couple where the groom is a widower; it mentions the bridal pair, from the beginning, but invokes the example of holy women, after the manner of the Gregorian nuptial blessing: 'the charity of Sarah, the penitence of Rebecca, the love of Rachel, the grace and charity of Susanna . . . . .' The sequence of ideas is the desire of the couple for priestly blessing, joining together, the Old Testament women, blessing on a good marriage, and everlasting joys. The third blessing is specifically for those who marry a second time, and is again from *LO*. The themes are: a remedy for human frailty (!), propagation of human race, the marriage of Ruth, Paul's reluctant condoning of marriage after the death of first partner, example in home-making to those who visit, and example of virtue in the Church. The Bobbio Missal seems to be a short version of *LO* and the Catalonian books, offsetting the grandiose and ideal setting of these other rites by something which appears to be derivative, and essentially domestic in character.

e. The Fulda Sacramentary

Although it is a tenth-century document, all the signs point to its reliance on these other sources. Its marriage rite[38] consists of a mass with special ceremonies inserted after the canon and at the end, in the way we have seen in *LO*, Roda, and Vich. The two collects are the two prayers in the Gelasian books, but the *super oblata* (NB so-called) is a simplified version of the Gelasian, the gifts being offered by both men and women! There is an additional prayer at this point, which is a new composition, closely linking the offering with the intention to be married, and asking for God's strength to persevere in the new relationship. The *hanc igitur* is the Gregorian prayer reworked to mention bride and bridegroom, and with more personal sentiments; it has an alternative, which is a heavy composition whose sources are not clear.[39]

After the canon the two Gelasian blessings occur, both the short introductory and the long blessing, which is touched up in places but substantially the same; it is bridal throughout (the priest blesses 'her' in the directions), but it is followed by a blessing 'over each', another new piece of work, which reproduces a familiar structure, though the style is somewhat different from what we have seen before—creation, reason for marriage, supplication for the couple, marital virtues, but with an underlying theme throughout of avoiding lust.[40] After the communion a re-worked Gelasian prayer follows, together with its second post-communion; then the couple come forward to the priest (with their support-parties), the priest veils the bride (only), and recites the two main blessings from *LO* (both of which appear in Roda and Vich, but separated).[41] Afterwards he gives the girl to the man, and tells them to abstain from sexual relations that night, because they have just received communion; and the rite ends with the dismissal.

The Fulda book may never have been used but simply put together as a private project by a monk interested in liturgical forms; but it is part of the Visigothic sphere of influence in the liturgical traditions of the Middle Ages. In this marriage rite we find a mixture of Gelasian, Visigothic, and 'local' features. The mass is basically Gelasian, even to the extent of including the Gelasian nuptial blessing, which is unique at this stage, but as if to compensate for a bridal blessing, a new prayer is added which is not found elsewhere. The mass ends with the Visigothic 'giving-away' rite preceded by two Visigothic blessings, but without any formula for the giving-away.

f. Local influence

The Visigothic marriage customs may have travelled into the mind of a tenth-century German monk with an eclectic approach to liturgy making, but they soon permeated what is now called French Catalonia,[42] as witnessed by three important texts from the High Middle Ages. The so-called Cahors Missal dates from the second quarter of the twelfth century, the same century in which the old town got its new cathedral.[43] The pre-mass rite contains new elements, similar to the Anglo-Norman rite of 'consent', which we shall examine later in this chapter; but the passionate temperament of the Midi made their public consent dependent on *love* (not *will*), and the priest gives the woman to the man (cf. *LO* and Vich). First, the ring is blessed, the *lex dotalium* is read out, the ring is given, together with the Anglo-Norman formula, and after a long blessing (found here in *LO* and Vich),[44] the tokens are blessed. The mass is of the Blessed Trinity, another Anglo-Norman feature, which we shall encounter again, but the rest is thoroughly Visigothic in essence: before the Pax the priest gives the girl to the man, a veil is placed over *both* (i.e. not just the bride, and the groom's *shoulders*) and the two Gregorian prayers are recited, the introductory, and the long blessing, preceded by the 'preface'-formula, as in Roda and Vich. After communion the prayer from Roda and Vich, 'God of Abraham . . . sow the seed of eternal life', occurs, and the whole rite ends with a short blessing, and advice to abstain from sexual relations.

The Cahors Missal mixes three features—Anglo-Norman material, which we shall see later, the Gregorian blessing, together with the Visigothic blessing of the tokens, preface-form at the main blessing, and the concluding rite. But unlike Fulda the entire rite hangs together well, for the mixture is judicious, and at no point is verbosity allowed to take over from sense.

Another marriage rite from the South of France, and also from the twelfth century, is a ritual belonging to the cathedral of Albi.[45] Unlike Cahors, there are no Anglo-Norman features at all. The rite begins with the blessing of the ring, using the Visigothic prayer of blessing the tokens, as in *LO*, Roda and Vich. The *carta sponsalicii* are read out at this point, probably a Visigothic custom, for there are suggestions in *LO* (as we have seen) that the contract belonged with the betrothal ceremony, of which the blessing of tokens is the survival. The mass is the Gregorian one (not of the Trinity, as Cahors), and before the Pax the two Gregorian prayers are recited, with the second in the preface-form (singular ending). After communion come two blessings, both from Roda and Vich, and the first also in *LO* (the long blessing). Then the priest gives the girl to the man with the formula found at the end of the *LO* A rite, the words given to Raguel at the marriage of Tobias and Sarah. This is the most important feature of the rite, for we have not seen this formula used since *LO* A. There are prayers for use at home which include (of all things) the offering of incense, surely a delight to some house-proud new bride; at the end the prayer, 'God of Abraham . . . sow the seed of eternal life', occurs again. Whereas in Cahors Visigothic influence is more in principle than in euchology, at Albi we have unmistakable use of material from *LO*, Roda and Vich, even to the point that the rites at the end of the mass begin to overshadow the conventional Gregorian material before the communion.

The Arles Pontifical of the thirteenth[46] century is in many respects similar to Albi. The tokens are blessed with the two formulae from Roda, Vich, and *LO* A, and the Gregorian mass follows. Before the Pax the couple come forward, the priest gives the girl to the man (as in Cahors), a veil is extended over both of them, and after invocation of the Trinity and some short *preces*, we have the Gregorian blessings, this time without the preface-formula. After the communion the rite inserts the short blessing from the Gelasian books, which is not in the least incongruous, but interesting as a piece of source-use by the compiler; then after a short blessing the priest joins the couple, and pronounces the 'Raguel' prayer, and dismisses them. Clearly dependent on the tradition represented by Cahors, Arles still goes its own way, simplifying the opening rite of blessing the tokens, probably because the ring was not yet in use at Arles, but keeping the same basic structure we can see in Cahors, as well as Albi; the Gelasian prayer is a point of originality, too.

What does this amount to? A gradual spread of the Visigothic rite of blessing the tokens/ring before the mass, and of 'joining' the couple with the 'Raguel' prayer at the end, and the inclusion of Visigothic blessings at the beginning and the end of the rite. None of them shows quite the degree of liturgical clutter of blessings before and after communion which we can see in Vich and, to a lesser extent, Fulda. On the other hand, a certain conflict is discernible between the two blessing-sections, before and after communion, for in both Cahors and Arles the couple are 'given' to each other by the priest just before the nuptial blessing before the Pax, and then at the end of the mass the priest 'joins' them with the 'Raguel' prayer.

g. *Local persistence*

In the Seminary Library at Gerona, in Catalonia, there is a local ritual which can be dated to somewhere in the second half of the thirteenth century; it contains a marriage rite which in one way typifies the rites of the time, but has one ingredient of considerable interest, to which Daniel Codina drew attention some years ago.[47] The two main 'strata' of the rite are by now almost expected: the old Gregorian Mass, with marriage-readings, together with the Spanish pre-mass rite of betrothal (consisting of the blessing of the ring, and the consent) and the 'giving away' right at the end (with extra short blessings). The peculiar feature is that the priest has to insist on the giving of the *dos* before the marriage can happen, an aspect of the rite which Codina traces back to the *Lex Visigothorum*, and which was enforced by a local synod at Gerona.

A group of rites from the diocese of Elne, just south of Perpignan, have recently been run to ground and examined by

Molin[48]; they consist of a fourteenth-century Sacramentary, and a late fifteenth and an early sixteenth-century Missal. They all have the same structure, except that, for some unknown reason, only the Sacramentary directs that banns should be given. The pre-mass rite has the usual blessing of the ring (but only one), together with a curious (and quite local) custom of blessing some bread, which only appears in the two later Missals. The nuptial blessing is given (in preface-form) *after* mass, with the veil over both bride and groom (shoulders only), and the veil appears to have had knots tied in it, perhaps to symbolize the union of marriage. The couple are given to each other with a special formula, and the 'Raguel' prayer is said, but no less than three times, and with the laying on of hands, another peculiarity.

The Avignon rite[49] of the late fourteenth century lays down instructions about the notification of banns, and the priest asks for the consent of the couple; they pledge their troth in the form, 'I give my body to you, as husband', to which the bride replies in a similar vein; they then say to each other that 'I receive you as my wife/husband', and the ring and coins are blessed. The ring giving is equally deliberate, and is followed by the giving of the *carta*, after which the couple kiss, as a sign of their troth, as the rubrics say. The nuptial blessing is given after mass, and is followed by the giving of blessed bread and wine, and the giving of the woman to the man by the priest. All in all, an austere rite, remarkably lacking in the blessings which are so freely multiplied elsewhere.

A fifteenth-century Bordeaux[50] rite starts at the door, and after an opening collect, which is a prayer for protection (nothing explicitly to do with marriage), and the consent-giving, involves kissing a cross, which is a peculiarity to this rite. The ring and '*arras*' are blessed, and the mass of the Trinity follows, but with the unusual epistle reading, Eph. 5.22–33, exceptional in the West until Trent, but a favourite in the Byzantine rites. The nuptial blessing takes place *before* communion.

To go on to the sixteenth century, the pattern adopted by Vich, together with the form of consent-giving at the beginning, appears to have solidified in the various local Spanish rites, though not without some variation. Palencia (1508)[51] starts the service at the church door, and has a group of Anglo-Norman prayers at the beginning, as do Salamanca

(1532),[52] Toledo (1554),[53] and Cuenca (1560),[54] but not Valencia (1514)[55] or Tarragona (1530),[56] both of which are in the Catalonian orbit. All of them have the explanation and publishing of banns, together with the consent and the ring-giving in the vernacular, and it is clear from the formulae that in some places two rings were in use, whereas others continued to use only one. The mass of the Trinity is used, except at Valencia (1514), which again holds out on its own, with the mass of the Holy Spirit. And Valencia (1514) and Tarragona (1530) keep to the later Visigothic tradition of placing the nuptial blessing after the communion, whereas the others have it in the Roman position. But all these rites place the 'Raguel' prayer after mass, and have a formula for the priest to 'give away' the couple to each other. Cuenca (1560) has a particularly fine blessing-prayer just before mass, punctuated with Amens in the traditional manner; and also directs the *iugale* to be placed across the bride and groom, as well as the veil over the head of the bride and the shoulders of the groom, during the nuptial blessing.

What are the 'Spanish symptoms'? There does not seem to be a uniform pattern for the position of the nuptial blessing, though the Spanish rites which are 'purer' place it at the end of mass, and often in a preface-form. It is in the giving-away of the bride by the priest at the end of the service that we have the surest sign of things Spanish, a tradition seen in *Liber Ordinum* and the Sacramentary of Vich. The way in which the consent is given and expressed varies, but the formulae are short and never reach the poetic lengths of the English tradition; and even though the early Spanish tradition knew great rhetorical heights in blessing-prayers, that tradition is soon mellowed and romanized, in contrast to the proliferation of blessing-prayers in the English rites of the same era. Nevertheless, the Spanish rites hold their own,[57] adapting to new needs, such as the giving of the consent by the couple. Ironically, it is in Catalonia, which in the eleventh century adapted more easily to the Romanizing movement (witnessed by Roda and Vich) that Visigothic peculiarities persist more strongly in the sixteenth century; unlike the rites of Old Castile, which were more resistant to Rome (witnessed by *LO*) initially, but which later on adopt a more conventional Anglo-Norman aspect. It is to this varied Anglo-Norman tradition that we must now turn.

3 The Anglo-Norman Synthesis

Liturgical development in medieval Europe was a complex affair, and no less so in the rites of Christian marriage. In this section we shall look at these rites as they appear in Britain and Northern France, because of the close liturgical connection between the countries from the eleventh and twelfth centuries.

a. The Pontifical of Egbert

The Pontifical of Egbert is a manuscript which dates from the tenth century, but probably reflects liturgical practice at the time of Egbert of York in the second half of the eighth century.[1] The Order of Marriage consists of a group of prayers almost identical to the set which comes after the nuptial mass in the Durham Collectar, which we saw in an earlier chapter; in fact, the similarity seems more than coincidental. All the prayers are short.

First comes the Aaronic blessing; then a collect-type blessing, followed by a short Trinitarian blessing, not specifically marital at all. The blessing of the chamber follows, together with a blessing of the couple, mentioning Tobias and Sarah, and after it the ring is blessed. The bed is then blessed, and the rite concludes with a Trinitarian blessing, which is adapted from a prayer in the *Missale Francorum* which has nothing to do with marriage at all,[2] and the blessing 'on your wife' (taken from Tobit) which mentions at the end future offspring. The first point of interest is that it is a complete domestic rite, since, as we saw earlier, the Durham rite breaks off half-way through the blessing of the bed.[3] Then there are no mass formulae, which poses the question, whether the marriage rite in Egbert was an exclusively domestic affair, or meant to be used in conjunction with a nuptial mass, as in Durham. The Leofric Sacramentary, which is ninth century, consists of a nuptial mass, probably with some set of 'marriage prayers' at the end, but it breaks off during the first of these.[4] Related to this question is the other curious feature of the Egbert book, that slightly later on there is another set of prayers *ad sponsas benedictio*, this time shorter.[5] It begins with the prayer which we came across in Roda and Vich, 'God of Abraham . . . sow the seed', and continues with the blessing of

63

the chamber (identical to the one in the previous set, except for the addition of one short clause); then comes the short blessing which appears near the beginning of the previous rite (but this time Raphael is mentioned as a protecting angel), and the rite concludes with an adapted form of the Aaronic blessing. The two sets of prayers are obviously related, and it is tempting to suggest that the second set is later because although it contains fewer prayers (and lacks a blessing of the bed), two of its prayers are longer. The marriage of Tobias and Sarah gives inspiration to the content of the prayers in both sets. Both are domestic, and both may have been intended for use at an entirely domestic rite, even though this is hard to match up with the direction attributed to Theodore of Tarsus (a century earlier) that weddings are to be blessed during mass.[6] But the most significant discrepancy between the two is the absence in the second of any mention of the ring, which suggests that when the rites were being written, either wedding rings were not in general use, or else the wedding ring was not yet expressed in liturgical prayer, or even (still) linked with betrothal.

Another important feature of Egbert is that all the prayers are short, unlike those which are to be found in *LO,* Roda and Vich. There are no traces of any influence from the Gregorian nuptial blessing. The most recent feature seems to be the ring-blessing, since it only appears in one of the rites, and when it does, the prayer is quite short. The prayer appears repeatedly in later rites, but filled out in order to give some rationale for the symbolism of the ring in marriage.[7] Like Bobbio (but in a different style), it reflects a missionary church, in which the nuptial mass is not fully established, and probably only used for those who specifically want it. There are signs of its subsequent use in Northern France.

b. *The Anglo-Norman Benedictionals*

Before looking at the Anglo-Norman marriage rites, it is worth discussing these collections of blessings, because they form an indirect literary link with some of the long blessings which we saw in *LO.* They are for use in conjunction with a nuptial mass, when a bishop celebrates.

The first is from the Lanalet Pontifical,[8] a tenth-century collection of episcopal prayers and services, and it is entitled 'the blessing of bridegroom and bride'. In four paragraphs, each with an Amen, the sequence of ideas is as follows: Adam and Eve (referred to by the Augustinian term 'first parents'),[9] divine blessing and divinely-intended companionship, together with the jussive subjunctive 'may (God) join you together' (cf. Tobit). The second paragraph refers to the sending of Raphael to the marriage of Tobias and Sarah, and asks for the same protection from evil in the couple being married now. Then we have—for the first time in a prayer so far—the miracle at Cana as a reason for Christ's interest in and blessing of the bridal pair. Finally, in the fourth part, marital promises are mentioned, a quiet time, health of mind, joy in the procreation of children, and after this life a share in the company of the angels.

We have not seen the like before: it is indeed a fine prayer, and we find it appearing again, with or without slight emendation, in the Claudius Pontificals, of the same century, the Missal of Robert of Jumièges, and in other English and French rites as the Middle Ages progress,[10] so that it eventually becomes part of the Sarum Manual, and so used by priests in a normal marriage rite. It usually occurs in an abbreviated form, consisting only of the first paragraph; but this is not until the twelfth century in the Pontifical of Lyre[11] (in Normandy), though it is possible that the shorter form is the original.

Another pontifical blessing is to be found in the Canterbury Benedictional,[12] from the eleventh century, which has similar themes as the previous blessing, but in a different arrangement. It has three parts each concluded with Amen. The first mentions Christ's presence at Cana, which provides the rationale for blessing the couple, and also the entire congregation; the middle section deals with marital virtues (concord, charity, continence, humility, discipline, practice of the faith), and the final paragraph invokes angelic protection, though not by any particular name, and refers to the expulsion of diabolical influence, the enjoyment of peace, procreation of children, and being blessed by God, 'so that here and in eternity they may be *crowned* by God'. We do not encounter the imagery of the crown at marriage elsewhere in the Middle Ages in the West. It could be an idea picked up by someone who had travelled to the East, particularly as the crowning refers both to the present as well as the future life. This prayer is not so theological as the previous one, and it does not appear again.

That both these prayers should appear at a similar time, and in the same tradition, is of some importance, when we are assessing the development of marriage euchology in their literary style and theological content. Both antedate the Norman conquest, though the second may have been brought by Lanfranc to Canterbury from Normandy, but the scribe's hand is clearly Anglo-Saxon.[13] Apart from their intrinsic interest, they demonstrate two features of development in these blessings, which we also saw in *LO* (and, to a lesser extent, Roda and Vich), the overt use of Scripture, angelic protection as a theme, and a distinct structure, of short paragraphs. Neither occurs in the Roman Sacramentaries. It goes without saying, of course, that these blessings are of both bride and groom. Their themes were obviously deemed sufficiently fine to be taken over by later rites and incorporated into them at a time when blessing-prayers were multiplying.

c. *Anglo-Norman 'ring at the end': tenth/eleventh centuries*

The Durham Collectar showed how the Gregorian nuptial mass was added to by the insertion at the end of the possibly older rite of blessing the ring and the chamber. This combination continues in the early Anglo-Norman books.

The Benedictional of Archbishop Robert contains the same form. If the 'Robert' to whom it belonged was Robert of Jumièges, then it is a mid-eleventh-century rite; but if (as is more likely) it is the Robert who was archbishop of Rouen, then this pushes the rite back to the beginning of the century.[14] The mass contains the Gregorian formulae, together with 1 Cor. 7.32–5 as the Epistle, and John 2.1–11 as the Gospel. After the long blessing the pontifical blessing from Lanalet appears, which mentions Christ's presence at Cana, and this perhaps explains the use of the unusual Cana-miracle gospel at the mass. The preparatory prayer which normally precedes the Gregorian nuptial blessing comes after communion (an odd position), and this leads into the after-mass rite.

The first prayer after mass is an entirely new one for the blessing of the ring; all it asks for is the blessing of God on the ring, 'that she who wears it may remain in your peace, live and grow old in your love, and have a long life'. There follows a curious sequence of pseudo-psalmic verses (*manda deus*),[15] which appears again and again, and which leads into the short ring-blessing from Egbert, the giving of the ring with the invocation of the Trinity, and Ps. 127. There follow three prayers: first the 'Raguel' joining-prayer of *LO* A; en elongated version of the prayer for Raphael's protection from Egbert, and the 'God of Abraham . . . sow the seed', also from Egbert.

No directions appear as to *where* the post-mass prayers are held, though the absence of chamber/bed blessings suggests that it all took place in church. The reliance on Egbert for new prayers is significant; but the use and adaptation inherent in these prayers and formulae marks off Robert as of prime importance in subsequent rites.

Another eleventh-century rite appears in the so-called 'Red Book of Darley', now identified as a travelling missal originating from the Benedictine Abbey of New Minster at Winchester, and written about 1061.[16] The rite is called the 'blessing of brides', which is a significant title in itself. The Gregorian prayers reappear, but (more conventionally) with 1 Cor. 6.15–20 as Epistle, and Matt. 19.1–6 as Gospel. After the mass the sequence is slightly different from Robert: the psalmic verses, a prayer beginning 'bless, Lord, these young people, and sow the seed . . .', the elongated 'Raphael' prayer from Robert, the 'Raguel' blessing, the blessing of the chamber, together with the short Trinitarian blessing, and the short blessing of the bed (these last three all from Egbert). The influence of the Durham Collectar, Egbert, and Robert is clear. Why the ring at the end, when the psalmic verses which invariably go with it in later rites (and which go with it in Robert) are at the beginning? Perhaps the use of the ring was not yet established in Winchester, or else the monk responsible for compiling the service did not want to give undue prominence to it. So comes to an end the experiment initiated by the Durham Collectar (and probably before) of appending the domestic rite to the Roman mass. Whatever went on at home depended on local custom, since prayers which are said in someone's home are more likely to be tailor-made for the occasion than prayers used in church. We note a tendency for the ring to become more constant in use, and also a move away from blessing the bed. The Church is slowly taking over; in the future these quaint domestic rites do survive, but they are no longer the substance of the rite, which they once upon a time obviously were.

d. *Anglo-Norman 'ring at the beginning': twelfth century*

Early in the twelfth century the Northern European marriage rite reaches its most definitive shape, in the Anglo-Norman tradition. It is impossible to find a central or local conciliar decree that requires the consent of the couple before the mass; the only evidence we have is far back in 1012 at a provincial synod in Rouen, where the priest's presence is required, and a serious undertaking on the part of the couple—but no more. However, from the twelfth century onwards all rites of this family place the ring-ceremonies at the beginning, together with some form of consent.

In the next two centuries there are many rites to look at. The first is from England; a manuscript written in Bury St Edmunds[17] between 1125–35, and subsequently used at Laon. The service begins at the church door, presumably to indicate the preliminary nature of the pre-mass rite. The ring is blessed with the two prayers we have already seen in Robert and Egbert, but they are both pluralized to refer to both partners. Then comes the innovation: 'after this blessing has been said, the man is asked by the priest if he wishes to have her as his lawful wife. This same question is asked of the woman.' (As the canon lawyers exert influence on marital consent, in particular Peter Lombard and (later) Thomas Aquinas,[18] the man and wife have to express their desire to marry each other *publicly*, and no longer assume it as an implicit aspect of the rite, or part of a rite of betrothal not under the Church's influence.) Immediately after this consent the man gives gifts to the woman, and the priest, first receiving her by the right hand from 'the person who gives her away' (N.B. not the priest himself), hands her over to the man and they join hands; if she is a widow, her hand should be covered, if a girl, then uncovered. This becomes the invariable practice of all subsequent rites of this family. The ring is now given, with the invocation of the Trinity; the ring is first placed on the thumb ('In the Name of the Father'), the index ('the Son'), and the middle-finger ('the Holy Spirit'), where it remains. The bridegroom says a new formula: 'with this ring I thee wed, this gold and silver I give thee, with my body I thee honour, with this dowry I thee endow.' This ring-giving formula becomes very important in subsequent British and North French rites.

After it the bride falls to her knees before her husband, as a sign of obedience.

We now come to a part of the rite which in England lengthens as the Middle Ages progress, a collection of short blessings before the mass. First come the psalmic (*manda deus*) verses; then an adapted version of the Gelasian preparatory prayer, followed by the 'Raguel' blessing. With candles in their hands the bride and groom follow the priest into church, while Ps. 127 is said (now an Introit), and at the altar steps four short blessings, which include the short version of the pontifical blessing in the Lanalet book; the prayers are slightly different in the case of older couples, a new provision. The mass is of the Trinity. This is again a new provision, and is ultimately responsible for pushing the Gregorian collect, *secreta* and post-communion into second place on *all* occasions. The popularity of the Trinity mass in the Middle Ages is the probable explanation.[19] In the nuptial blessing the bride and groom prostrate themselves, and the two Gregorian prayers follow, but the long one is pluralized at the end, and with 'both' inserted before mention of eternity. A new prayer is inserted at this point, mentioning the joining of bride and groom.[20] We do not again encounter it. Clearly inspired by the 'Raguel' blessing (but extended), it was probably added here to give extra force to the nuptial blessing, and to ensure a blessing of widows, who were denied the Gregorian blessing. After mass there is a short blessing of the couple, and a blessing of a common cup. This may be a eucharistic substitute, or else the result of bringing domestic traditions into the public liturgy, or else (less likely) a borrowing from Jewish practice. All three reasons are worth consideration. At home afterwards the chamber is blessed in a single prayer, followed by another blessing of the couple.

For English (and Northern French) marriage liturgy, the Bury order is the most important in the late Middle Ages, as little changes from now onwards, except the expression of consent at the beginning. But note the important growth-points as well as the points of decline. The ring is blessed, but it is not given until after the consent is expressed and the woman given away; it is almost as if the ring is a dramatic emblem, and its being given depends on consent. Then there is the collection of short blessings before the mass which forms a block of intercessory material. As this section of the rite develops, so too does the nuptial blessing within the mass, with its prostration, and the new prayer which follows it. But after mass the old domestic rite is a paltry affair, and may have been optional.

Another early twelfth-century rite is Martène's *Codex Victorinus* which Molin-Mutembe place in Avranches, but which Martimort suggests may come from Mont Saint-Michel.[21] It has the same structure as Bury, but with some interesting differences. No mention is made of starting at the church door, and the priest must inquire 'if anything is contrary to the Law of God', i.e., if they can marry. The ring is blessed with the same two prayers, and the *contract* is read, the first appearance so far. The same sequence follows, with the giving of the ring, and several short blessings, at the end of which appears (for the first and only time) the recitation of the Benedicite, surely an endurance-test for any young couple at their marriage. A very short blessing is inserted after the long nuptial blessing during mass, and an adapted version of a Gelasian prayer is added at the end, which stresses fidelity, and the fact that the couple are now joined together. There is also a blessing of a common cup, as in Bury, and other domestic prayers follow.

The other rites from this and the following centuries tell a similar tale, some with a longer pre-mass rite than others, some with more fuss at the nuptial blessing than others, some with a common cup (or bread) at the end, and some with more or less to do at home afterwards. They may antedate the developments noticed in Bury and *Codex Victorinus*.[22] An Irish missal[23] from the mid-twelfth century has the whole service before the altar, and only one blessing-prayer of the ring, but it inserts after the (plural-ending) nuptial blessing in the mass *two* extra blessings, one from the Gelasian book, and the other from Lanalet (the pontifical blessing in its full form). These may also be compensations for widows, who were, of course, denied the nuptial blessing itself.

Two other English rites from the twelfth century are worthy of mention. The first is the second (and later) rite contained in the so-called Magdalen Pontifical.[24] The pre-mass section takes place at the church doors, and for the first time we have a Latin text of the consent: 'N, do you want this woman', and, if he answers yes, 'do you wish to serve her in the faith of God as your own, in health and infirmity, as a Christian man should serve his wife?' The priest receives the woman from whoever gives her away; he also receives the ring and the *denarii sponsales* (marital money), and blesses the ring with two prayers. The bridegroom gives the ring to the bride, in the formula used at Bury. The other is the so-called Ely Pontifical,[25] which has a similar order to Bury, but with the reading of the *dotalium* and the Lanalet pontifical blessing before the mass begins. The prayers at home consist of a blessing of the chamber, another blessing of the couple, and a blessing of their bodies.

e. Later French rites, thirteenth–fifteenth centuries

With the decree of the Fourth Lateran Council in 1215 that banns should be given on three Sundays preceding marriage,[26] we notice an immediate effect on local rites, but continued variety over the way in which consent and the giving of the bride to the 'groom are expressed. The basic structure of the service, however, remains unchanged, consisting of the pre-mass rite of the ring and accompanying prayers, the mass itself, with the nuptial blessing, and (on occasion) prayers at the end of mass, such as those over bread and/or wine, and blessings at home.

The Roman rite,[27] which dates from the second quarter of the thirteenth century, like other Norman services resembles English rites, but there are important differences. After publishing banns for the third (and last) time, the priest declares that the girl should be given to the man. This may be a rationalization of the (old) rite of betrothal and the (new) practice of calling banns. Then the priest asks the man if he wants her, but the formula is longer than we have seen earlier:

> Do you really want this woman as your wife, to guard her in health and sickness, as long as she lives, as a good man should keep his wife, and to join her faithfully with your body, and all your possessions?

Apart from the alteration from 'Christian' to 'good', the significant new feature of this interrogative is the mention of the sharing of goods. The priest now says, 'on this condition, I give her to you', a dramatic and solemn liturgical act, which gives him a definite role in the transaction. The ring is now blessed, with the psalmic verses, and the Egbert prayer in its longer form, and the man pronounces the ring-giving formula, 'with this ring'. After the 'Raguel' prayer, joining the couple together, the procession moves into church for four short blessing-prayers. The mass follows immediately, with a pall spread out over the couple during the canon, during which they prostrate themselves, and the (plural-ending) Gregorian nuptial blessing prayer is recited. There is a blessing of bread and wine after mass, and a blessing of the chamber and the couple (their bodies) afterwards.

Molin-Mutembe are captivated by the first part of this rite, with the priestly giving of the bride to her husband, and they single out this rite as exemplifying what they call the 'Norman' manner of giving, which persisted throughout the province of Rouen and the diocese of Senlis for the remainder of the Middle Ages; it even travelled with the Normans into Southern Italy, as witness the Pontifical of Sora, in Campania, which dates from the beginning of the thirteenth century.[28] I would myself prefer to describe these features as 'Anglo-Norman', since we have evidence of them in England, e.g., in the Magdalen rite. The use of the canopy is probably an adaptation of the Spanish veiling, but whereas the latter was usually spread over the bride, and only the groom's shoulders, the canopy has a more egalitarian symbolism, and we encounter it again in Northern France, Britain, and Scandinavia.

The Meaux rite of 1280[29] takes us much further on in the thirteenth century, and in the environs of Paris. Here the giving is of Molin-Mutembe's 'full' variety, expressed before (or after) the ring-blessing, but 'passive', i.e., the priest asks the questions, the couple do not say any more than 'yes' in the first giving. Once again we are at the church doors, but no mention is made of banns, though they will have already been called. The priest asks each if they want the other, and then gives the man to the woman, saying, 'I give him over to you as your married husband, that you may keep him, in health and sickness, and serve him faithfully according to the precepts of the Church'; he asks of the other, 'do you receive him?' and he says the same for the giving of the bride to the groom. The ring is blessed, and the man says a similar formula. The pre-mass rite comes to an abrupt end, as there are only two blessings (a lean rite by comparison with English services at this time), of which the first is, expectedly enough, the 'Raguel' prayer, joining the couple, and the second is a short Trinitarian blessing. Two curious features of the nuptial mass are that the preface is the Gregorian one, but adapted in a somewhat didactic fashion to stress indissolubility, and the nuptial blessing (like Vich, in preface-form) comes at the end.[30]

Also dating from the end of the thirteenth century is the service from St Vedast of Arras.[31] The giving is of the 'full' type, active and mutual, i.e., both partners make the consent themselves. The service begins by alluding to banns, and the possibility of impediment. No actual forms appear in what is said between the priest and the bridal pair, except the priest's command that they consent publicly. The rest of the service is even barer than Meaux—one blessing before mass (the 'Raguel' prayer)—but the nuptial blessing is in the form of a preface, and with plural ending.

A different service altogether is that of St Maur-des Fossés, which dates from the second half of the thirteenth century.[32] It begins with a full rite of betrothal in which the priest has to hear from the families assembled how the marriage is to be arranged, details about the dowry and *'omnium quae ad ista pertinent'*. He then asks the couple if they wish to be married and joins their hands 'on the declared conditions'. The banns are to be called. The marriage rite itself begins with the blessing of the ring, and asks for the last time if there is any impediment to the marriage. The consent is once again required of the couple, and the priest asks them if they will remain together, in a formula similar to what we have seen before, but with a significant addition: 'Do you promise before God that you will have N. as your wife, and that you will keep faith and fidelity with her, and that you will protect her in health and sickness and all other circumstances; and that you will not change her or dismiss her, for better or for worse?' Familiar also is the way in which the ring-giving is broken up according to the finger on which it is placed, 'with this ring, I thee wed' (thumb), 'with my body I thee honour' (index), 'the dowry as it has been settled and arranged I give thee' (middle finger). The mass follows without any intervening blessings, with a pall once more extended over the couple during the canon. The domestic rite after mass is indeed full; after the blessing of the chamber comes the 'Raguel' prayer, in an unparalleled position, which is followed by three short blessings, of the bed, and of the couple. It is tempting to see the survival of a number of older elements in this rite, as well as some new features. The simplicity of the pre-mass rite (no blessings at all), the incorporation of the rite of betrothal into the rite of matrimony, and the fuller domestic rite—these could be features which have survived from earlier times. But the promises and the words said in the giving of the ring are obviously new. In the next century we find two other rites from the North of France (Cambrai 1364 and Barbeau, end of fourteenth century)[33] which contain the betrothal rite; both have the 'Raguel' prayer in its now traditional position (straight after the giving of the ring), and Barbeau has a full domestic rite at the end.

Another exceptional rite is the so-called Pontifical of Auxerre,[34] which Martimort dates at the beginning of the fourteenth century, belonging to a later bishop of Laon. It almost looks as if it came from the twelfth century, for it lacks any interrogatives at the beginning, and simply starts at the church door with the blessing of the ring, the giving of the ring (but just with the invocation of the Trinity), the 'Raguel' prayer, and one short blessing. The nuptial mass follows immediately, with the two Gregorian prayers, and nothing else. Afterwards appears a curious rite indeed, 'the blessing of bride and groom in their chamber'. This office begins with the 'Raguel' prayer (again), and continues with another short blessing, mentioning Raphael's presence at the marriage of Tobias and Sarah, and concludes with the Aaronic blessing, and a short Trinitarian blessing. Is this meant to be used afterwards at home, or is it the survival of an old domestic rite which was used for couples who did not want a nuptial mass in church? The separate title of the service and the reappearance of the 'Raguel' prayer strongly suggests this; and the archaic nature of the rite as a whole gives support to such a view. In any event this whole rite shows that not every marriage service in the fourteenth century was prepared to keep up with the times.

The Lyon rite (1353–8)[35] is another interesting composition. It also begins at the church door with the *blessing* of the ring, which is now followed by a notice by the priest concerning the banns. The priest then asks the couple for their consent, which is followed immediately by the *giving* of the ring, and the 'Raguel' blessing, and another blessing, mentioning Raphael's presence. At the end of the mass the priest advises the couple to abstain for three nights, and then pronounces the formula, 'receive her in the name of the Father . . .' and the 'Raguel' prayer, but with the mention of 'joining' omitted; this is very similar to the formula used in Roda and Vich three centuries earlier. An unusual feature of the domestic rite is a different prayer over the bread (of Southern origin), but most unusual of all is the concluding blessing at home, which is a catena of Old

Testament characters, and is taken from the Roda/Vich betrothal rites.[36] The Lyon service appears to be a Northern one, into which Southern features have been introduced. Molin-Mutembe date it in the fifteenth century, but Martimort is probably correct in placing it originally in the mid-fourteenth century,[37] thus increasing its importance.

Two other interesting fourteenth-century rites are those of Amiens and Barbeau.[38] Amiens has a consent-formula which provides the inspiration for subsequent sentiments:

> N. do you promise and swear by all that you have well and loyally to stay by her, and for better or worse not to leave her, and to give her the faith and loyalty of your body and all that you have, healthy or sick, and protect her as long as God grants you both to live?

Barbeau, however, gives us probably the earliest verifiable example of an *active* consent, a vow:

> I take you as my wife, and I espouse you; and I commit to you the fidelity of my body, in so far as I bear for you fidelity and loyalty of my body and my possessions; and I will keep you in health and sickness and in any condition which it pleases our Lord that you should have, nor for worse or for better will I change towards you until the end.

In both these cases, we have the beginnings of a vernacular tradition, in which the Latin background of the older consent-formulae are still visible. Barbeau's type of formula never secures universal popularity in France, but England makes a great deal of it, as we shall see.

The last two Northern French rites, Rouen 1455 and Lyon 1498,[39] continue the trend we have already noticed, the establishment of the first part of the rite. Rouen opens with mention of the banns, and the consent (which is made interrogatively, as Amiens), but at the moment when the couple join hands, the priest recites a formula of great theological significance for the future: 'I join you together in the Name of the Father . . .' The ring-blessing comes next, with the formula said by the man, and then the 'Raguel' prayer, and five short blessings. The priestly hand-joining formula occurs here for the first time, and becomes popular in France in the sixteenth century and later especially in Normandy. The Lyon rite,[40] like other French services of this period, is thin on blessings before the mass, but includes the handing-over of the marriage *carta* before the ring is given; but it has the first appearance of Matt. 19.6 pronounced by the priest at the hand-joining. It also puts the nuptial blessing into preface-form. None of the Southern features noted in the earlier Lyon book survives; but after the blessing of the food at home, the priest recites the Genesis creation formula, 'Go and multiply. . .', a neat order for a celibate to make!

Northern French rites from the thirteenth until the end of the fifteenth century are varied in content, but fairly uniform in structure. Points of variety include how the consent and promises are expressed, whether to have several short blessings before the mass, or just one or two, and what is to be the content (if any) of the domestic rite afterwards. There is little variation in the nuptial mass. The survival of earlier features in the Auxerre book and the Southern elements in the Lyon (1353–8) rite show conservatism on one hand, eclecticism on the other. But apart from these minor points of detail, and the odd eccentricity, the local rites are relatively stable, as witness the great similarity between Rouen thirteenth century and 1455. Lyon 1498's use of the Matthean pronouncement (as we shall call it) becomes popular in the Midi, and important in the next century.

f. British rites from thirteenth century to the eve of Reformation

Evidence for British marriage services in this period is paltry by comparison, but we have enough to go on, and we note a similar tendency for attention to focus on the pre-mass rite, but with the difference that the short blessings multiply.

The first few are local services from the thirteenth and fourteenth centuries. The Pontifical of Anianus of Bangor[41] (from the later thirteenth century) begins at the church door with the reading of the *dos* (contract), and the giving of the consent, which is simply rubricked, without a formula. The couple join hands, and the ring is blessed and given, with the invocation of the Trinity. A short blessing follows: the 'Raguel' prayer, and Ps. 127 during the procession to the altar. Four short blessings precede the nuptial mass, in which the nuptial blessing (unusually for Britain) has the plural ending. The prayers at home include one which goes right back to the Durham Collectar.

A later thirteenth-century rite comes from the Missal of Hanley Castle, in Worcestershire.[42] Like Anianus, it begins with the reading and giving of the *dotalium* (contract), and the giving of consent by the couple. The ring is blessed in the full form, with psalmic verses (*manda deus*), and the two traditional prayers; it is given with the invocation of the Trinity, and the traditional formula, 'with this ring', but this includes both a gold piece and some pence (representing the *dos*). As in the other northern rites, all this happens at the church door, and there then follows (in a unique position) the long Lanalet blessing, the 'Raguel' prayer, and two other short blessings. The procession moves into church to the strains of Ps. 127, the couple holding lighted candles. Two prayers precede the mass, one short blessing, and an adapted (elongated) version of the Gelasian prayer which appears in its shorter form in Lyre. The manuscript breaks off in the middle of the mass. Little real change can be detected from this rite, compared with Anianus; of peculiar note are the two long prayers, from Lanalet and Lyre.

The Benedictine monastery of Evesham had a book containing a marriage rite from the turn of the thirteenth–fourteenth centuries, and which probably points back to liturgical practice as much as a century earlier.[43] The service begins with the publishing of banns, and the priest asks the man if he wants to marry the woman, and if he will look after her 'in weakness and in strength'. The *dos* is then nominated and the woman is given to the man. A later hand inserts at this point a form of promise, by each of the partners: 'I receive you as my wife, from this hour and for as long as we live, and I stand by this pledge'. This is an interesting formula which was probably written in English and put into Latin for the purposes of the book. The ring is blessed, and it is given with the invocation of the Trinity and the (by now) traditional form. Like Hanley Castle (not far geographically from Evesham), the blessings begin with the long Lanalet blessing, and continue with the 'Raguel' prayer, two short blessings, and Ps. 127 during the procession to the altar (with candles). Another group of blessings follows, which includes the Gelasian prayer, as well as the first paragraph of the Lanalet prayer, the full version of which has already been said earlier! The nuptial blessing in the mass has the plural ending, and there are prayers to be said at home afterwards. Evesham seems to depend on Hanley for the two unusual prayers,[44] one in the same unusual position, and the fact that this prayer is (in part) duplicated suggests that the long version was subsequently inserted as a result of influence from Hanley, as it is unlikely that a new prayer would be added in the middle of a section. These are, of course, only conjectures, but it is more than a coincidence that two rites so near in time and geography should both contain rarely-placed prayers.

Another fourteenth-century rite is contained in the Pontifical belonging to an abbot of Westminster.[45] It begins with the reading of the *dos*, and in the opening directions there are hints of the consent-formula, that the man 'receives the woman as wife in the faith of God, to care for her in health and sickness'. The ring is blessed, and given with the invocation of the Trinity, and the formula, 'with this ring I thee wed, and with my body I thee honour' (these last words are written in red, and they may be a later addition). A collection of blessings follows, including the two used in Bury for those who are older. The mass is the same as before, and there is a blessing of wine and the bedchamber at home afterwards.

We now travel north of the border to Rathen in the county of Buchan, which yields us a fifteenth-century Manual.[46] It begins with banns, and both consent *and* promise before the ring-blessing. The consent suggests what we shall see in the great Manuals of England: 'do you wish to have this woman as your wife, to love, honour, keep and protect her . . .'; and the vow is the same as Sarum.[47] The ring is blessed and given, with invocation of the Trinity, and 'wyth this rynge I wede the', as in Sarum. The usual group of blessings follows, which includes the Lanalet blessing (in its shorter form) but tucked away at the end of the group just before mass begins. There is nothing unusual after this, except a fairly full provision of prayers for use at home afterwards, including the Durham prayer, 'May the hand of God', which we saw in Anianus.

The Welsh Manual,[48] from the fifteenth century also, seems to be somewhere between Anianus and Rathen in its development. The *dos* (contract) is read out, and the priest asks them if they want to be married, 'do you want to have this woman as your wife, and to love and keep her, as a husband should his wife?' They join hands, and the Sarum vows follow, including the wife's promise to be 'boner and buxsom in bedde and at bord'. The ring is blessed, and it is given with the formula, and invocation of the Trinity. A group of blessings follows, including the Lanalet prayer, in its shorter form. The mass has the nuptial blessing, with a pall spread over the bridal pair.

We now come to the three great Manuals, which we shall deal with together, because of their close interrelation. We shall take Sarum as the 'norm', and indicate variations in York and Hereford in the course of the discussion.[49] The text probably goes back to the middle of the fourteenth century, subsequent additions in the tradition being confined to small notes here and there but altering the rite very little. The priest begins with a final banns reading, and here the manuscript notes indicate an increasing rigour against priests who conduct weddings before the last banns have been read. The priest then asks the couple if they wish to be married: 'Do you wish to have this woman as your wife, and to love her, honour her, keep and protect her, in health and in sickness, as a husband should his wife, to keep from all other women except her, as long as your lives shall last?' The question of the woman includes 'obey and serve'. York has the same (one manuscript translating 'honour' as 'wirschipe'[50]); Hereford has the simpler form which we saw in Anianus, although one manuscript has an even simpler form, 'do you want this woman joined to you/man coupled to you?' At this point York, and only York, has the priest saying, 'who giues me this wyfe?', and in all three, the couple join hands; this is the only appearance of a priest's question at this point. The priest gives the woman to the man, and the vows are now said by each. Here is the text of the man's:

> I take the N. to my wedded wyf, to haue and to holde, fro this day forwarde, for bettere for wors, for richere for pourer [one manuscript adds 'for fayrere for fowlere'], in sycknesse and in hele, tyl dethe us departe, if holy chyrche it woll ordeyne, and therto y plight the my trouthe.

And the woman promises:

> I take the N to my wedded housbonde, to haue and to holde, fro this day forwarde, for better for wors, for richer for pourer, in sycknesse and in hele, to be bonere and boxsom, in bedde and atte bord, tyll dethe vs departhe, if holy chyrche it wol ordeyne, and therto I plight the my trouthe.

A very late manuscript comments that 'bonere and boxsom' means 'meek and obedient';[51] York adds 'at bedde and at borde' in both vows after 'to haue and to holde'; and all manuscripts add after 'tyll dethe us departhe' the words 'if holy kirk it will ordayn'. Hereford, on the other hand, begins each with 'I undersynge ye', leaves out 'fro this day forwarde', and the woman promises 'to be buxum to ye' after 'in sekeness and in helye'; but a later manuscript has 'take ye to' instead of 'undersynge ye for'. Sarum clearly influences the others, but Hereford shows signs of its own earlier (simpler) forms. The expression 'have and hold' dates right back to Anglo-Saxon times, and appears in alliterative poems, where the context is property or weaponry, and in subsequent preaching.[52] The ring is now blessed (all three Manuals using both the customary prayers), and then it is given. Sarum has as follows: 'With this rynge I the wed, and this gold and siluer I the geue, and with my body I the worshipe and with all my worldley cathel I the endowe', and the ring is placed on the fourth finger, with the invocation of the Trinity, starting with the thumb, in the manner traditional by now. York, however, begins by placing the ring on the bride's hand with the invocation of the Trinity, and concludes the action, 'with this ryne I wedde the, and with this golde and siluer I honoure the, and with this gyfte I dowe thee'. Hereford starts with the vernacular formula, but it has two versions; the main one is 'Wyy yys rynge y ye vvedde, and yys golde and seluer ych ye geue, and vvy myne body ych ye honoure', and the variant is 'Wyth yis rynge I ye spowse, and with yis gold and seluer I ye dowe, and with my body I ye honowre'. We note the same variety in the giving of the ring as we saw in the vow and the consent. They all express the same sort of ideas, but variation seems to stem from local dialect-rhythms, rather than a desire to translate a Latin original.

All three Manuals place the customary pre-mass blessings (with the psalmic verses and Ps. 127) at this point. Each varies slightly: Hereford has nine blessings in all, with Sarum coming a close second, with eight, and York lagging behind with six. No unusual prayers appear in these sets—the 'Raguel' prayer and the short version of Lanalet appear in all.

It is in the mass that we come across a peculiarity of some importance and considerable bafflement. The nuptial blessing takes place with four (two in York) clerks holding a pall over the couple (probably the result of French influence).[53] But each directs that the second clause (the Ephesians analogy) should be omitted when the bride has been married before.[54] The traditional custom was to withhold the entire nuptial blessing from widows, and in the twelfth century both Hildebert of Tours (d. 1133) and Hugh of Amiens, Archbishop of Rouen (d. 1164), refer to the nuptial blessing as privileged and priestly.[55] But it is not until the thirteenth century that we find any hint in a liturgical text of the Ephesians analogy being omitted, and that is in the Norwegian Manual (a rite largely dependent on England),[56] which describes this clause as 'the prayer of virgins'. All three Manuals state at the beginning of the clause, 'here begins the sacramental blessing', and mark its ending in similar terms. Whereas other books, including Evesham, warn that the nuptial blessing cannot be repeated, these English books, together with the Norwegian, isolate the Ephesians analogy as containing *the* blessing. They cite Aquinas and others in support, and state that there are four places in which blessings occur at marriage, before the mass, during the mass, at the end of mass, and at home, but they insist that the *second* is the most important, and is therefore restricted. But some restriction! Obviously, the English (and Scottish, Welsh and Irish) rites loved marriage blessings, as witness the proliferation in the pre-mass rite, since for them these prayers were of particular importance; in the interests of maintaining the balance of all the blessings, before, during, at the end of, and after mass, the traditional nuptial blessing is recited at *every* marriage, but an esoteric reason is used to distinguish its use for virgins and widows. Nonetheless, the reason is of great interest, for it shows that some English liturgical minds in the late Middle Ages were aware of the fact that marriage blessing prayers contain many themes, images, and intentions, but only the Gregorian nuptial blessing uses the Ephesians analogy of Christ and the Church.

Each Manual has a post-mass set of prayers for use at home, Hereford with seven, Sarum with six, and York with three, thus reproducing the same league-table of blessings which we noted in the pre-mass prayers. The Hereford set is in the same sequence as Sarum, but it adds a short preliminary prayer; it was no doubt influenced by Sarum (see Appendix II).

g. *Conclusion*

We have seen the radical change in the structure of the British and Northern French rites at the beginning of the twelfth century, when the marriage prayers and ring-blessing are placed before the mass (which is now compulsory), whereas hitherto, they had followed the mass (which was perhaps originally optional). In this later development, the following conclusions can be drawn:

i. There is a move away from the reading of the *dos* coupled with an informal declaration of consent (Molin-Mutembe's 'common' type, with 'passive' giving), to a formal giving of consent and pledging of troth (Molin-Mutembe's 'full' type, with 'active' giving).

ii. The developing part of the rite (the banns-notice, consent, vow, and ring-giving), makes for a substantial section of the service in the vernacular, since the only Latin parts were the blessing of the ring and the invocation of the Trinity. This is a gradual process, which starts at Bury in the twelfth century, and reaches its height at Sarum in the fourteenth.

iii. The consent-form appears originally to have been made up of a Latin minimum. This would explain the resemblance early forms have, as, for example, Bury, Irish, Rouen, and Amiens. Molin-Mutembe are right in seeing different ways of expressing consent (and vows), although the precise distinctions they attempt to make seem somewhat contrived. Conservative rites, like the Norman ones, stick to passive consent, but others advance to a fuller form, with a vow.

iv. The vow first appears in Northern France in the fourteenth century, and, if the English Manual tradition goes back into that century, simultaneously in England, spreading quickly through the British Isles in the fifteenth. Whereas the French formulae vary in length and style (Barbeau's text which we quoted is but one example), the English are more uniform, Evesham being the briefest, and exceptional in this regard. Both the French and the English vow-formulae rely on earlier (Latin-inspired) forms of consent; but whereas the French are more like mini-speeches, the English flow more freely, as they are made up of the kind of short contrasting phrases which would be easy to pick up from a priest, which may, indeed, be one reason for their persistence. The background of the Anglo-Saxon alliterative poem which I have suggested confirms me in the conviction that the English vow is a separate development, independent of the French, a mature example of vernacular devotion, with its rhythms and didactic features, as witness the relatively few variants as they appear in local dialects.

v. British rites know nothing of the sacerdotalism of some of the French rites (e.g., Rouen, thirteenth century) in which the priest hands over the woman to the man; the priest is the instrument of the Church, but the couple make their own consent. This reflects much of medieval theological thinking.

vi. The ring-giving formula, which again makes its first appearance in England at Bury, spreads quickly through both Northern French and English rites. It varies as time goes on, as local custom demands (e.g., whether to include gold and silver pieces, as well as the *dos*), and it is translated, adapted, and retranslated for different vernaculars. Like the consent-formula, it was probably originally written in Latin in the twelfth century, but as time goes on it undergoes more changes as it enters local vernacular forms.

vii. British rites differ from many French in the efflorescence of their marriage blessings, particularly in the pre-mass section of the service; this is in contrast to Visigothic and Visigothic-influenced services, which confine the blessings (which tend to be fewer but longer) to the latter part of the mass. This English development is a peculiar one, reaching its height in the Manual tradition, where—to safeguard the nuptial blessing for all weddings—a small section has to be deleted in the case of widows.

Undoubtedly, it is the English Sarum rite which represents the apogee of the North European medieval marriage service. In spite of its length, with repeated blessings and obtuse reasoning over the nuptial blessing, it nonetheless contains the richest expression of marriage in vernacular devotion, for it not only develops the consent and the ring-giving formula, but produces that masterpiece of medieval vernacular liturgy, the marriage vow. Other rites take note of this, as we shall see. Furthermore, liturgical symbolism is not allowed to get out of hand, for the English rites take the French lead in using a large pall, or canopy, to be extended over *both* partners, instead of the Visigothic veil, which was placed over the bride, but only over the shoulders of the groom. (The post-Vatican II Roman rite allows for both options.) The same sort of 'balance' is seen in medieval iconography, which more often than not depicts the moment when the priest joins together the hands of the couple when they make their consent to be married.[57]

4 Scandinavia, Germany, Italy

The territories covered in this concluding medieval Western section hardly make good bedfellows. They appear together, however, for reasons other than expediency, for the first two (Germany and Scandinavia) do not make any substantially original contributions to the evolution of the rite, but give a series of variants, which have much in common with the Anglo-Norman kind of rite. Italy does not make an original contribution either (except in Milan), with the result that as late as the sixteenth century we are faced with Italian marriage rites that are as bare and austere as those from the same era in Spain are elaborate and rich.[1]

a. Scandinavia

We have not much to go on, but what we have is significant enough. Many years ago Dom Basilius Binder drew attention to the importance of the Scandinavian rites,[2] but this was before the appearance of Helge Faehn's edition of the Norwegian Manual,[3] which shows a highly developed Anglo-Norman type of marriage service. To this we must immediately turn.

The book contains two thirteenth-century marriage rites, MS B from the middle of the century, and MS O from later on in the century. They are very similar in their structure, except for one significant item, the absence in B and the presence in O of the vernacular material found in English rites of the time, namely the publishing of the banns, the consent, and the giving of the ring. Turning firstly to B, we discover the service beginning in conventional fashion at the church doors. The ring (or *argentum* = gold-piece) is blessed with the two traditional prayers, but with the psalmic verse (*manda deus*) placed between them. The ring is given with the traditional formula, and the procession moves into church with Ps. 127, where there follows a very English-looking series of no less than six short blessings, beginning with the 'Raguel' prayer ('joining' the couple), the mass of the Trinity, and the two usual prayers at the nuptial blessing, but the MS breaks off during the long blessing, so that we do not know whether or not it had the plural ending, nor indeed what followed it.

The later version, the O manuscript, is more developed, indeed the most highly-developed in Scandinavia or Germany for many years to come. The service starts at the doors, and the ring is blessed first of all, as in the twelfth-century Bury rite. The banns are read out, and consent to marry is asked of each partner, in a form again reminiscent of Bury. Then comes an innovation: the priest exhorts the couple to keep to each other, 'whatever chances to befall you while you both live, you shall keep these laws of God and not disturb this union'. We do not encounter this sort of formula until the Reformation; it resembles the kind of 'declaratory' formula which we shall meet in different ways later on. Then there is another feature, this time an import, for the priest 'hands over' the woman to the man, in a form which seems to be a direct translation from the thirteenth-century Rouen rite. But the ring is 'given' as in the Bury rite. All this (apart from the ring-blessing) is in Old Norse, but in a style that reads strangely, as if the scribe were working from another scribe's draft, and translating from another language (Latin), rather than in the mature flowing style of a living vernacular tradition.[4] It is mainly English, but the Rouen gem is deliberately inserted at the appropriate point (though it does not appear again in Scandinavia).

We must not regard these thirteenth-century Viking Christians as slightly cultivated savages, for King Haakon's Court was known to be a sophisticated one, in which French literature was deliberately encouraged as much as English; moreover, the Nidaros Province not only contained the whole of Norway, but Iceland, Greenland, the Faroes, the Western Isles, and 'Sodor and Man'; and Nidaros had by the end of the thirteenth century a magnificent Early English Gothic Cathedral.

The rite continues in the usual manner, with the procession into church (but with candles this time), and no less than seven short blessings, including two (at the end of the series) which other rites occasionally prescribe for use with older couples,[5] though there is nothing in them that seems particularly appropriate for such circumstances, except the absence of the procreation-theme. The mass of the Trinity follows immediately, and the nuptial blessing appears in the plural-ending version, with *ambo* ('both') as in the Bury order; the plural version is to be found in other British thirteenth/fourteenth-century rites, such as Anianus of Bangor and

Evesham, but it is rare thereafter.[6] Also like Bury, it inserts another prayer after the nuptial blessing, with the theme of protecting the couple against adversities; and, once again like Bury, it has a series of four prayers for use at home afterwards, for blessing drink, the bedchamber, and the couple. Obviously Bury (or something closely resembling it) is behind the Norwegian Manual, but the most interesting feature is the vernacular material, which probably represents a subsequent strain, basically English, but incorporating Northern French (the 'giving') and home-grown (the 'declaration') features. The vernacular material presents difficulties. It is easy for a Latin prayer to travel from one tradition to another, but, as the twentieth century knows well, it is much more difficult for a mixture of official and popular piety in liturgical prayer to come from one language and reappear in another, well-translated and highly polished. Old English and Old Norse are closer than their modern counterparts, but by the thirteenth century they were sufficiently diverse to make the process extremely awkward.

We now have to take a leap of two centuries, to the south of Jutland, to the island of Als, to the parish of Notmark, to a Manual edited by Knud Ottosen, and dated by him to the 1470s.[7] Even though there is a gap of two hundred years, the marriage rite is bald by comparison. The ring is blessed at the church doors, the *dotalium* may be read out, consent is asked for (no text, or details), the hands are joined and the ring given, all in Latin. Five short blessings are given, divided by two psalms and the procession into church. The mass of the Trinity is said, but the Epistle is Rom. 11.33–6, which is unusual. At the nuptial blessing the pall is used, and the blessing contains the plural ending, which is usual in Scandinavia,[8] as we shall see. The domestic rite afterwards begins with the *Asperges*, and contains three short blessings.

We would be correct in regarding this local parochial rite, in the diocese of Odense, as very plain, if an examination of the Manual traditions of all the other Scandinavian rites of subsequent years did not reveal a similar austerity, and no vernacular material. Uppsala (1487) does give a simple twelfth-century Anglo-Norman looking form of consent, and the nuptial blessing has the pall, but the text is in the singular ending, although it begins in the preface-form; the late fifteenth-century Lund Pontifical (Lund was at the time the metropolitan see for Southern Sweden and Denmark) has a lacuna between the ring-blessing and *manda deus*, but indicates a form of ring-giving based on Bury (and, supposedly a form of consent beforehand); the nuptial blessing lacks pall, preface-formula and plural ending; but, most interesting of all, the pontifical prayer after the nuptial blessing is identical with one found in an early thirteenth-century Reims Pontifical, itself a variant of the eleventh-century Canterbury Benedictional prayer.[9]

Skara (1498) and Hemsjö[10] (both in Sweden) give identical services; they begin by asking for impediments, but with no set form, and the ring is blessed and given, and two sets of three short blessings are divided by Ps. 127; the mass of the Trinity follows, with the nuptial blessing in plural version. In the next century Slesvig (1512) and Roskilde (1513)[11]—two important rites—reproduce a similar scheme, but (like Uppsala) with fewer short blessings (Slesvig has only two before the mass), the nuptial blessing with the plural ending (Slesvig, curiously, places this *after* communion); and a form of *benedictio thalami* (blessing of the bedchamber) after the mass.

The Åbo (1522) and Linköping (1512)[12] services show some developments. Åbo lays down banns to be read three Sundays before the marriage, and begins the service by asking for consent in terms similar to Uppsala: *Vis tu N. ipsam tibi recipere in uxorem; et habere eam tam in prosperis quam adversis?* (Do you want to take N. as your wife, and to have her in prosperity and adversity?); to which the man replies: *Ego te recipio N. exnunc mihi in uxorem in nomine domini* (I take you from now onwards as my wife in the Name of the Lord). The ring is blessed, and given, in Latin, and (unlike Uppsala) no less than seven short blessings are pronounced, again divided by a psalm. The mass of the Trinity follows, with the nuptial blessing (but with *singular* ending), and with the pall extended over the couple: and the bedchamber is blessed afterwards.

The Linköping service lacks any interrogation at the beginning, but like Notmark simply blesses the ring, gives it, and blesses the couple in a long series of short prayers, again divided by a psalm. The mass of the Trinity follows, but the nuptial blessing is given *after* communion, as Slesvig, and there is also the additional prayer which appears in the Norwegian Manual and Bury, for the protection of the couple. The rite ends, again, with the blessing of the bedchamber.

What are we to make of these Scandinavian rites? They certainly are uneven, when compared to the more systematic progression of the rites in England and France, and even allowing for the paltry evidence that we have, they do seem to be late in taking on any vernacular material at the beginning; quick to elaborate short blessings before the mass; but, like the Anglo-Norman rites, they keep (and elaborate) the domestic prayers at the end. Christianity came to Scandinavia later than other European countries, so that when the Church marriage service arrived, it would have had no Christian domestic rite to contend with, as compared with Anglo-Saxon England, in the Pontifical of Egbert, or pre-Carolingian France, in the Bobbio Missal. Added points of interest are the presence of the nuptial pall in the Norwegian Manual, Notmark, Uppsala, Åbo, and Linköping, and the North French symptoms in the Norwegian Manual and Lund. The most baffling aspect comes in the absence of vernacular material, and the appearance in only the Norwegian Manual, Uppsala andAbo of any formal expression of consent; but perhaps this just was not a Scandinavian concern, and could well have been a *deliberate* omission, rather than the result of isolation.

b. Germany

In the tenth-century Romano-Germanic Pontifical the manuscript tradition is universal in giving the Gregorian mass with 1 Cor. 6.15–20 and Matt. 19.1–6 as the readings. The Leonine nuptial blessing appears in a special mass in the Bamberg eleventh-century manuscript, on the first wedding anniversary, which is a neat way of ritualizing a special occasion, and at the same time keeping in circulation an old liturgical text which has been replaced by something better. The (Gregorian) nuptial blessing in the marriage mass itself is nearly always in the singular form, except the twelfth-century St Florian version.[13]

When does the Anglo-Norman pre-mass rite at the church door make its first appearance in Germany? Lüdtke has drawn attention to a Ratingen-Düsseldorf rite,[14] dating from around 1200, in which the three Gregorian prayers appear, followed by a familiar-looking sequence: the psalmic verse, Ps. 67, the blessing of the ring, Ps. 127, the 'Raguel' prayer (joining the couple together), and six short blessings. Perhaps this series was meant to precede the mass, and was added to the manuscript after the (much earlier) Gregorian mass prayers.

The best known rite with this structure is from the Silesian Ritual of Henry I, Bishop of Breslau (1309–19).[15] It is much more carefully worked out, and begins with the blessing of the ring, and then immediately with a short blessing of the couple; the priest asks for any impediment, and then for the consent of the couple (no form given); Ps. 127 is said, two short blessings follow, the couple kiss each other, another short (Trinitarian) blessing is pronounced, and the mass follows immediately, but it can be of either the Holy Spirit or the Trinity; at the nuptial blessing the singular-ending version is used, and the pall is extended over the couple; and afterwards, the bedchamber is blessed. When is the ring given? No directions appear, but we can probably assume that it was given immediately after the consent. A curious feature of this rite is the presence of a short blessing of the couple after the first blessing of the ring. Perhaps Henry was imitating a local service, or else trying to make sense of the beginning of the rite, in blessing the man and the woman before they make their consent to marry each other; the Reformers develop a similar practice. The consent formula was probably brief like those of the Anglo-Norman family in the preceding century. The position of the ritual kiss is interesting and probably a local practice.

Our next rite is that of Köln in 1485,[16] which gives us an example of a marriage rite without the celebration of mass, a feature of later medieval German service-books discussed by Binder, and the result of local pressure to make the marriage rite a 'proper service', but without the mass, because it was not always thought appropriate to celebrate the Eucharist at weddings.[17] Köln's service comes in three parts. First, there is the blessing of the ring, with the psalmic verse, and the two ring-blessing prayers. Next, the blessing of the bridegroom and bride, which consists of Ps. 127, and a group of short blessing-prayers, beginning with the 'Raguel' prayer, and ending with the Lanalet prayer, but substituting *copulavit* (joined together) for *creavit* (created) when referring to Adam and Eve, and a short blessing-prayer; then comes the 'Last Gospel', and a concluding versicle and response. The third and final part of the rite is for the 'leading of the bride' into church; it begins with Ps. 127, and some versicles and responses, and ends in a special blessing of the bride only, referring to her being 'outside' the church doors, and asking for her to be filled with divine grace.[18] The source is the Anglo-Norman marriage prayer before the mass, but the bridal blessing at the end is new. This last part of the rite was used after the consummation of the marriage. The absence of the mass is the most interesting feature.

The Magdeburg Agenda (1497)[19] has an even barer scheme, consisting simply of a short blessing of the couple, followed by the Gregorian nuptial blessing (with plural ending). Meisen (1512),[20] however, is more conventional; the priest asks for consent, and then for impediments, in the vernacular; and then declares the couple married in this form: *matrimonium inter vos contractum deus confirmet: et ego illud in facie ecclesie solennizo: In Nomine* ... ('May God confirm the marriage which has been contracted between you: and I solemnize it in the face of the church: In the Name of ...'). When the bride is 'enthroned' (i.e., 'introduced')[21] in the church, two short prayers are used, one specially for her, and another taken from Scripture. The next section is called the 'blessing of the bridegroom and bride', and it begins with the reading of the Last Gospel, Ps. 112, the preliminary prayer to the nuptial blessing (Gregorian), but without the blessing itself, some versicles and responses, and four short blessings, the first clearly inspired by the Gen. 1.28 motif of creation, joining together, and procreation to 'fill the earth'. It is unclear when these two rites were used; perhaps the first one was used for every couple, and the second was an additional set of prayers for the more devout. The second rite may have been tacked on at the end of a mass, as is directed in the Naumburg (1502) rite,[23] which resembles this one in many respects.

The Schwerin rite (1521)[24] is again similar in structure, but more detailed. The 'order for contracting marriage in the face of the Church' begins with directions to the priest concerning the circumstances under which marriages may be contracted. The consent is a formal statement by both man and woman, in the vernacular, which may be said either entirely by each, or at the prompting of the priest, who then declares the couple married in a form similar to Meisen, but compressed so that it is the priest who 'confirms' the marriage, and he may make this declaration in Latin or the vernacular. The 'blessing of the bridegroom and bride in first marriages' takes place at the end of mass, and consists of Ps. 127, followed by a group of short blessing-prayers. Finally, the 'way of introducing the bride after marriage' is a simple procedure; it may happen on the day after the wedding (so, presumably, after the marriage is consummated), with the priest reading out a verse from Scripture, and sprinkling her with holy water. Later on in the same century, Augsburg (1547) and Ingolstadt (1564)[25] have identical structures; after instructions that second marriages are not to be blessed, the couple join hands, Ps. 127 is said, and a series of short blessings follow, Augsburg using six, one of which is the Gen. 1.28 prayer from Meisen, and Ingolstadt has four, two of which are new compositions. The notable features of these German rites are the quasi-priestly 'declaration' of marriage; the loose connection of the mass to the marriage service; the absence (except in Henry of Breslau) of any reference to the marriage ring; and the custom of blessing the wife after the marriage has been consummated, a reappearance of a negative view of sexual relations. It is obviously impossible to get behind these local customs, but I suspect that in the non-eucharistic rites, we have a survival of an older tradition (antedating any popular nuptial mass) of an *ad hoc* domestic service, consisting of a series of short blessings which have been added to in order to emphasize the public and legal nature of marriage. In the Pontifical tradition (echoed by Henry of Breslau) we perhaps see the 'ideal' practice of marriage which is based on the mass, and to which later features are added. But the later local books probably more accurately reflect the Church grappling with the need to ritualize marriage in the simplest possible way and safeguard its legal aspects. The three examples of entirely new prayers (in Meisen and Ingolstadt) are likewise remarkable, as is also the ill-fated blessing of the bride in the post-nuptial 'introducing to church' in the Köln rite, a prayer which does not appear again.

c. Italy

Italy was not immune to the kind of changes we have seen in the rest of Europe, but it lagged behind. For convenience's sake, as well as out of proper respect, we shall deal first with the Ambrosian rite. Magistretti's edition gives a faithful-looking version of the now familiar Gregorian mass, with collect, and other prayers, and the nuptial blessing (singular ending) with its preparatory prayer before the communion.[26] This seems to be the use of the Church of Milan at the time of the Gregorian Sacramentaries, in the ninth century. Cattaneo has made a full study of the Milanese rite,[27] and identifies two slightly different traditions in the tenth and eleventh centuries, manifested in the so-called Sacramentary of Lodrino (from St Stephen's, Milan), and the Sacramentary of St Ambrose in Milan. They agree on such points as the readings (1 Cor. 7.25–31, and—unusually for the West—John 2.1–11); and the Gelasian–Gregorian preface. But for the other mass prayers, excepting the nuptial blessing, Lodrino prefers Gregorian prayers, whereas Milan has Gelasian; the extra prayer, peculiar to the Ambrosian mass, is the *oratio super sindonem*, before the Offertory, and here Lodrino employs the Gregorian preparatory prayer to the nuptial blessing (we have already seen the nuptial blessing on its own),[28] but Milan adapts a Leonine prayer. But there are no rings yet. We have to wait until the year 1216 before we have firm evidence, and here it is charmingly placed in a *Liber Consuetudinum* of Milan, which mentions the use of a ring, or a crown, or a girdle, or a scarf, or a veil, as possible (and recognized) signs of marriage; how these were handled liturgically is unclear. Subsequent aristocratic evidence marshalled by Cattaneo suggests the same story we have seen already, a preference for the ring, blessed and given with promise to marry, before the mass, according to Roman usage.

There is a Sacramentary which is dated to 1402 which lacks the readings, but gives similar prayers to Lodrino; but the real change comes after the nuptial blessing (described as *benedictio sponsae*), when two Gelasian prayers—one of them the 'extra' final blessing—are added as *benedictio sponsi et sponsae*.[29] Subsequent editions of the Milanese rite up to the time of the Council of Trent tell a similar story, but the extra blessings disappear, and are replaced by one only, probably in the interests of brevity. The trends in these late books are towards simplification of the mass formulae, though keeping the traditional lections and the special *oratio super sindonem*. The combination of Trent and Charles Borromeo takes the Ambrosian rite in a new direction in the sixteenth century.

We have already discussed the thirteenth-century Pontifical of Sora,[30] which was the first Italian rite to include the ceremonies at the door with the consent, in the Norman pattern, and the influence this book had on local Italian rites in the period afterwards. Castello takes this over in his 1523 *Liber*

Sacerdotalis, which popularizes this tradition even further, with the result that at long last in 1614 the Tridentine *Rituale Romanum* establishes a brief form of the pre-mass consent and blessing of ring; these we shall discuss in a later chapter.[31] For the mass prayers, however, we note an eccentric variation in the editions of the *Missale Romanum* printed from 1474[32] up to the time of the Council of Trent, with new prayers, which are more explicitly marital in their content and imagery, and even borrowing terms from the nuptial blessing; there are also experiments with additional blessings after the nuptial blessing (increasingly in the plural form), as well as at the end of the mass; and a pre-mass series of prayers, blessing the ring (the two prayers we have seen in the Anglo-Norman books), Ps. 127, and short blessings of the couple. Thus, apart from the Ambrosian tradition, and the influence of the Normans, Italy's marriage rites of the Middle Ages remained austere, only cautiously ready to absorb ideas from other places; this story is typified in the recent study made by Amiet of the Northern Italian Valdotan rite.[33]

d. Postscript

By way of summary, we can now see in the medieval Western rites a great deal of variety, and a considerable degree of development. The formative factors appear to be as follows:

i. An early domestic rite tradition, represented in England by the Pontifical of Egbert, in France by the Bobbio Missal, and, remotely, in Germany by such non-eucharistic rites as Köln.

ii. A subsequent inclusion of the Gregorian Mass almost everywhere, the natural consequence of the authority of this book throughout the West.

iii. Two separate developments of 'marriage ceremonies', in the Spanish rite at the end of the mass, and in the Anglo-Norman rites before the mass.

iv. The pre-mass section of the service becomes increasingly encumbered by vernacular material and short blessing prayers, in the Anglo-Norman tradition counter-balancing the nuptial mass, and in parts of Germany becoming sufficient *without* the mass, whereas in England (e.g. Sarum) the need is felt to emphasize the *importance* of the nuptial mass by insisting on the uniqueness of the nuptial blessing in one particular section.

v. At the end of the Middle Ages, in France and Germany, the priest's role becomes authoritatively expressed in the rite, through the introduction of '*Ego*'-type formulae.

vi. Consent to be married is either passively expressed, or actively given in the form of a vow, or, as in England, both; and it is probable that England led the way in establishing the principle of vernacular material at this point in the rite, and even of developing a vernacular tradition, instead of working from a Latin original.

vii. Wifely obedience is often (but not always) expressed in consent and vow, thus differentiating the roles—a feature *not* shared by the Eastern rites.

viii. The multiplication of pre-mass blessing-prayers in the English tradition spreads to Scandinavia, and continues to flourish, emphasizing the pastoral nature of the service, that the newly-married couple need intercession for their life together in the future, in all its aspects, and that this needs to be given liturgical expression immediately after they have pledged each to the other.

ix. Spain develops the use of rings at an early stage, using two as early as the eleventh century, if not before; and whereas rings continue to be used sporadically elsewhere, in later medieval Germany they do not yet appear in the liturgy.

x. The old rite of betrothal is seldom made into a liturgy (except in some French rites), and because by its very nature it is a form of consent to be married, its demise was *partly* the cause of the development the rite of consent before the nuptial mass. Spain, once more, shows vestiges of antiquity in the way it spreads the marriage over betrothal, domestic blessing (now a domestic *preparation*), and the wedding mass.

xi. After the growth of the Sacramentaries liturgical leadership is taken from Italy by the Northern countries, in different ways; but the parent eventually shares some of the fruit of the offspring.

3   *The East*

1 The Byzantine and Armenian Rites

The Eastern rites of marriage take us into a world very different from the West, in which prayer forms and symbolism are much richer, the mixture of folk-lore and Christian ceremony more complete, and there is considerably less influence from legal minds. In all the Eastern rites the two-stage process of betrothal and marriage is still to be seen, although the two rites have in most cases long since been performed together. But documentary evidence (except for the Byzantine rite) is sparse, partly because the early texts are lacking, and partly because the necessary work has not yet been done on editing older manuscripts. Even so, there are hints here and there of what might be 'older' strata in the services.

a. The Byzantine rites

One of the encouraging signs of recent liturgical scholarship has been the growth of proper critical study of the older texts of the Byzantine services, led by the Pontifical Institute of Oriental Studies in Rome; we now understand much more clearly the diverse nature of the forces which shaped the Byzantine services throughout the Middle Ages. Some work has been done on the marriage rites (over and above the collections of manuscripts of Goar and, more recently, Dmitrievski), particularly in the researches of Raes, Baldanza, and Passarelli.[1] What is of considerable significance is that the rite reached a developed shape at a comparatively early date, and that subsequent generations did little more than add subsidiary elements to what is undoubtedly a great work of art (see Appendix 2 for chart).

The earliest Greek order of marriage is from the Italo-Greek Barberini 336 manuscript of the eighth century.[2] The betrothal consists of two prayers, which are the backbone of the later rite; they are priestly blessing-prayers, and support the priestly character of the marriage ceremonies alluded to by the Eastern evidence of the fourth century. The first is a short prayer recalling the betrothal of Isaac and Rebecca, and asking for God's blessing on the couple in their undertaking to get married in the future. No explicit consent is in the rite, and does not appear for a long time. The deacon tells the congregation to bow for a blessing, and another short prayer follows, built on the Ephesians analogy. The surprising aspect of this short rite is that we find no allusion to the signs of betrothal, e.g., ring or piece of silver or gold, which are actually mentioned by Chrysostom.[3] Perhaps customs varied from place to place. In any event, the themes of these two prayers build on what we know of the Eastern Fathers, whether in Chrysostom's praise of Rebecca, or in Basil's delight in the Ephesians analogy. The marriage rite is expectedly longer, and is entitled 'the prayer for marriages', as later manuscripts also call it. The service begins with a short litany by the deacon, into which are introduced three special petitions for the marriage, praying for their life together in the future, and for the presence of Christ at the wedding. The service is made up of three priestly blessings, round which later rites add various ingredients. Interestingly enough, Ps. 127 (which Gregory of Nazianzus quotes, and to which Chrysostom may allude) does not appear in the rite at all, until the tenth century; but it may have been an optional part of the rite, or else not placed in the text because of its priestly/diaconal character.

The first of the three blessings has a venerable feel about it, and is quoted in full in Appendix 1. I have suggested elsewhere that this may be the earliest Byzantine nuptial blessing.[4] It certainly embodies much of the teaching which we have gleaned from fourth-century writers, with the connection between creation and marriage, as well as the imagery of 'fitting together' and the 'yoke', not to speak of the Eastern custom of 'crowning'.[5] The prayer could have been familiar in some form to Chrysostom, Gregory of Nazianzus, and Basil of Caesarea. It is biblical, to the point, and refers to both partners throughout; most important of all, it has a logical structure, like the Talmudic blessings.

The couple are now crowned, and their hands are joined; and the priest prays another prayer, which is a more 'theological' composition:

Lord our God, who in the economy of your salvation at Cana in Galilee deemed to show marriage worthy of your appearing, even now guard these your servants [N and M], whom you have pleased to join together, in peace and harmony. Show them that marriage is honourable, keep their marriage-bed undefiled, be pleased to keep their life together without taint; and with pure hearts to carry out your precepts, and to reach abundant old age . . .[6]

But it does not mention crowning. This makes me suggest that the previous, and possibly older, prayer (which *does*) was originally connected with crowning; and that this second prayer was added, as a supplementary prayer of intercession for the couple. The third is a blessing over the common cup, and feels very much like a concluding prayer,[7] referring to the crowning that has taken place, and asking for the blessing of the Spirit on the couple. Traditionally this common cup has been interpreted as a eucharistic substitute;[8] I would identify it as an example of Jewish influence, for the total decline of eucharistic participation at marriage was a later development; even if it is not Jewish, it may well be a throw-back to early domestic customs, as in the later medieval West. What interests Baldanza[9] is that (only) Barberini 336 gives an *alternative* to the first of the three blessings, which is a somewhat mannered production, made up of biblical quotations, the second part of which reappears as a second prayer in a later manuscript. He suggests that it was written by Greek monks in Italy in order to defend marriage against those with Marcionist or Tatianist tendencies; but this seems a little far-fetched. More likely is the supposition that the second prayer was written in the eighth century by someone who wanted to write a much longer and biblicist marriage blessing, but was unable to dislodge the traditional (and much shorter) prayer.

Although Barberini 336 is Italo-Greek, we have more than conjecture to go on in order to establish its essentially Byzantine origin, for Theodore the Studite quotes from it in two letters written in 808 and 809. In both he quotes the second part of the *first* prayer, 'stretch forth your hand from your holy dwelling-place . . .'[10] In a subsequent letter Theodore connects marriage with the creation and blessing of Adam and defends the practice of crowning, connecting it with the reception of the Eucharist at marriage itself.[11] It is interesting that Theodore should on both occasions quote from the same prayer, the one which may be the oldest, the one which to him was the most significant.

The rite of betrothal was subjected to little future development, largely because from the eighth century imperial legislation and social customs brought it closer and closer to the marriage rite, so that from the tenth century it was rare for the two rites to be celebrated separately, and very rare for them not to take place on the same day; Coislin 213 (1027) is a Constantinopolitan rite, and the marriage service in it follows immediately after the betrothal. The two main prayers which constitute the earliest stratum of the rite (Barberini 336) are first of all prefixed with a short litany which has some special biddings for the couple (Sinaiticus 957—ninth/tenth century), and the ring formulae are added after the early prayers (Sinaiticus 958—tenth century); two rings (gold for her, silver for him) become usual from the eleventh century. The rite proper concludes with a lengthy blessing, invoking the betrothal of biblical characters, and asking for blessing on the betrothal of the couple; the second part is a catena of allusions to the use of the ring as a pledge, including Joseph in Egypt. This charming and lengthy composition first appears in Sinaiticus 973, which dates from 1153. The use of candles at the beginning is first met in Patmos 105, in the thirteenth century, long after the fusion of the two rites.

So much for the early Byzantine rite, with its obvious differences from the various Western services.[12] The additions of later centuries do not obscure the basic simplicity and theological richness of this rite. Sinaiticus 957, from the ninth/tenth centuries, is an Eastern text, not directly part of the Palestinian family of Greek liturgy, which reproduces Barberini 336 word for word, except that it does not contain the prolix alternative to the first blessing-prayer, and 'life-giving communion' (reserved?) is given after the second prayer. In the tenth century, and back in the Italo-Greek tradition, Grottaferrata G.b. VII adds quite a bit. The service is called a *leitourgia*, and follows on straight 'after all have communicated': Ps. 127 comes at the beginning, and then a *velatio* (surely the result of Latin influence, for it does not appear again); a short litany and the first prayer, as before, but followed by an epistle (Eph. 5.20–33) and a gospel (John 2.1–11);[13] then comes another litany, and a new and lengthy prayer, made up of biblical material, citing married couples from the Bible, and asking for God's blessing on the man and woman. The crowning follows, and for the first time we have proper 'formulae', with verses from Pss. 8 and 127, which could conceivably be what Gregory of Nazianzus and Chrysostom were referring to, and were left out of Barberini 336 and Sinaiticus Graecus 957. The service ends with a cup-blessing prayer which is new.

Sinaiticus Graecus 958 (tenth century) shows a similar restlessness, which is interesting to observe in its tradition, Palestine/Constantinople, and thoroughly non-Italian. On the altar are placed the crowns, together with the common cup. The service takes the same form as the earlier two, but with some significant insertions. There is an epistle and a gospel, as Grottaferrata G.b. VII, but these come *after* the crowning, and not before; the presanctified gifts are administered just before the common cup (a neat juxtaposition); and two new blessing-prayers (both long, and biblical) are added, sandwiching the joining of hands. In the next century Coislin 213 (which is dated 1027, and comes from Constantinople) has the presanctified gifts as well as the crowns and common cup placed on the altar at the beginning; it is not as complicated as Sinaiticus Graecus 958, lacking an epistle and gospel, adding one prayer to the old three of Barberini 336, but inserting the presanctified gifts just before the cup-blessing. Two subsequent Constantinopolitan rites taking us into the twelfth century keep this structure, avoiding the complexities which we have seen in Italy and Palestine. A similar unevenness in these different traditions within the Byzantine rites is discernible in the Eucharist and the Easter Vigil.[14]

Later ages add, as one would expect. Thus the formula used at the crowning which we first saw in a text in Sinaiticus 958 (tenth century) is polished in Patmos 105 (thirteenth century); and in the fifteenth century it comes into the passive terms known today, 'N. *is crowned* in the name . . .', like the baptismal formula known long before. A troparion first appears after the blessing of the common cup in Patmos 104 (thirteenth century), extending the imagery of crowning to the saints and martyrs, who have conquered eternally, and who rejoice with the congregation at the wedding; an introductory stanza is added at the end of the fifteenth century; and then, almost as if the priest and couple should do something while this is sung, there first appears elsewhere at the end of the fifteenth century the quaint custom of the priest leading the couple by the hand in a circular walk, to symbolize the eternity of the love in which they now share. Another ritualizing of something which has to happen—taking off the crowns—begins to appear in the fifteenth and sixteenth centuries; originally, this took place at home, in the bedchamber, but by now the link between church and home in matters liturgical was much more tenuous. The concluding blessings at the end are from the twelfth and thirteenth centuries, and simply serve to punctuate the rite, without adding anything drastically new.

Two other features deserve mention. First, the practice of communicating from the presanctified elements begins to die out later on in the Middle Ages, and Symeon of Thessalonica (d. 1420) feels the need to defend the custom.[15] It is easy to see why, especially since at the same time the marriage rite is frequently directed to take place after the Eucharist, as Grottaferrata G.b. VII directed in the tenth century when the presanctified liturgy was gaining popularity at weddings in the first place. Here is surely the tension between marriage as a big social occasion and a celebration of the Christian family; we have travelled a long way from Chrysostom, Gregory, and Basil! The other feature is the one which has long concerned Roman Catholic scholars: where is the expression of consent?[16] We have already alluded to the custom of inserting very short questions asking for the couple's willingness at the beginning of the betrothal rite, in the twelfth century. Rome insisted from Trent onwards that Uniate rites should contain a valid form of consent, and it was through Ukrainian mediation in the seventeenth century that the Russian Orthodox Church (under the Latinizing influence of Peter Moghila) incorporated a series of formulae along these lines, which it still does today; but they are fortunately singularly un-Latin in their style. Greece, and other Byzantine rites, followed suit, according to local customs.[17]

The 'liturgical unit' appears to be the nuptial blessing, which tallies with the kind of teaching about the need for priestly blessing which we saw as early as the fourth century, so that even when the ring-giving ceremony is introduced from the tenth century onwards the ring is not 'blessed', but a prayer is composed for the use of the priest after the ring has been given (and, in time, *both* rings). Ironically, it is one of the comparatively late prayers ('Blessed are you, Lord') which Baumstark suggests was inspired by a Jewish model;[18] we come across a similar Jewish use of 'Blessed' in the Armenian rite, probably copying the Byzantine.[19] But behind all the later overlay stands out clearly the simple and supremely beautiful rite of Barberini 336 which, together with the other parts of the service which we may conjecture are ancient (the readings?), takes us back to a particularly developed age of Christian experience, thought, and practice. Subsequent additions on the whole demonstrate flexibility, rather than unthinking accumulationism.

The nuptial blessing-prayers, like many others from the (so-called) Lesser Eastern Churches which we shall be looking at in due course, have the same structure, and appear to be modelled on an 'original' pattern. A useful comparison can be made to illustrate this observation; the first prayer of Barberini 336 is strikingly similar both to the additional prayer which now comes first in the blessing series, 'Undefiled God'[20] (which was inserted in Grottaferrata G.b. VII in the tenth century), and to the concluding prayer[21] of the betrothal rite (which first appears in Sinaiticus 973, 1153). The progression of ideas is as follows: address, creation, creation of man and woman, marriage, supplication for the married couple, marital virtues, protection from evil, and children; and such themes can be illustrated by reference to biblical characters. It seems, compared with the various medieval Western prayers, to be a standard structure. But more important than this basic community of ideas is the strongly positive view of marriage, and the enjoyment of the things of the flesh when blessed by God; all this the Byzantine marriage liturgy reinforces. You could never find a Troparion invoking the joy of the saints and martyrs at a wedding in any medieval Western rite! Moreover marriage is about *both* partners, an insight given symbolic expression in that the couple are crowned, instead of the bride alone being veiled. It is not for nothing that even though the Byzantine rite makes little fuss of the rings (when compared, say, with later medieval France or England), the fact that two rings first appear in the East shows that the Byzantine under-standing of the marriage relationship was not only highly developed but given liturgical expression. Perhaps the choice of lections clinches the matter, if we are looking for a distinc-tively Byzantine view of marriage compared with Western ones which we have already seen. The gospel reading appears always to be John 2.1–11—Christ at the wedding in Cana—a tradition that may probably go right back to the fourth century, if we take Gregory of Nazianzus' remarks seriously; and the epistle is usually Eph. 5.20–33—the Christ–Church analogy. So in-stead of hearing Jesus' pronouncement on indissolubility and

Paul's chauvinism on wifely obedience, Byzantine-rite Christians got married with a liturgy that did not encourage them go home to bed feeling slightly guilty.[22]

b. Armenia

Armenia was the first Christian nation, the result of Gregory the Illuminator's mission to that country in the second part of the third century. Since that time Armenia has known rather more political vicissitudes than other countries, and its liturgy has experienced several influences, though liturgists are nowadays (thankfully) reluctant to regard the Armenian rite as a junk-store of everyone else's fringe-practices.[23] Three influences are discernible: the general liturgical development of most rites in the fourth century; Byzantine influence in the seventh, eighth and ninth centuries; and Latin extras at the time of the crusades.

When it comes to marriage, however, we do not have much to go on. Faustus of Byzantium tells us that during the time of Nerses the Great (364–72) it was the custom of priests to bless the crowns used during the marriage liturgy; we know from other contemporary sources that consent was required before marriage, though how precisely this was expressed is unknown; and we can probably assume that betrothal was also blessed by the Church at a similar time.[24] All this does not add up to much, except that the crowns are actually *blessed*; and this evidence, coupled with other suspicions, leads Ritzer into suggesting that the liturgical use of crowns in the East originated in Armenia, which seems very unlikely, given the use of 'crowning' in the eastern Mediterranean from the fourth-century sources discussed in a previous chapter.[25] I would myself suggest that the crowning ceremony came from much older pagan practices, was reinforced by biblical traditions and Jewish practice in the Old Testament and Apocrypha, and slowly wormed its way into Christian respectability; throughout the East nothing firm points to Armenian origin (if any one country should be isolated, then probably Syria), and if Armenians actually 'blessed' the crowns, this suggests little more than the hint we have in Chrysostom that the crowns used at marriages were specially reserved for these occasions.

The first real Armenian marriage rites known in manuscript form date from the ninth to the twelfth centuries, and are to be found in Conybeare's collection.[26] The series consists of a rite of betrothal (which appears separate from what follows), and the 'Canon of Marriage', which is made up of some readings, chants, and prayers, during which the couple are blessed, and crowned, and the crowns are removed. Byzantine parentage is obvious, but the proliferation of readings marks a real difference. These lections are from MS D, a late thirteenth-century collection: Prov. 3.13–18; Gal. 5.14–18; Ps. 118; Matt. 24.30–5. The prayers which follow are novel in character and are from MS A, a ninth-century text: the deacon prays a special bidding, asking for protection through the power of 'the cross' (which is a small cross the couple keep as a sign of betrothal); and then the priest makes a prayer for the blessing of the betrothal through the cross, that they may be preserved faithful in their commitment to get married; towards the end, mention is made of the future marriage, 'let the interchange of this cross between them be deemed an inauguration and sure foundation of the base of the edifice of holy matrimony; that they may receive the crown of comeliness upon their heads, and give praise . . .' The most interesting feature is the use of the cross, perhaps introduced instead of the Byzantine ring.

The 'Canon of Marriage' is a similar mixture: three New Testament readings, Eph. 5.22–33; Matt. 19.1–9; John 2.1–11 (cf. Byzantine rite), are followed by a short litany without special biddings; the priest makes a longish prayer, which seems to be a longer variation of the old Barberini 336 prayer quoted earlier: creation, creation of man, procreation, incarnation of Christ, Cana and its miracle; supplication for the couple, in love, fruitfulness, old age, and eternity, which is quaintly referred to as 'the bridal chamber above'. Of all the Armenian prayers this is the finest from a literary, symbolic, and theological point of view, and reinforces the emphasis on Christ's presence at Cana which we see in Byzantine euchology as well; it may go back much earlier than the ninth century.

The manuscripts diverge now, A giving a somewhat prolix prayer, again asking for blessing and protection, increase in children and holiness, whereas D prays for similar purposes, elaborating on marital virtues and 'the crown of comeliness'. A later manuscript adds a special ceremony to the crowning, with the priest binding on a diadem, praying confidently about the goodness of marriage, and invoking Old Testament characters.

On the seventh day after marriage the crowns are removed, after Ps. 44, John 2.1–11 (again), and one of the marriage prayers. But MSS D (later thirteenth century) and N (eleventh/ twelfth century) have another psalm, no reading, and two prayers, the first of which is short and to the point (and probably earlier), the second being a much longer affair, praying for all the aspects of marriage which have not so far appeared, e.g. making the couple one flesh, as well as repeating similar themes, e.g. the miracle at Cana.

From these diverse manuscripts, we can see a three-stage marriage, consisting of betrothal, marriage with crowning, and the removal of the crowns a week later. The next manuscripts come from much later, but they all involve the material we have already seen, in addition to some quite new features, which include the blessing of robes, the hand-joining, and the common cup. When these ceremonies (some of which have died out) were introduced is uncertain; and a case could be argued in favour of pushing at least the domestic customs (e.g., the robes) back even as far as the Conybeare manuscripts. However, these later texts are from the last two centuries, and consist of the Constantinople 1807 Maschdoz of the Armenian Church; the Venice 1839 Uniate form; and the Vienna 1905 Uniate rite (which seems to be simplification of Venice 1839).[27] The easiest way of looking at them together is to identify six stages.[28]

The Betrothal makes up the first three:

i. The presentation and blessing of gifts, including ring, necklace, ear-rings, 'sarus', and veil, in 1807 rite; all this has been abandoned by both the Armenian and the Uniate Armenian communities, through duplication; it was obviously a domestic rite in origin, a sacralizing of folk-lore; when it was introduced is unknown—Islamic influence sometime in the Middle Ages, or even Jewish? In the 1807 rite the ring is regarded as a symbol of consent; and it also uses the betrothal prayer from the ninth century MS A. Similar readings to those in MS D reappear in both 1807 and 1839.

ii. The blessing of robes, with readings and hymns, together with a prayer of blessing, in 1807 reaching portentous length, and even mentioning such Christian monarchs as Constantius, Thiridates, and Theodosius; a beautiful composition, florid in style, universal in scope.

iii. The joining of hands, performed by 'stretching forth' the hand, which Raes suspects is taken from Islamic custom;[29] the first part of this rite appears to have originally taken place at home (as it does in 1807 and 1839), and it is concluded by a particularly fine prayer, which appears in all texts, and opens with a quotation from Basil of Caesarea's definition of marriage as 'the uniting of those who are separate';[30] 1807 has a sharing of a common cup (no marital allusions in the accompanying prayer); the party proceeds to church, where the priest hears the confessions of both partners (not in 1905); the rite concludes with a form of consent, which Raes dates to fourteenth-century Latin influence.

The Marriage follows immediately:

iv. The crowning[31] takes place during the Eucharist (though this latter seems increasingly optional, and unwelcome) after a series of readings (five in 1807 and 1905, no less than seven in 1839), the last two of which are Eph. 5.22–33 and Matt. 19.1–9, and a short litany, without marital biddings; the crowning happens in the same position as the Byzantine rites, with two blessings, which in 1807 and 1905 seem to be reworkings of the corresponding prayers in MS A of the ninth century; 1905 places the common cup blessing at this point, again in common with Byzantine practice, but this seems to be a restoration/revision, and not a survival.

v. The common cup is blessed and shared at home, but in Venice 1839 only.

vi. The removal of the crowns follows in all three texts, 1807 implying that this takes place at home, and giving three readings (including John 2.1–11), together with the symbolic use of the unsheathed sword, surely a sacralizing of chivalry; the later two rites omit this, and the readings; but all three use some version of the MS A prayer after the crowns have been taken off.

Clearly the 1839 is the most cluttered of the three, and we notice a reforming tendency in Vienna 1905. But in spite of the later overlay, the early stratum represented by the Conybeare texts is still visible, forming the backbone of the rite. Probably for reasons of national temperament, and the smaller nature of the Armenian liturgical orbit (compared with the Byzantine one), we also notice a greater degree of flexibility and adaptation in the rite.

The Armenian marriage services take us into a mixed world, but one which is basically Byzantine. The use of the cross as a symbol in the prayers, in blessings, and, above all, in the primitive betrothal rite,[32] is a peculiar feature. Furthermore, the adaptation of folk-lore (the blessing of the bride's attire) marks off this rite as distinct from the Byzantine. And the proliferation of readings certainly adds another dimension. Theologically, however, we are still in the Byzantine world, with Eph. 5 and John 2 as the foundations for the popular liturgical understanding of matrimony, though this does not prevent subsequent ages from providing additional euchology of a more pastoral character, praying for home-life in practical terms, so that the married couple may be protected from the more explicitly adverse circumstances that their future life may have in store for them. The tree has roots which are firm and plain for all to see, even though some of its branches and fruit seem strange.

2 Other Eastern Rites

The so-called Lesser Eastern Churches are by no means less interesting in their marriage rites than the Byzantine orders, but limitations of space (and the absence of the kind of detailed historical evidence which it has been possible to use in the previous section) mean that our discussion of these churches will have to consist of a description of the principal parts of the rites, together with some observations on the kind of liturgical style and theological themes of their prayers.

a. The Coptic rite

We can go back as far as the fourth century to find evidence for enforcing liturgical celebration of marriage.[1] Our next witness is a series of prayers from the tenth/eleventh-century Euchologion of the White Monastery,[2] where, after one blessing of oil, there appears a series of four prayers, the last incomplete: a blessing of the crowns, a blessing of oil for anointing the couple at marriage, and a blessing of bread and then wine. The themes of the prayers are rich and biblical, and the prayers for the crowns and the oil bear some similarity to the corresponding prayers of the later Coptic rite. But what of the bread and the wine? The wine prayer breaks off during the first sentence, and it is tempting to suggest that Cana would have figured prominently during its course; all the other prayers recall Old Testament characters, and have the same conclusion, for 'blessing and goodness . . . healing and forgiveness of sins'. It is hard to dismiss this as a eucharistic substitute, particularly as the common cup was established in the Byzantine rite in the eighth century (Barberini 336). The context is also unclear: is it a domestic rite, or are we in church? No directions are given; and, of course, the rite cannot be said to typify Coptic practice, even though it is good and strong evidence for ceremonies known in more detail in later books. In the writings of Patriarch Cyril III ibn Laklak (1235–43)[3] there is a description of marriage procedure, involving the presence of priests at betrothal, a dowry, special marriage gifts, including a cross and a ring; the marriage service takes place in church (not at home), and includes a censing of the couple, as well as the crowns, and the celebration of the Eucharist. It is not until the time of Gabriel V (1409–28) that the Copts got a uniform liturgy, whose marriage rite is reproduced by Denzinger. It is in all essentials the same as the two later orders in his collection, Rome 1763, Renaudot 1619, as well as Raes' modern text; upon which our discussion is based.[4]

The bride and family proceed to church early in the morning for the betrothal, and there the priest meets them, carrying candles, and with musical instruments. The bride is escorted to a special place at the head of the female division of the nave. The groom arrives and is conducted to a corresponding position in the male division of the nave. After a thanksgiving prayer, and censing, there are two readings (1 Cor. 1.1–10 and John 1.1–17), which lead into three intercessory prayers (nothing to do with marriage), and the creed. Three prayers for the betrothal come now, all of which have an ancient feel to them, a suspicion shared by Raes,[5] and they contain Greek words which suggest strong Greek influence at an early stage in the development of the rite; they are all about the same length, only the third is explicitly about betrothal, though the other two allude to it. After a thanksgiving, which again shows signs of Greek influence[6] (it has a eucharistic pattern, beginning with creation, and praying for the couple in the life of the Church), the wedding attire is blessed; this consists of a multicoloured tunic, a cincture, and a white veil, all rich in symbolism. The groom's party and the priest go to the bride's place in church, where the attire is put on, the groom presents the gift of the cross to the bride, and the priest places a ring in the hand of the groom, who puts it on the bride's finger. The priest covers them with a veil, and a hymn follows. Strangely only the ritual of Gabriel mentions the ring.

The marriage rite follows immediately, though once upon a time it would have been held after an interval. The two latest texts (Rome 1763 and Raes) begin with the priest asking for the consent of the couple, and the service continues in the same manner as the betrothal, with a thanksgiving and censing. After no less than four readings (Eph. 5.22—6.3; 1 Peter 3.5–7; Acts 16.13–15; Matt. 19.1–6), there is a special litany, with twelve petitions, all directly concerned with marriage, and carefully worked out so as to produce a sequence of ideas which we may by now assume to be conventional: creation, creation of woman, blessing and marriage of patriarchal couples, the incarnation, Cana, presence of God now in blessing those about to be married. Graecisms abound, as in the earlier prayers. Three marriage prayers follow, again on the same lines, the first praying for the couple to become one flesh, the second for the multiplying of blessings, including offspring, the third for protection in the future. Once more Greek words appear, and the symbolism of three is obviously deliberate, and comparable with the *three* betrothal prayers, and the *twelve* petitions in the litany.

There now comes a special rite, peculiar to the Coptic tradition; it was suppressed during the nineteenth century,[7] probably because it was unpopular, or else because no other rite did it: the blessing and anointing with oil. The prayer used for blessing the oil is intriguing, for it resembles the *first* prayer over oil in the White Monastery book which comes immediately before the wedding rite, and has no specific allusions to marriage, and may, indeed, have been used for the sick, which is what it implies at the end;[8] the *second* prayer in White Monastery is the one which tries to give a rationale for anointing at weddings. The main theme from the first prayer which comes in these much later texts is the 'prophets, priests and kings', a motif that can be traced right back to Hippolytus.[9] Reliance on White Monastery seems obvious, but the presence of *two* oil-prayers remains a mystery.

I think that the reliance on the prayer in White Monastery which is not explicitly marital, and therefore more immediately 'borrowed' from the oil-prayer for the sick, strongly suggests that the tradition of anointing married couples in Egypt is not much older than the tenth/eleventh century. If we are looking for a reason behind the practice in principle, then I would suggest connecting the oil with the crowns, an extension of the king-symbolism, even though that symbolism is absent from the prayers which accompany the crowning.

The crowns are now blessed and placed on the heads of the bride and groom, in a prayer which works out the symbolism of the crowns more fully than anything we have so far seen, linking the crowns with all kind of marital virtues and protection from ills; and future life in the Church is included. The bride and groom are blessed, and special hymns follow, rejoicing in the marriage, and the happiness of the couple. The Eucharist used to follow with the anaphora at this point, but it is now no longer celebrated. In olden days the crowns were removed at a special short ceremony seven days after the wedding, although now this is usually performed two days afterwards. The symbolism of the seven may be connected with the ideal of seven whole days of continence; the reduction may be a concession to human frailty. Raes alludes to a special *imlak* ceremony, relating to the consent of the couples, which has been described by Kopp,[10] and comes at the beginning of the rite of betrothal, and which may be the result of Islamic influence; if it is, the formulae show that it has been thoroughly christianized.

The Coptic rite is an interesting compendium of mixed material. Although the *imlak* and ring ceremonies come at the beginning of the betrothal, the priestly blessing is still central, and the marriage rite works up to the crowning as the great climax of the service, determining much more the content of hymnody and euchology than the Byzantine and Armenian rites. Of particular beauty and dignity is the blessing of the crowns:

> Holy Lord, who crowned your holy ones with untainted crowns and joined things heavenly with things earthly in unity, now therefore, our Master, bless these crowns, which we have prepared, in order to place them on your servants; may they be for them the crown of glory and honour. Amen. The crown of blessing and health. Amen. The crown of rejoicing and good fortune. Amen. The crown of jubilation and gladness. Amen. The crown of virtue

and justice. Amen. The crown of wisdom and understanding. Amen. The crown of strength and might. Amen. Grant lavishly on your servants who wear them the angel of peace and the bond of love, deliver them from every wicked thought, every wrong desire; and free them from all the hurtful and evil assaults of the devil; may your mercy be over them, hear the cry of their prayer; set fear of you in their hearts, rule their lives, so that they may live to a long old age, may they rejoice in gazing upon sons and daughters, and whoever they bring to birth may they be useful in your one and only holy Catholic and Apostolic Church, confirmed in Orthodox faith. Rule them in the way of truth through the well-pleasing grace of the Father of your good and holy Spirit, now and always.[11]

Such a prayer is of great value, for it is clearly based on the earlier version in White Monastery, and also reflects a deep theological and pastoral reflection of marriage, offered to God for his blessing and strength.

b. The Ethiopic rite

The Ethiopic rite is a cousin of the Coptic, as is manifested by the marriage service, which is the same in all essentials, except for a few peculiarities.[12]

The blessing and giving of the gifts at the beginning of the betrothal rite can be carried out either solemnly or simply, the difference being that the solemn form means that the entire marriage service takes place during the celebration of the Eucharist. This is probably a conservative feature; the 'popular' desire not to have a Eucharist has not resulted in its never being performed, but simply reserved for those who want it. There is no *imlak* rite, another instance of conservatism.

The marriage rite begins with censing, as does the mass, but the bride and groom sit together, and the priest performs a curious ceremony, which seems to be almost a 'tribal' custom. He cuts a small piece from the groom's hair, and places it on the head of the bride, and then repeats the procedure from the bride's hair, and places it on the groom's head. After the first part of the Eucharist the priest asks for the consent of the couple, in a form which appears to be influenced in principle by Latin practice, though the form and language are thoroughly Ethiopic; the ring is blessed and given. The Eucharist then continues, with the blessing and giving of the robes after the first part of the celebration. The crowning comes right at the end, using similar formulae to the Coptic rite, but the couple process round the church three times before leaving. The Ethiopic rite thus shows a slightly independent development from the Coptic, keeping some older features (e.g., closer link with the Eucharist), and adding some of its own (e.g. the cutting of the hair).

c. The Syrian Jacobite rite

Early evidence is even thinner, but we do know that betrothal had to be enforced in the thirteenth century, in the Nomo-Canons of Bar Hebraeus, where the presence of a priest and witnesses is insisted upon, as are the use of a ring, the use of the cross, and the priestly blessing; the marriage service involved crowning in church, again by the priest.[13] So it was still separated from marriage for much longer than in the Byzantine rite. The Syrian as well as the Maronite and Chaldean rites are much more lengthy than anything we have seen before, and witness to a strong tradition of prayer and hymn writing.[14]

The betrothal rite shows the interest of parents, dating from the time when they simply married off their children, but it also manifests the important role of the priest as the president, even the mediator, of the marriage. Originally the betrothal took place long before the wedding, but nowadays it normally happens on the eve of the wedding. The priest goes to the home of the groom, and asks, in the presence of witnesses, if he is willing to take the woman as his wife. On an affirmative reply, the priest goes to the home of the bride, and asks her for her consent to be married to the man. The priest blesses the ring, and places it on the finger of the bride, and the blessing-prayer is the most lush we have so far encountered, reducing to the second place anything that the medieval West could ever invent; it is based on the image of Christ as the spouse of the Church.

An intermediary rite takes place called the 'joining of the right hands', which has puzzled liturgists, because its significance seems unclear, and it has been positioned *before* the betrothal in the 1872 order. It does not appear to be practised everywhere, and may simply be a more recent *alternative* to the betrothal, which has survived as an addition, by process of accumulation. For in it the priest asks for the consent of the couple, in their presence, and at greater length than in the previous rite, where he is a 'message-boy', going from one house to the other.

The 'nuptial blessing' (i.e., the marriage), as it is called, comes next in the scheme, and modern texts precede the rite with detailed directions about what the couple must do before they are married by the priest. The rings are blessed (although Uniate Syrians insert formal expression of consent first, inevitably!) with great solemnity, involving the singing of special chants, and a rich prayer which recalls the marriages of the Old Testament, and an incense-prayer, which directs the symbolism of the perfume towards the couple, in their life of love and peace and fragrance in the years ahead. In another prayer comparison is made with the use of rings in the Old Testament, as we saw in the previous section in the Byzantine rite,[15] and the rings are finally placed on the fingers of the bride and groom.

Next comes the blessing of the crowns, as follows: after a long *Sedro* (proclamatory prayer, with psalmic material, chanted while the censer is swung), in which the crown-theme is strong and developed from biblical material, the epistle (Eph. 5.20–33) and gospel (Matt. 19.1–11) are read, and the crowns are blessed in a lavish prayer which recalls Cana as well as the Ephesians analogy. Then the priest places a crown on the head of each one with a brief formula, declaring that it symbolizes the blessing of God coming from heaven on the head of its wearer. A blessing of the couple follows, praying for protection in the years to come. The priest addresses the couple, and then removes the crowns (although once this was done some days after the wedding).

It is difficult to unravel the various strands in this rite. The rite of 'joining hands' may be later than the betrothal ceremony, and it is tempting to suggest that the use of *two* rings in the marriage rite is later than the use of *one* ring at betrothal. Of considerable interest, however, is the imagery of the hymnody and the prayers, which dwells again and again on the joy of the occasion, and the rich biblical precedents of marriage. Like the Armenian and Coptic rites, the Syrians once had a blessing of bridal robes (as Bar Hebraeus describes) during the betrothal, but this has long since disappeared. All in all, the Syrian rite of marriage is a fluid affair, ready to adapt to new circumstances. Unlike the Coptic rite, where early features are discernible, it is hard to identify different traditions within the scheme, though I would suggest that the central core of the blessing and imposition of crowns goes back to a very early age.

d. The Maronite rite

The Maronite and Chaldean rites are now being taken seriously by liturgists who are anxious to find Jewish origins and influences. They are similar and distantly related in their marriage rites; but the Maronite has a strong strand of Latin influence, as one might expect, and predictably in that part of the service where the Latins imposed on the Maronites a formal expression of consent by the couple. But similarity with the Syrian rite is stronger, and it may even represent an earlier but independent development from a similar original tradition.

The rite comes in two parts—the 'Testament' (corresponding to the betrothal), and the 'Crowning', the marriage proper.[16]

The 'Testament' happens in the house of the bride, where the whole wedding-party meets. The priest asks the couple whether they want to be married, and they then join hands, and the priest prays a prayer for them, with a strong accent on the Holy Spirit. Older texts had a special formula said by the priest after this prayer, declaring the binding nature of these vows, but this has disappeared, to great advantage, since it reads like an intrusion to the rest of the service. The rings are blessed, together with the cincture, the robe, and the bridal jewellery, thus taking us into the orbit of the Armenian rite, as well as the Copts; the imagery of the prayer is, like the Armenian, concerned with the adornment of the whole world, in praise of the creator,[17] and has nothing to do with the Church as the bride. The older texts added before the ring-blessing a formula of anointing with oil, quite different from the Coptic, and recalling the woman who anointed Jesus' feet, and praying that the bride will follow this example, and thus be granted forgiveness of sins;[18] this custom has (like the Coptic) been suppressed, but its rationale here is nonetheless ingenious. The presence of two rings may be a Byzantine influence, as also in the case of the Syrian rite. At any rate, this preliminary 'Testament' is clean and clear, without being bald and cerebral.

The 'Crowning' is longer, as one would expect. The wedding-party proceeds to church, with lighted candles, the bride dressed in the special attire which had been blessed previously. The corporate nature of the service comes across in that it takes the place of one of the seven daily offices. The proceedings begin with an introductory prayer, and the deacon censes the cross, the altar, the clergy, the people, and the crowns, while the priest prays for forgiveness in a fine prayer which mentions the final reconciliation feast in heaven, the marriage of the Lamb. A fine *Sedro* follows, recalling the creation of Adam and Eve, and asking for the blessing and strengthening of the couple in the years ahead of them. Then comes a hymn of such beauty that it should be given in full, since it evokes all that is positive and biblical in the Eastern Churches' understanding of marriage:

> Alleluia and glory to you, Lord, Christ, Spouse who was invited to the wedding in Cana of Galilee, who blessed the bridegroom and bride and made their goods abound; in your mercy may your right hand, filled with all spiritual goodness, be placed also on the bridegroom and bride, and bless them at the same time, so that they may sing your glory, and that of your blessed Father and Holy and life-giving Spirit, Alleluia, Alleluia![19]

After a dialogue between deacon and priest, in which the deacon tells the priest to bless the couple and their party, the same epistle and gospel as in the Syrian rite are read (Eph. 5.22–27; Matt. 19.3–6). Then the priest and deacon go to the entrance to the chancel, where a table stands on which are placed a cross, candles, the Gospels, the rings and the crowns. The priest asks for the consent of the couple, in a form different from the 'Testament', and he joins their hands, wrapping his stole round them, a very Latin touch. The rings are blessed in the same manner as before. Then he blesses the crowns, places one on the head of the groom, with a special 'male' prayer, mentioning Abraham, Isaac, and Jacob, and the other on the head of the bride, with a corresponding 'female' prayer, mentioning Sarah, Rebecca, and Rachel. At this point, a crown is also placed on the heads of the paranymphs, which may be a very ancient custom. A hymn attributed to Ephraem comes now, dominated by the theme of Christ as the spouse, and the members of the Church of all types and ages, as the jewels adorning the Bride. The husband and wife are again blessed individually, while the priest stretches his right hand over them in words reflecting a traditional view of their roles. The crowns are removed, and the service ends with a blessing. The rite here described is the modern one; the text in Denzinger is fuller, but incomplete.

The Maronite rite combines several elements; the Latin influence is the most obvious in the duplication of the content and ring material. Most striking is the 'Christ-Spouse' imagery in many of the prayers and hymns. In view of what we have suggested in the previous chapter regarding Jewish influence, it is tempting to identify the hymn quoted above as expressing this tradition; but it undoubtedly pushes the Cana symbolism into much greater prominence than we have seen hitherto.

e. The Chaldean rite

The early history of this rite can be traced back to the Synod of Catar (676), which insisted that a girl cannot be betrothed or marry without the consent of her parents, the use of the cross, and the blessing of the priest.[20] In the following century the regulations of Metropolitan Iso ebokht (775–90) mention the exchange of rings, by the priest, but allow marriages to take place without the presence of the priest where one is not available. Patriarch Timotheus (d. 823) declared invalid any betrothals contracted without the presence of a priest; and the code of Patriarch Iso bar Nun (823–8) mentions the use of the cross, the blessing of *Henana* (ash in water) and the ring. At the turn of the thirteenth century the betrothal rite seems to have been performed with the help of virgins, and consisted of the priest's prayers, the blessing of the chalice, holy water, the ring, and the cross. When it comes to the marriage rite itself, little is known of its early history, though there is evidence of a domestic rite, which may antedate the church ceremony, in which the blessing pronounced by the priest may have contained allusion to Matthew 15.34, the feast at the end of time.

The recent texts tell a much longer and involved story,[21] and in many respects the Chaldean rite of marriage is the most complex of all the Eastern Churches. There are six stages in the scheme, and they tell the tale of folk-lore freely mixed with public liturgy:

i. Consent. The priest sends a woman to the bride, offering her a ring. If she accepts, the marriage can take place.

ii. The joining of right-hands. This is similar to the Syrian rite, not surprisingly. When the undertaking has been made to get married, the priest blesses the couple, in prayer which mentions Adam and Eve, Abraham and Sarah, Isaac and Rebecca, and ends with a request for the intercession of the Virgin Mary. The sign of the cross is made on their hands.

iii. Betrothal. This rite begins with a long chant, made up of material from the psalter, and it is followed by a series of blessings, the first two extremely long, with such symbolism as 'embrace, Lord, the bridegroom and bride with the fire of love and mercy . . . wash, Lord . . . with the prayer of the sinner . . .'. More chants follow, in a similarly lavish tone, one of which includes such a tell-tale theology as, 'the rite of betrothal is well ordained among Christian people. The priest there is the mediator between the parties; the ring there seals the promise; the chalice filled with wine there is blood and water, and the cross a living witness; the holy water contains the blessing which one receives for the expiation of the sins of the people. Blessed is he who originally gave us this rite and made it come down to us to perform'.[22] Here is liturgical history indeed! The priest blesses the couple with a chalice, with water; then he blesses the ring by placing it in the chalice; then he places the ash in the water, making the *Henana*, and gives some to each of the couple to drink. The ring-blessing is addressed to 'Spouse-Christ', a theme even stronger here in the Chaldean rite than in the Syrian.[23]

iv. The blessing of the robes is a relatively simple office, consisting of chants and prayers, each kind of attire having its own blessing. At the end the priest blesses the crowns. (Uniates reverse the order of these sections, in order to give prominence to the betrothal.)

v. The crowning is the longest, even in its earlier forms. After an introductory prayer various psalms are sung, and prolonged chants follow, all of which are made up of psalmic material, and dwell on the theme of joy in the Church, the bride of Christ; for example, 'in your mercy, guard the bridegroom and bride from all evil, O Our Lord, multiply in their way your grace, so that with a joyous soul and a healthy body they may look to glorifying your divinity.' The epistle and gospel (Eph. 5.21—6.5 and Matt. 19.3–11, again) follow, and a very long blessing-sequence comes next, attributed to Ephraem, in which first the groom and then the bride are blessed, while the priest stretches out his right hand; the themes of these prayers are the blessing of God, protection in the future, and their life together—a most pastoral (if prolix) production. The two paranymphs each get a blessing, one for the male, the other for the female, and the service ends with a doxology to Christ the Spouse, and the sign of the cross. The wedding-feast is supposed to follow now.

vi. The making of the bedchamber. This is a simple rite, again consisting of prayers and chants, some involving the divine presence, as on any home; others refer explicitly to the new home that is being built. The imagery is as lush as ever.

The parentage of these rites with the directions quoted from earlier material is obvious, and so are the similarities with the Syrian and Maronite rites. But there are significant differences. First of all, the use of the cup of wine is attested as early as the ninth century, one century after it is known to have been used in the Byzantine rite (Barberini 336);[24] however, it is possible that the Byzantine rite derived the custom from the Chaldeans, and not *vice versa*, which would strengthen the theory that the practice is a Jewish one (it is certainly no eucharistic substitute); but this is only conjecture. Another feature, which we have seen in the Armenian rite, is the use of the cross, and most peculiar of all is the *Henana*, whose precise significance is obscure; is it a symbol of the heavenly and the earthly mixed in one, thus reinforcing the human (frail) aspects of marriage with the divine (eternal)? The formulae do not make it clear, which suggests that the practice antedates the prayer-forms by many years. The hymnic tradition probably dates from the changes made in the Chaldean liturgy under Iso-yahb, who was Patriarch in the seventh century. The full domestic rite at the end may be a survival from the earliest times, duly filled out with later hymnic material. The Chaldean rite is the quaintest of all; its pastoral, theological, and liturgical aspects take us into a very different world, but it is real, authentic, and probably quite ancient.

f. Postscript

It has not been possible to make more than suggestions concerning many aspects of the Eastern rites, and so this chapter has been less scientific than others, although we have taken care to indicate the difference between an assured conclusion, based on textual evidence, and varying degrees of probability, as yet unconfirmed. Nonetheless, the following general observations can be made on these rites:

i. Each rite is distinct, but the way we have dealt with them suggests some groupings, Byzantine with Armenian, Coptic with Ethiopic, and the three old Syriac rites. But in spite of their distinctiveness, all seven use the *crowning ceremony* as the climax of the wedding service, investing it with various kinds of symbolism, according to local tradition and liturgical flair. It supplies the foundation of much prayer and hymn writing. Nothing corresponding to the Western veiling is used, except briefly, and without much liturgical significance, in the Coptic rite,[25] where, however, both partners are veiled equally and there is no distinction between them. At Constantinople in the ninth century the crowning by the priest[26] is made the only legal form of marriage in the 89th 'novella' of Emperor Leo VI.

ii. Each rite is made up of *betrothal and marriage*, as originally two separate rites, which have in the process of time got closer together. This may be a contributory factor towards the gradual inclusion of 'consent' material, in addition to the obvious Latin influence noted in the Maronite rite.

iii. But although it is important, it never challenges the essential, historic importance of marriage as performed during a *public liturgy*, consisting of readings and prayers, and dominated by *priestly blessings*, not as some sacerdotal magic but as the offering to God of the needs and aspirations of the couple as a particular church sees fit to express them.

iv. We note that the Eastern rites are less closely connected with the *Eucharist* than the Western medieval rites, but this is because the Eastern Churches know nothing of the development of the Low Mass (which is essentially what the medieval Western eucharistic rite became).

v. Different rites freely incorporate various elements from *folk-lore* (e.g., Ethiopic hair-cutting) as well as more strictly *liturgical* features (e.g., Chaldean penitential ash). Both these strands are significant in the evolution of any rite; and both are less stable as history takes its toll (e.g. the Syrian Jacobite blessing of robes, and the Coptic anointing with oil).

vi. Sometimes the *domestic* rite (e.g., various Byzantine rites, and the Chaldean) may point to a very early domestic service which was not conducted in the church at all; but such hints as we do have probably reflect a concern to bridge the gap between Church and home from a subsequent age, long after the church ceremony was well-established.

vii. Most important of all is the *spirituality* of marriage[27] that permeates all these rites, derived strongly from an emphasis on Eph. 5, and John 2; the combination of the love of bride-groom and bride compared with Christ's love of the Church, and the presence of Christ at Cana. If some of the enthusiasm for the former occasionally overreaches a more sober dispo-sition towards this analogy (e.g., Maronite and Chaldean chants to the Spouse-Christ), it is nonetheless at the heart of much prayer and hymn composition; Jesus was present at an ordinary wedding, and blessed the proceedings, hence the use of the wine-cup, in drinking (Byzantine) or blessing (Chal-dean). To invoke that presence on couples about to get married seems to be a most biblical and positive view of marriage and sexuality.

4 *Reformulations*

1 Luther and Calvin

a. Antecedents

Luther and Calvin dominate the Reformation period in theology and also in liturgy. Luther got himself married, so that he was committed to marriage in terms both existential and theological; in this respect he differed from his medieval counterparts. Both Luther and Calvin were anxious to purify and reform what they had inherited from medieval Catholicism, and they are both—in different ways—brutal with the marriage service. But they were following in an already existing tradition, even though their ideas were more carefully thought out than their predecessors. For instance, the two orders used in Strasbourg in 1524 and 1525[1] betray a conservative revision of the Catholic 1513 Agenda, a typical German marriage rite; in 1524 the vernacular material appears without much change, and after the vows and ring-giving there is an anthology of scriptural material, from Genesis and 1 Corinthians; this is followed by prayers, including the Lord's Prayer, and an interesting adaptation of the nuptial blessing from the old mass. The 1525 form is very similar to 1524, but is longer, and more obviously reformed. Some later South German orders followed the Strasbourg tradition. More radical were the forms of marriage in the 1529 Zürich rite and Farel's 1533 book.[2] Zürich opens with a short exhortation, the Matt. 19.3–6 reading, a brief form of consent, and then four prayers, all of them rich in biblical allusion (the last three are attributed to Leo the Jew); and a fifth prayer asks for God's blessing on the couple, mentioning the Old Testament patriarchs. But the rite is bare of symbolism. Farel's service opens with a full scriptural anthology, the couple are declared married (after brief forms of consent) by the reading of Matt. 19.3–6, and the service concludes with one prayer for the couple, and a blessing. Many of the old customs have disappeared, including the ring. But both these rites show the path to be taken by Luther and Calvin in the future; the centrality of Scripture, and the lush use in new prayers of biblical images of creation, procreation, and the marriage of Christ and the Church. This last image they make much more of than their medieval predecessors.

'Many lands, many customs, says the proverb': thus begins Luther's introductory words to the 1529 'Order of Marriage for Common Pastors'.[3] When faced with many diverse practices in German Catholicism as it was being gradually adapted by his followers, his pragmatic attitude comes to the fore; he is determined to leave local secular customs unchanged, provided they do not intrude on the spiritual needs of the rite as he sees them. He observes: 'Some lead the bride to the church twice, both evening and morning, some only once' (obviously referring to the practice we have already seen of the marriage, followed by 'introducing the bride into church' on her own). He waxes sarcastic about such survivals, offering defensively his own suggestions for change, but expecting local clergy to have their own mind about what they should do 'when we are requested to bless them before the church, or in the church, to pray over them, or also to marry them'. However marriage is to be described, it is 'a worldly estate', not a sacrament, but it must be celebrated in church. He is positive about it: 'it should be accounted a hundred times more spiritual than the monastic estate, which in truth should be considered the most worldly and fleshly of all' (he ought to know—he was one himself!). But he also recalls Augustine: young people should be taught of its importance, since it is 'a divine creation and command', so that disgraceful behaviour at weddings should not be allowed; and he seems to imply that the bridal procession to church was often degraded—it was originally intended for people who 'desired the blessing of God and common prayer, but not tomfoolery or a pagan spectacle'. He repeats the combination of 'the blessing of God and common prayer', before he describes his rite in detail.

He is, predictably, strong on God's grace to protect marriage from adultery, and his rite is simple and pithy, with a strong dose of the Bible. The banns must be published, and again 'common prayer' is the way the marriage rite is described. The service itself comes in two parts. At the church door, the priest asks straightforwardly, 'Hans, dost thou desire Greta to thy wedded wife?', and 'Greta, dost thou desire Hans to thy wedded husband?' The couple give each other rings (*two* rings, therefore), without any blessing or formula, and the priest joins their right hands, saying the words of Matt. 19.6,

'What God hath joined together, let not man put asunder.' The priest then declares them married, recalling the couple's desire, expressed in public and symbolized in the joining of hands and the giving of rings. The wedding procession then goes into church, to the altar,[4] where the priest solemnly reads Gen. 2.18, 21–4 and then turns to the bride and 'groom and reads a selection of biblical passages from Genesis, Ephesians and other books. But the first reading is clearly the most important, and has a solemn liturgical character. After the readings, the priest shall spread forth his hands over them and pray thus:

> O God, who hast created man and woman and hast ordained them for the married estate, hast blessed them also with fruits of the womb, and hast typified therein the sacramental union of thy dear Son, the Lord Jesus Christ, and the Church, his bride: We beseech thy groundless goodness and mercy that thou wouldst not permit this thy creation, ordinance, and blessing to be disturbed or destroyed, but graciously preserve the same; through Jesus Christ our Lord. Amen.

Compared with other blessings we have seen from elsewhere, this is indeed a meagre prayer. But a number of points can be said about it. It is biblical, with the themes of creation and procreation, the Ephesians analogy, and the indissolubility of marriage. Although the priest stretches out his hands for this, the final prayer of the rite, the prayer is a summary of the Scripture passages previously read. For Luther, this final prayer is closely associated with the biblical material; in terms of liturgical genre, he is doing to the marriage rite what he does with his other public services; word and prayer are connected, indeed inseparable.

The earlier part of the service is clearly inspired by such non-eucharistic rites as the 1485 Magdeburg Agenda, and Bryan Spinks is correct in identifying this kind of form as the god-parent of Luther's service;[5] not that Luther needed a precedent; he would not have scrupled to go his own way in any case; but we can be sure that non-eucharistic marriage rites in Catholic Germany made the work of Luther and his colleagues easier in this respect. The form of consent is passive, not active, and gives no really detailed expression of commitment; but then the anthology of Scripture passages easily makes up for this. The rings are dealt with tacitly, again in common with some late medieval German practices; and the scriptural formula of 'joining' (known in some later medieval rites[6]) is of crucial importance, but it is a *comment* on what *has* taken place, not the imparting of grace hitherto absent. In the blessing-prayer, Luther refers to marriage as typifying the sacramental union of Christ and the Church. After 1520 he no longer regarded marriage as a sacrament; he is here using the term in the strictly Pauline manner, which, in our view, was shared by Augustine. Due to his efforts to be both primitive, biblical and liturgical, his rite marks an important step in the direction of simplicity and reform. It is the first main attempt in the West to rethink marriage liturgy since the vernacular material had begun a few centuries before, but even here the material was added to an already-existing service, and haphazardly at that. Luther's rite is a rationalization of Western medieval thought and practice, along his own lines, but two things are lacking: joy and a congregation. The shape of Luther's rite, consisting of consent, solemn reading, and solemn prayer, is the one which dominated subsequent Lutheran rites, and even where local composers added their own prayers, Luther's somewhat lugubrious prayer reappears, either as an alternative to an already established one, or as a later addition to one written by an indigenous Lutheran worthy. The commonest variations are to prefix the service with either a bidding to prayer for the couple, as Mansfeld 1580, or a preface explaining the reasons for marriage (the Prussian 1568 Agenda actually reaches no less than *nine* reasons). Prayer themes are often heavily biblical, as, for instance Frederick II (1563), where Old Testament characters get a good innings in some exceptionally verbose compositions, to be padded out further by a rite which (under Frederick IV, 1601) inserts as many references to Adam as any marriage rite known hitherto! Not all Lutheran books followed these trends initially; we also have evidence of the early use of material at the end of the rite from the old nuptial blessing, e.g., the 1540 Agenda of Electoral Brandenburg.[7]

Luther's rite arrived in Denmark with Bugenhagen in 1537, but it was soon extended by Peder Palladius, the first Lutheran Bishop of Sjaelland, whose visitation articles make interesting reading. The service should take place at the end of public worship on Sundays; children born before the marriage are 'legitimized' by being present in church at their parents' wedding (an interesting adaptation of medieval custom— association of the 'pall' at nuptial blessing); and he insists that candles be lit in church in order to make the service as festive as possible (there was a Low Church move from Germany to stop this). His rite has *three* questions to the bride and groom, first for willingness, then for commitment to lifelong union, finally for assurance that neither is betrothed to another. Palladius inserts *kirke* (church) before 'congregation', to heighten the ecclesiology, and he makes provision for a collect, epistle and gospel after the service, in the *brudemesse*. This pattern survives throughout subsequent Scandinavian books (except Sweden), for we find it with only slight adaptations in Oslo in 1862, and Reykjavik in 1869.[8] However, it eventually earned criticism in a much changed world; Bishop Mynster, Kierkegaard's old enemy, disliked the third 'question' (which had long since ceased to be of any relevance), and the Danes put out a draft revision in 1890, which was passed in 1897; the questions are now only two, and there is more scope for scriptural material, as well as greater choice in the nuptial prayers at the end of the rite, which are more joyous in their style and positive in content; the old *brudemesse* has disappeared. The same trend is noticeable in the Danish 1912 rite.[9] Palladius' enrichment of Luther is under the surface, even extended, although his 'public' ideal setting for the rite has been compromised by reality in the meantime. Sweden settled down to a similar rite, but the Manual of Olavus Petri in 1529 represents an attempt to keep many of the old customs, including the blessing of the ring, and the pall spread out over the couple. Olavus Petri probably did not know Luther's *Traubüchlein*, but even if he had, he would have gone his own way.[10]

So ends the Lutheran tale, which is one of adaptation as well as following the 1529 rite of the Reformer. But the structure remains the same, the only major difference being the insertion of a short 'address' at the beginning, which many of the German sixteenth- and seventeenth-century rites do, as well as the Danish. Even though the eventual form of the Lutheran rite is a privatized one, hymnody came to its rescue, notably in the magnificent compositions in the nineteenth century of the Danish hymn writer, Grundtvig, whose blend of natural imagery, biblical piety, and human tenderness marks off his hymns as among the finest in Western Protestantism, certainly *the* finest for use at weddings.

A significant variant, and one of vital importance to Cranmer (though admittedly not to the rest of Germany), is the tradition represented at Köln under Hermann von Wied, in the

1538 *Encheiridion* and later in the 1543 *Consultation.*[11] Luther's rite is obviously in the background, but there are differences, probably the result of Bucer and Melanchthon. The biblical reading is incorporated into the introduction, following the Brandenburg-Nüremburg order of 1533, with 'three reasons' for marriage; a prayer precedes the vows; the vows are active, again as Brandenburg-Nürnberg; and Luther's marriage-prayer at the end has an alternative, taken from the Cassel order of 1539. Here we have signs of combining Calvinist features (biblical material at the beginning, prayer before the vows) with an enriched Lutheran foundation. Cranmer uses some of this material, as we shall see later.

c. *John Calvin and Calvinism*

John Calvin was a Renaissance lawyer in his approach to matters of theological and pastoral concern, so that when we come to his directions for marriage liturgy, we do not encounter the impatience of Luther; indeed, Calvin's whole scheme is carefully composed, and was not subjected to the kind of amplification and extension that Luther's rite received when it travelled into other realms. His rite as it appears in the 1542 book, *La Forme des Prières et Chantz Ecclésiastiques*, owes a certain amount to Farel's 1533 service in Strassbourg,[12] but Calvin's is more thoroughly worked out, as the difference in the titles of the service shows: Farel has 'Declaration du sainct Mariage', whereas Calvin has 'La Forme de confirmer les Mariages devant l'église des fidèles'; which is enough to show that Calvin sees *Christian* marriage as the concern of the Christian assembly. The service should take place during public worship, before the sermon, but not on days when the Eucharist is celebrated.[13] The service is preceded by directions concerning the need for the minister to conduct the service, and the procedure to be followed regarding the publication of banns; Calvin's view of marriage is biblical and positive: the minister's job is to 'approve and confirm the marriage before the whole assembly, and to show them the dignity and excellence of the state of marriage . . . .' (shades of Eph. 5, and the Gregorian nuptial blessing!).

The marriage service is in three main parts, the biblical catechesis, the consent, and the prayer for the couple. The biblical catechesis opens with 'Our help is in the name of the

Lord ...', as Farel's rite of 1533. Then the minister reads a lengthy exhortation, explaining the origin and purpose of marriage—creation, creation of man, creation of woman, procreation, obedience of wife to husband, indissolubility, fidelity, sanctity of the human body, marital virtues. It is a beautiful collection of biblical texts, and in all the explanatory material which this (and subsequent) centuries produced, Calvin's exhortation ranks among the finest.

The consent comes in the form of a series of direct questions. In an early 1542 book,[14] the minister asks, 'Do you desire to live together in the holy estate of marriage, and to witness and confirm this here before God and his church and his congregation?' This question gets lengthened in the proper 1542 rite, copying Farel's 1533, to greater literary and theological advantage. The minister asks for impediments; he prays for the couple, in their desire to be married, that God may confirm their intention. Then he asks each partner for consent and pledge, first of the groom:

> Do you N, confess here before God and his holy congregation, that you have taken and do now take for your wife and spouse N, here present, whom you promise to keep, loving and caring for her faithfully, as should a true and faithful husband his wife; living piously with her, keeping faith and loyalty with her in all things, according to the holy word of God, and his holy Gospel?

and then of the bride:

> Do you N, confess here before God and his holy assembly, that you have taken and do now take N for your lawful husband, whom you promise to obey, serving him and being submissive to him, living piously, keeping faith and loyalty with him in all things, as should a faithful and loyal wife her husband, according to the word of God, and his holy Gospel?

The minister then prays for the gift of the Spirit on the couple:

> Father of all mercy, who by your grace called you to his holy estate of Marriage, for the love of Jesus Christ his son, who by his holy presence has sanctified marriage, making there the first sign before his Apostles, give you his Holy Spirit, to serve him and honour him in this noble estate.

The minister then reads Matt. 19.3–6,[15] and informs the couple in exalted terms that God has indeed joined them together, and that Christian marriage is about certain virtues.

The third part of the rite—prayer for the couple—follows immediately. It consists of two prayers, a long one, interceding for the couple, and a short blessing. The long prayer is of great interest; it shows no sign of reliance on any medieval text (it is taken straight from Farel's 1533 rite), but it still follows the pattern which we have seen so often before: creation of man and woman, supplication for the couple, the gift of the Spirit in fidelity and strength in future difficulties; marital virtues known and perceived as the blessing of God; their life in the future as a witness to the gospel.

There is much in this little service. The biblical catechesis comes first, and the later reading from the Bible serves to exhort the couple in their vows of marriage; in this, Calvin differs from Luther, who gives an equal prominence to the Bible, but its function is to ratify more than to exhort. Then the promises appear to be based on the medieval vows; they take no further the traditional view of wifely obedience, but add biblical warrant at the end. And like Luther's, they are passive: the minister asks, and the couple reply affirmatively. Calvin, however, interjects prayer-material before and after the promises, in order to emphasise divine grace and human resolve, and (presumably) to take attention away from any magical notion of priesthood. We shall come across such a prayer as this in Scottish Reformed and English Free Church rites.[16] Finally, the service reaches its climax in a long prayer for the couple, which proclaims the divine origin of marriage, as well as alluding to its difficulties, in a composition of great literary value and theological merit; but the rings have disappeared.

Subsequent editions of the book show practically no differences in the rite, except that it is usually called *la manière de célébrer le mariage*; and (occasionally) *la liturgie du mariage*.[17] More recently, the same structure persists, but with a certain variety. For instance, the use of rings has been reintroduced, but without actually 'blessing' them, and also the joining of hands by the minister; both these practices can be traced back to the Palatinate rite of 1563, where Lutheran origin is obvious. Under English influence, the French Reformed Church has turned the vows into active form, with the couple making the promises themselves, rather than merely answering the minister's questions.[18] And there is also variety in the way prayers have been written, though in no great differences from Calvin's classical composition, until recent times. A peculiar feature in all of them is the emphasis on the Holy Spirit, which follows from Calvin's theology of grace.[19]

Eugène Bersier's rites,[20] for his own church, in 1878, and his 'projet de révision' for the rest of the French Reformed Church, do not show much that is new; rather a desire to give the Calvinist rite a more congregational focus, including the presentation of a bible to the couple at the end, a custom which was already established in France, and persists today.

d. Conclusion

Luther and Calvin both produce a vernacular rite, taking pruning-shears to the practices of their immediate past which we now call medievalism. Luther keeps the more 'liturgical' features, e.g., using different parts of the church, keeping the ring, as well as the symbolic joining of hands; but his rite is bare, and it is left to local authorities to exercise their freedom in enriching this rite, as Luther himself hoped, perhaps rather more than took place in the event. Calvin, on the other hand, throws out much, even the ring, and the joining of hands; but from a theological point of view his rite is richer in its euchology, and it is avowedly congregational, even though the ideal soon passed into oblivion, as the rite gradually settled down to being an 'Occasional Office'. The stress on the need for divine grace in his prayers, and the more expanded nature of the promises give us a more fulsome service than Luther. As we saw in a previous chapter, the promises made in German and French medieval rites differed somewhat in length and scope, so that Luther's reticence and Calvin's full style both echo in different ways their Catholic predecessors. Subsequent cross-fertilization and local adaptation (e.g., Denmark) of the two traditions makes up for deficiencies;[21] Lutherans fill out promises and provide for prayers which are better suited to the occasion, whereas Calvinists introduce the ritual use of the ring, doubtless from popular pressure. The fundamental difference between the two traditions is the place of the Word; Calvin follows a more 'pure' liturgical principle in placing this *before* the vows, but Luther follows his own ideas, positing the Word in the latter part of the rite, to come close to the prayer. As we shall see a little later, the place of the Word becomes a problem, for psychological as well as liturgical reasons. The role of the minister continues to pose questions, and in the Lutheran tradition in Germany, debate centred on whether he 'pronounces' or 'confirms' the marriage. Much as late medieval theologians emphasized the importance of consent, the liturgical setting and content of the old rite continued to make the Reformers wary; what theologians and Councils say is one thing, what liturgical texts contain (e.g., priestly 'joining' formulae, whether in prayers, like the 'Raguel' form, or in declarations 'ratifying' the union) is a different matter.

2   The Anglican Prayer Book Traditions, 1549–1929

a. 1549

Dean Perry once observed that 'probably no service in the Prayer Book has undergone fewer changes since the Middle Ages than the form for the Solemnization of Matrimony'.[1] So we come to another liturgical Rolls-Royce, the marriage rite of the First English Prayer Book, which gives to all Anglican marriage rites for the next four hundred years a definitive shape; 'shape', indeed, is a definitive word, for through it we can discern the motives and theology of the first compilers, and, when compared with its Reformation counterparts in Germany, France and Switzerland, as well as with its medieval predecessors, the venerable and magnificent service can be seen in its true light, as a synthesis.

1549[2] comes in two parts (the preliminary banns reproduce the Sarum Manual in all essentials). The first part takes place in 'the body of the church', instead of at the church door; the second takes place 'at the aulter', and leads into Holy Communion, which should either follow immediately, or at some point on the day of marriage. Similarity of structure with Sarum is obvious, but at second sight the composition begins to look quite different.

The first part begins with a long exhortation, explaining the reasons for marriage, and giving the congregation a final chance to give an impediment to the marriage. This reproduces Sarum, in principle. Reeking of Reform, the explanation begins with a statement that the gathering 'in the face of his (God's) congregacion' is to join together the wedding couple.

Marriage was begun 'in paradise, in the tyme of mans innocencie'; Christ was present at Cana; and Paul commends it 'to be honourable emong all men'. It therefore must not be undertaken without proper consideration, and at this point Cranmer borrows a passage from Hermann von Wied's Canons of 1536, a document he would have known well. The three reasons for marriage which follow are those which were common coin in the West since the time of Augustine; the procreation of children, a remedy against sexual frustration, and companionship. Wickham Legg tried to argue some time ago that these three reasons were in some sense 'original'; he marvelled that they seemed to appear in a similar exhortation in the Paris Ritual of 1654 and were not the two books possibly deriving their material from the same source?[3] But Geoffrey Cuming (following Brightman) rightly points out that 'references to Paradise, Cana and the causes of matrimony are to be found in the Parson's Tale in Chaucer's *Canterbury Tales*';[4] and similar parallels occur in other reformed books. Peter Lombard had described marriage as a remedy against sin, and among the sources suggested by Brightman is one from Luther, 'or is hereafter for euer holde his peace'.

The priest then gives the couple a chance to lodge an impediment, in words taken largely from the York Manual. Now comes the consent, which appears in the full form of the medieval Manuals, linguistically dependent on them, but with new features as well.

First, the agreement to marry:

> N. Wilt thou haue thys woman to thy wedded wyfe, to lyue together after Gods ordeynaunce in the holy estate of matrymonie? wylt thou loue her, coumforte her, honor and kepe her, in sickeness and in health? And forsakyng all other kepe thee onely to her, so long as you both shall lyue?

This is straight from Sarum, except for 'after Gods ordeynaunce . . . matrymonie', a neat denial of the sacramental status of marriage, taken from Luther. The question to the woman is the same, except that she is asked if she will 'obey him, and serue him' before 'loue, honor and kepe him'. Instead of the York form, 'who gyves me this wyfe?', the priest asks 'who geueth this woman to be maried to thys man?'; the other Manuals asked no such question at this point. Cranmer deliberately turns attention away from the priest to the couple.

Then the vow, the couple joining hands:

I, N., take thee N. to my wedded wife, to haue and to hold from thys day forwarde, for better, for wurse, for richer, for poorer, in sickenesse, and in health, to loue and to cherishe, till death vs departe: according to Gods holy ordeinaunce: And therto I plight thee my trouth.

Similarity with Sarum, and to a lesser extent with York, is obvious. But as in the consent, so in the vow do we find again a reference to marriage as 'Gods holy ordeinaunce', replacing 'if holy chyrche it woll ordeyne'. Reformed influence on the theology of the rite is clear, but it lies hidden behind a medieval covering. When it comes to the woman's vow, the couple loose hands (an innovation from earlier practice which was perhaps designed to emphasize the mutual aspect of the vows), and the woman promises 'to loue, cherishe, and to obey', instead of the quaintly explicit 'to be bonere and buxum in bedde and atte borde'; and she gives her troth. Cranmer perhaps could not take brash medieval references to sexuality!

The ring is now given, but—like Luther—it is not blessed, and—unlike Luther—there is an accompanying formula, again taken from Sarum, hardly without a syllable being changed:

With this ring I thee wed: This golde and siluer I thee geue: with my body I thee worship: and with al my worldly goodes I thee endow. In the name of the father . . . .

The 'golde and silver' are described as 'other tokens of spousage', the word 'tokens' presumably being a deliberate defence against any superstition of a Catholic or traditional nature. The absence of any blessing is sure testimony to the intention of Cranmer; the ring 'conveys' nothing, but is only a token of troth pledged between man and wife. The old formula here bears no hint of sacramentality, and thus proves acceptable.

We now come to the first example of prayer-writing in the new marriage service, and it speaks volumes. The couple kneel, and the priest prays a longish prayer for God's blessing, taken from three sources. The first part is from the old medieval blessing of the ring, except that instead of blessing the ring, it prays for blessing upon the couple. The second is taken indirectly from the marriage of Isaac and Rebecca (those old euchological warhorses of yesteryear): 'that as Isaac and Rebecca (after bracellettes and Iewels of golde geue of thone to thother for tokens of theyr matrimonie) liued faithfully together: So these persons maye surely performe the vowe and couenaunt betwixt them made, whereof this ring geuen, and receiued, is a token and pledge'. Here again is a defence of the use of a ring and precious pieces, but it is done retrospectively, as the vows have been made. The third part concludes the prayer, and it is taken from one of the many short blessings of Sarum.

At this point, and only at this point, the priest joins their hands once more, and says, 'Those whom God hath ioyend together: let no man put a sunder' (Matt. 19. 6; N.B. not Coverdale's translation). Luther again, but with a difference; in the medieval rite the corresponding formula was the old 'Raguel' prayer ('joining' the couple), but it came immediately after the ring-giving and the psalmic verses, *manda deus* (which have disappeared altogether, and to great advantage). The thrust of the 'Raguel' prayer was to emphasize the role of the priest, in the eyes of the Reformers; and to some of them, the prayer's source in the Apocrypha would hardly commend it for use in Reformed liturgy in any case. Cranmer follows Luther in using Scripture, but like Calvin (who does not use the short Matthean formula but instead has a reading of the whole passage) he places a prayer for the couple immediately after their consent. In other words, Cranmer is anxious to put the scriptural formula from Matt. 19.6 in its proper place, *after* a prayer, not before it, in order to express a Reformed theology of the marriage rite: the couple make their vows, on which the Church prays for divine blessing. And as if to hammer the point home, the priest now declares the couple married, in a formula taken straight from Hermann's *Consultation*: 'Forasmuche as N. and N. haue consented together ...', but inserting 'golde and siluer' after the giving of the ring; he ends by 'declaring' ('*So spreche ich*' in the German original) that 'they be man and wyfe together'. Only now does the priest actually bless the couple, in a prayer based heavily on a medieval blessing: 'God the father blesse you + God the sone kepe you: god the holy gost lighten your vnderstanding ...' The sequence of thought, motive, and applied theology in this scheme so far is of the utmost importance in showing up Cranmer for the Reformer that he was.

The second part of the service begins with a psalm which is either 127 (128) or 67; the alternative has not appeared before and may be a tactful provision for couples who are unlikely to produce children. During the psalm the priest and the couple 'goe into the quier', and at the end of it the priest stands 'at the aulter' and, facing the couple, leads the congregation in the *Kyrie Eleison* (which is new), the Lord's Prayer (which is not), and five *preces* (from Sarum). Four prayers follow, each a masterpiece of conflation. The first is a prayer of blessing, made up from two Sarum prayers, one asking for the 'seed of eternal life', and the other alluding to the presence of Raphael at the wedding of Tobias and Sarah. The second prayer is for childbearing, and it may be omitted where appropriate: taken from the preparatory prayer to the Gregorian nuptial blessing, and the nuptial blessing itself, it prays for 'thy blessing on these two persons, that they may both (*sic*) be fruitful in procreation, and also liue tigether so long in godly loue and honestye, that they may see theyr chyldrens chyldren, vnto the third and fourth generation'. Cranmer has moved away from the pre-mass blessings in Sarum, and gone forward to the centre of the nuptial blessing; but his prayer is defensively for *both* the couple, and not the woman only, since he is anxious to dispel any traditional notion (Catholic or folklore) that marriage is about the change in status of the woman. The third prayer reinforces this principle, for it is a catena of material from the old nuptial blessing, keeping the sequence of ideas, but again for both the man and the woman. It is quoted in full in Appendix 1.[5] The dependence of the first part on the Gregorian nuptual blessing is clear, and its sequence determines what follows: prayer for the man, with the insertion of material from Eph. 5.25, 29; prayer for the woman, with material from the latter part of the old nuptial blessing; but the defensiveness reappears at the end: 'O lord blesse them *bothe*'. The last of the four prayers is a translation of another short pre-mass blessing, on the theme of Adam and Eve (the short version of the Lanalet prayer);[6] there are no significant alterations, but it is called a blessing in the rubrics, and has a printed cross in the text.

In the Communion, which follows immediately, there is either a Sermon, or (an allowance for the homiletically less-gifted) an exhortation, which is taken from various biblical sources; the first part is addressed to the man, and includes such passages as Eph. 5.25ff, Col. 3.19, 1 Peter 3.7; and the second is addressed to the woman, and includes such passages as Eph. 5.25ff (those relevant to the wife), Col. 3.18. 1 Peter 3.18. The use of the Ephesians material is from Hermann's *Consultation*, and the idea of reading various passages from Scripture at the end of the service seems to be inspired by Luther. The direction that the couple must receive communion is not accompanied by any proper; but, then, there is enough Scripture in the exhortation, and Cranmer's intention was probably to link the marriage with a 'normal' public Eucharist. Future developments see the rite becoming as privatized as its medieval counterpart.

What, then, of Cranmer's marriage rite? It is at root a service which is thoroughly Reformed in theology, but in post-medieval dressing, with a dash of Luther and Hermann here and there. There is both continuity and discontinuity. For those who wanted no marriage service at all, or a bare one, it is called '*solemnization* of matrimony', and yet it is not defined as a sacrament. For those who want to keep the ring, it is still there, but now placed on the *left* hand (not the right, as Sarum[7]), and it is placed 'on the book' before being given, though it is not blessed.[8] The rite is much more involved than any corresponding service of the Reformation, and we really are left to wonder what Cranmer would have made of it had the rites of medieval England been as paltry as were many of the German ones. Unlike Calvin, it comes in two distinct parts, with nave and sanctuary distinguishing them, and it is (on paper) linked with the Eucharist, whereas Calvin explicitly forbids marriage to be celebrated on those occasions when there is a Eucharist. Unlike both Luther and Calvin, but like the Zürich rite, Cranmer opts for several marriage-prayers; and, like Strasbourg in 1524 and 1525, he uses medieval sources.

It is possible, too, to see a logic between the progression of ideas in the opening exhortation and the way those ideas are prayed about in the prayers later on, and in this way it becomes didactic, along with many Reformed liturgies (compare Luther's concluding prayer, closely linked with the Scripture passages immediately preceding). All in all, it is a remarkable production, a veritable landmark in the development of marriage liturgy. While its theology is avowedly sixteenth-century Reformed, in that the contract makes up the first part of the rite, and the priest prays over the couple in pronouncing the Church's blessing on that union, its outward appearance is traditional, rich in euchology, and in biblical and theological themes.

What has disappeared, apart from the blessing of the ring? Many things: the sacramental position of the nuptial blessing, which is now spread like butter over an intercessory section of the service; repeated blessings before and after the Eucharist, though the service has enough as it is, certainly competing well with Catholic rites on the Continent at the time; liturgical paraphernalia, such as candles, sprinkled water, the ring placed on thumb, index, and second finger before resting on fourth, the pall at the nuptial blessing; and, of course, the sacramental role of the priest, who now witnesses the exchange of vows, and gives the blessing, in no sense 'joining' the couple, since God is supposed to do that. What is left, whether of relic, adaptation, or intended restoration is surely more complex than the primitive Church could ever have dreamt of; but I doubt if Cranmer had this specifically in mind when he set out to fashion his new rite from medieval tradition, Reformed thinking, and Lutheran insight.

b. 1552–1662

Gregory Dix surprised many when he suggested some time ago that 1549 was only a *ballon d'essai*, intended to prepare the ground for a much more explicit and thorough-going revision in 1552, and that all along Cranmer's theology was decidedly Swiss.[9] The alterations which were made to the marriage service in 1552 certainly support such a theory, which is backed up by what little Bucer had to say of criticism of the 1549 rite in the *Censura*. Bucer's remarks are, on the whole, laudatory.[10]

> The address which stands at the beginning of this order is excellently godly and holy: nevertheless at about the end of it three causes for matrimony are enumerated, that is children, a remedy, and mutual help, and I should prefer that what is placed third among the causes for marriage might be in the first place, because it is first.

The reversal which he suggests takes some time to filter through the minds of liturgical revisers, and certainly makes sense to priests preparing couples for marriage today. But his Continental chauvinism reveals itself in his praise for the custom of giving-away the bride, which he finds 'admirably suitable for Christian people', but which the Continental revisers had abolished. Moreover, he takes no objection to the use of the ring, and other 'tokens of spousage', provided that their significance is 'explained to the people'. Placing the ring 'on the book' is for him a sign that 'we ought to offer and consecrate all things to God, to whom they belong, before we use them'; he goes on to quote the medieval rationale for the ring on the fourth finger, because a vein 'runs from the heart to finish there'; and he regards as right and proper that the invocation of the Trinity should be included at the ring-giving. He admires the recommendation that newly-weds should receive communion, 'for Christian people ought not to be joined together in matrimony except in Christ the Lord'.

In the face of these reflections, Cranmer could hardly take the revision much further; those very aspects of the old marriage service which had either been abolished abroad, or were to be questioned by other Reformers (the ring, the invocation, the Eucharist), are upheld by Bucer himself. What, then, happens in 1552?[11]

The opening exhortation is hardly altered; the second reason for marriage now includes the explanation that it is for those who 'haue not the gift of continencie'. The giving-away and consent are almost identical to 1549; but the ring-giving omits reference to pieces of gold and silver, and instead, the preceding direction adds (after laying the ring on the book) 'with the accustomed duty to the priest and clerke', a neat liturgical expression of the wedding fee. The prayers which follow are all in the same order, but the references to pieces of gold and silver (and bracelets, etc., after the example of Isaac and Rebecca) are deleted; and the short Trinitarian blessing before the Psalm is smoothed (but still called a blessing), so that each member of the Trinity no longer does a separate job. In the first prayer after the *preces*, references to Raphael, Tobias, and Sarah are left out, but the remaining prayers are unaltered (except that the last one is no longer described as a blessing); the concluding exhortation of Scripture passages together with the recommendation about communion are similarly unchanged.

1552 takes the rite along a slightly more Protestant path, but the theology is exactly the same as 1549. The only major changes are the omission of pieces of gold and silver, together with material from the Apocrypha, both of which would please a Protestantizing party. If Gregory Dix is right about Cranmer and the Eucharist, then there is an equally strong case for the same conclusion about the marriage service. 1549 keeps some traditional features of a 'popular' rite, but with a view to their eventual abolition, and although the custom of giving precious pieces would have been hard to erase, we may similarly guess that prayers which mention angelic protection might well have been an aspect of popular piety which needed careful handling.

The next Prayer Books do little to the service. 1559[12] reproduces 1552, hardly altering a syllable, even keeping the reference to communion at the end; but since the alternative for Queen Elizabeth I would have been the English version of Calvin's Genevan services,[13] complete with its English translation of his marriage rite, any desire to return to 1549 was impracticable. The Hampton Court Conference at the beginning of James I's reign partly raised objection to the use of the ring, and after the initial heat had abated, the Conference did agree that 'the words of marriage (should) be made more clear', but nothing was done for the 1604 Prayer Book.[14] The ill-fated and much under-estimated Scottish Prayer Book of 1637[15] reproduces the English rite, maintaining the use of the ring, to which the Presbyterians (following Calvin) objected strongly; other changes include the retention of 'Church' for 'Congregation', and a stronger insistence on the Eucharist at the end of the wedding, both being features hardly likely to endear the book as a whole to the predominantly Presbyterian country of Scotland; there are also signs that some 1549 traditions were envisaged, which would be in line with the rest of the book.[16] Scottish 1637 is clearly a more High Church book as a whole, representing classical seventeenth-century Anglicanism in a way that is not true of 1662; but the marriage rite embedded there from 1549 (however slightly changed) was intended to be Reformed in its theology by its author, even though its opponents (and some of its users) a century later might have been unaware of it.

Enthusiasm for the nuptial Eucharist seems to have long been only theoretical. It appalled the Presbyterians, North and South of the border, and it is one of the points referred to by Richard Hooker in his *Laws of Ecclesiastical Polity*:[17]

> To end the public solemnity of marriage with receiving the blessed Sacrament is a custom so religious and so holy that if the Church of England be blameable in this respect it is not for suffering it to be so much but rather for not providing that it may be put in use.

Naturally, he defends the format of the 1559 service, as one of the exponents of the Elizabethan Settlement, and in his treatment of the marriage service he delves into the history of the ring-giving, going back to the medieval Manuals, as well as to Tertullian himself. His historical treatment of marriage is significant; he gives many patristic references, and shows interest also in post-Talmudic Judaism, the Seven Benedictions and all.[18]   Under the Commonwealth the Westminster Directory came into use, together with a thoroughly Calvinist marriage rite, which we shall discuss in the next section. Among the many options open to the new reign at the Restoration was Hamon L'Estrange's *Alliance of Divine Offices* (1659),[19] in which the 1604 rite is set out and defended, together with those points which the Puritans found contrary to their liking. Not only does he defend the use of the ring, but he actually suggests, 'why doth not the woman give somewhat to the man ... ?', thinking of a ring, perhaps Luther's. He was ahead of his time, and while he takes no objection to 'with my body I thee worship', he concedes that language had developed over the century, giving some amusing examples of other etymological conundra. He quotes Clement of Alexandria, no less, to commend the practice of extending the hand over the couple at the final blessing. The eucharistic link is also praised. But L'Estrange's interests were hardly those of the majority. At the Savoy Conference the two extreme groups were the Laudian party, led by Cosin and Sanderson, whose project is contained in the Durham Book, and the Presbyterians, led by Baxter and Reynolds; Baxter was charged with producing his own project, subsequently nick-named the 'Savoy Liturgy'. The Durham Book consists of the 1559 Prayer Book rite, with many annotations which have been brought together by Geoffrey Cuming in his edition of the collection,[20] and they divide into certain categories. First there are small points, which are linguistic or clarificatory, and they occur throughout the rite; for example, after the man has given the ring to the woman, he must 'hold it there' while he says 'with this ring ...', and the word 'departhe' is altered to 'doe part' in both vows; ironically, the bishops recommended updating 'worship' to 'honour' after 'with my body'[21]. Then there are those which are clearly meant to take us back to 1549, such as the reintroduction of 'other tokens of spouseage, as gold or silver, or bracelets';[22] Cosin liked this, quoted Bucer in defending it (as did L'Estrange), and used his Durham experience to note that 'it is a general Custom still to observe this Order in the North ...'. There are some innovations, such as the suggested direction by Wren (indirectly following L'Estrange?) that the priest should 'lay his hand upon their Heads' during the *first* prayer after the ring-giving (not the final blessing, as L'Estrange wanted) and the couple should kneel down. At the end, however, non-eucharistic practice rears its head, for Cosin suggests that the Communion 'shall begin, if any be that day appointed'; Wren had observed that one of the objections to Communion at weddings was that it was usually celebrated when marriages could not be conducted. They clearly would like a Eucharist, but realize that it is impracticable; it is one thing to have a wedding at a time when the Eucharist is normally celebrated in the locality, but another altogether to have a wedding and tack a Eucharist on to the end of it because the wedding is *per se* a special occasion.

However, the liturgizing group represented by the Durham Book did not win their rearguard action. Gold and silver pieces do not reappear, nor does the priest lay his hand over the heads of the couple, though we may guess that both these practices continued in some areas anyway. But the agreed alterations for the 1662 book[23] included a few of their proposals, as well as others. The opening exhortation is smoothed over, so that in a few places it reads more clearly. The vows are altered to 'death us do part'. The ring must be held by the man when he says 'with this ring'. The couple must kneel down for the marriage prayers after the ring-giving (previously they had only knelt down when they arrived at the chancel for the second part of the rite). The concluding prayers at the holy table are touched up, the first prayer changing 'sowe the seed of eternal lyfe in their *myndes*' to the more familiar and intimate '*hearts*'; the prayer for children changes the somewhat quaint 'third and fourth generation' to a petition that children should be 'christianly and virtuously brought up', altering a fine biblical (and medieval) image to a moralistic and pompous sermonette: the long prayer deletes references to Rachel, Rebecca, and Sarah, which had been suggested by Cosin, thus taking the prayer further away from the Gregorian nuptial blessing[24] and probably to great advantage. At the conclusion, however, comes the most drastic change, but one which probably brought the rite into line with how it was actually most commonly celebrated. The catena of scriptural material follows immediately after the final blessing, 'if there be no Sermon', and the service ends with the suggestion that '*it is convenient* [my italics] that the new married persons should receive the holy Communion at the time of their marriage, or at the first opportunity after their marriage'.

1662 is obviously a compromise. If any party were the losers, they were the Puritans. Such alterations as there are included one or two along Laudian lines, as well as small points of greater clarity which cannot really be assigned to any theological or churchmanship group. The most significant theological point is that while the rite is still at root a Reformed one, the role of the priest is given greater accentuation, in line with seventeenth-century Anglicanism. The main literary alteration is the omission of the Old Testament women from the long nuptial prayer. The most important pastoral point is that the link with the Eucharist is virtually severed, and the English marriage rite has *de iure* settled down to what it had probably been *de facto* for long, an 'Occasional Office', with all the privatizing tendencies that this involved.

A last liturgical question-mark before the long reign of 1662 finally got under way came in 1688 and 1689 with the so-called 'Liturgy of Comprehension',[25] a set of proposals to bring the Puritans and the Establishment together. Recently edited by Timothy Fawcett, the marriage service contained in it is of considerable interest, the changes being intended to appease the objectors. The ring is to be kept, but 'is here used only as a civil Ceremonie and pledge', and at the ring-giving, the man says 'by this our marriage we become One according to God's holy Institution. And this I declare in ye presence of Almighty God, Father …'. This passage was much debated, and, of course, the offending words 'with my body I thee worship' have gone. Some objectors were apparently ready to allow the use of the ring to be optional. The prayers are also slightly altered, and the 1688 original text even deletes the *preces*, which Methodism was to do later, (as well as to experiment with the ring-giving formula). The most significant change, however, is concerned with the conclusion. Taking the bull by the horns, in the face of strong protests against nuptial Communions, and probably lack of enthusiasm to have them anyway, this book still recommends newly-weds to go to Communion 'as soon as they have Opportunitie', and indeed they may have a Eucharist straightaway if they 'signify beforehand'; but the printed text rounds off the service by inserting the second of the 'Table Prayers' from the Communion ('O Almighty Lord and Ever-lasting God', from Sarum Prime), together with the Com-munion blessing, 'The peace of God ....' (This 'Table Prayer' already appeared at the end of the 1662 Confirmation rite.) In other words, Cranmer's rite, which was originally intended to lead straight into a Eucharist, and incorporate a sermon (or else a scriptural exhortation), simply comes to an abrupt halt with the exhortation itself when there is no Eucharist; and in order to put a liturgical full-stop to such a truncated rite, the new proposal adds a prayer and blessing both of which relate to the whole congregation. Of course, the Liturgy of Comprehension did not get anywhere near winning the day, but its marriage rite provides material for later Methodism, as well as another ill-fated rite, that of 1928.

c. 1662–1929

So the Church of England settled down to its Prayer Book, and at least on paper, nothing in the way of revision was passed by Parliament until the 1965 Alternative Services Measure; but that did not stop speculation or actual re-casting of services in sister-provinces. Charles Wheatly's *Rational Illustration of the Book of Common Prayer* contains a sublime and didactic account of the 1662 marriage rite, together with the kind of use of ancient authors and precedents which one expects from such a High Church divine.[26] He remarks, amusingly enough, that the old York Manual's inclusion of 'for fairer for fouler' in the vow was intended 'to prevent any Objection, I suppose, that might afterwards be imagin'd from either Party's declining in their Comeliness or Beauty'. He takes time over explaining the significance of the ring, aware of its history, and more aware of the need to defend its use in Reformed England, even citing Jewish practice in support.

In Scotland the English Prayer Book appears to have been used both by nonjuring Episcopalians, and also by Anglicans who 'qualified' under the Toleration Act.[27] Nonjurors seem to have adopted the custom of blessing the ring silently, which they doubtless took from medieval sources, rather than from the Eastern rites, which were dear to their hearts but which knew no ring-blessing. But there is also evidence, probably among the 'qualifying' group, that the ring was abandoned altogether; this was probably due to Presbyterian influence. Those couples who did go to Communion after their wedding went together, in procession, and were greeted at the church door, at their 'kirkin', as it was called; and at Communion they consumed the elements simultaneously.

The Proposed American Prayer Book of 1786,[28] however, provides a somewhat heavy-handed reduction, though this may reflect a desire for a speedy rite in an unsettled and mobile setting, as well as influence from Wesley's 1784 American book which we shall see in the next section. The Americans went much further than Wesley, though they kept the ring; they proposed compressing the exhortation right down to the opening sentence, denoting the purpose of the gathering, and the final sentence, asking for impediment. At the vows the words, 'and thereto I plight/give thee my troth' are to be omitted; and the ring-giving points to future paths, leaving out the offending words, 'with my body I thee worship'. The service continues until the end of the first part, and there breaks off altogether, leaving out psalm and marriage-prayers entirely. When this draft became official in 1790 two small alterations were made; the 'troth-clauses' were restored to the vows, and the Lord's Prayer (which otherwise would have disappeared without trace) was placed in a new position, immediately after the ring-giving, perhaps to reflect a supposed Cranmerian view of the rite, as near to the vows as at all possible, in the same way that Cranmer's baptismal and eucharistic rites place it after the baptism and the communion, respectively. Subsequent American revisions maintain this order; it is a landmark in the evolution of the Cranmer 'shape', and we shall meet it again. Wesley had already introduced it; and it shows that the second part of the rite had for many become meaningless. American Episcopalians were in no mood to love, cherish, and obey the English Establishment.

During the nineteenth century there was much agitation for liturgical revision from various groups in England. Winstanley and Bevan in 1828 had fought for the abolition of the words 'with my body I thee worship', as well as the repeated references to the marriage of Christ and the Church, which were said to be unhelpful; and they also wanted to leave out the prayer for children and the exhortation at the end. What might be left would be remarkably similar to America and Wesley. In the same year Hull agreed with Winstanley and Bevan, and openly praised the American 1790 book.[29] Bishop Maltby of Chichester gave a Primary Charge in 1854, and among the matters dealt with he noted universal dissatisfaction with the marriage and burial offices, observing that Dissenters could not use them (we shall discuss their rites in the next section).[30] And in 1854 a confidential group, which seems to have been strongly Evangelical, met under the chairmanship of Carr Glyn, and recommended 'omissions and alterations in the Occasional Services' as among those matters which they 'chiefly desired'. Ironically, the Reformed Episcopal Church reflected these trends, and in many respects reproduced the American rite in their 1888 Prayer Book.[31]

From another quarter altogether, Anglo-Catholics wanted the insertion of a solemn blessing of the ring, the recasting of the opening exhortation, with the deletion of 'unnecessarily and brutally coarse' language;[32] but, perhaps surprisingly, it was not until after the turn of the century that their various altar-books make any provision for a nuptial mass proper.

In a class of its own, but loosely connected with the Prayer Book tradition, is the rite of the Catholic Apostolic Church, which in 1880 produced the final edition of the *Liturgy and other Divine Offices of the Church*, although their marriage rite reached its full development quite early on in the history of this Church.[33] The framework is basically Anglican, but the new features are of great interest, and manifest this Church as deserving more attention than it has hitherto received. The opening exhortation is much the same as 1662, but the three 'reasons' are omitted (cf. the 'Dunkirk' book, which we shall see in the next section). After the address to the couple asking for impediment, there appears a new prayer, couched in biblical imagery, praying for their marriage (compare, in principle, Calvin), and this is followed by a reading (Gen. 2.18–24—an Eastern choice). The forms for consent, giving-away, and vows are much as 1662, but the vows include reference to the life of the Church ('to uphold in the faith of Christ's Church and in the ways of God's commandments'). The ring is given with a slightly rearranged formula which ends, 'and I receive thee to the fellowship of my honour', which is presumably a rewriting of the offensive 1662 'with my body I thee worship'. The Prayer Book prayers and blessing follow as usual, and then the priest helps the couple to their feet again, joins their hands, and says, 'I join together this man and this woman in holy matrimony, and I pronounce them to be man and wife, in the Name . . . Amen. Those whom God hath joined together . . . Amen.' Here come together the late medieval Norman (and Catholic Tridentine) priestly formula, followed by part of the Prayer Book's declaration, which in its turn is followed by Luther's (and the Prayer Book's) Matthean pronouncement, all in one. After two blessings, with the Peace between them, Psalm 45 is used (new in this position), and the Prayer Book order of *preces* and prayers follows. The first prayer (included in Appendix 1) is a superb blend of medieval and Byzantine imagery. At the end the priest 'shall address such words of exhortation to the newly-married as he shall consider convenient', and the service concludes with the Grace.

A proper for the Eucharist follows, complete with a collect, epistle and gospel (again Byzantine: Eph. 5.22–33; John 2.1–11), a special blessing before communion (compare, in principle, Roman practice), a post-communion prayer, as well as propers for use at the gradual and post-communion. In practice the Eucharist normally followed straight away, though the special form could be used separately from the wedding itself. All in all, this is a most interesting rite, which tries to enrich the Prayer Book tradition both by exalting the role of the priest, and by setting the entire rite within a proper liturgical context, with the reading of the Word and the Eucharist. By this, as well as by adapting material in the exhortation (rewriting the introduction and leaving the priest to address the couple in his own words), the Catholic Apostolics anticipate much of the twentieth century's liturgical thinking and practice, as well as reflect the changes being made in British Methodism.

Returning to the authentic fold of Anglicanism, the long trek to 1928 begins in 1909 with the publication of the Royal Letters of Business[34] relating to the Ornaments Rubric and modifications to services; such changes to the marriage rite as appear are of great interest. The second 'reason' ('carnal lusts') is omitted from the exhortation, following Wesleyan Methodists; one or two clarifications are made to rubrics; the prayer for children is rewritten; there is a recommendation for rewriting the concluding exhortation; and the service is rounded off with the prayer, 'O Almighty Lord and Everlasting God' (as the 1689 Liturgy of Comprehension), and a short blessing. The three main bodies of proposals which subsequently came out represented the three main groups concerned with revision, the Green Book (the Anglo-Catholic Church Union), the Grey Book (the Liberals, led by William Temple), and the Orange Book (broadly speaking, the Alcuin Club)[35]. The Anglo-Catholics left the marriage service almost unchanged (no ring-blessing, the word 'obey' remaining), but pressed for a proper nuptial mass, in which Cranmer's long blessing would be inserted between the 'Canon' and the communion. The Liberals wanted a rewritten introduction, the omission of the promise to 'obey', adapted prayers, an epistle (1 Cor. 13.4-7) and gospel (John 15.9-12), followed by the Eucharist from the offertory onwards, a radical proposal indeed; the rite could end with the 'Comprehension' Collect and the Aaronic blessing, when no Eucharist took place. The Alcuin Club went for the middle ground between extremes, and because they had the best scholarship and could get on with the influential Liberals, theirs were the proposals which eventually made up the substance of the rite in the 1927 Report, which was (for the marriage service) identical with the Book as it appeared in 1928. Much heat had earlier been generated by the proposal to leave out the word 'obey', with the Bishops Gore and Frere showing opposition, and Wickham Legg even wrote a pamphlet in which he mustered much evidence from late medieval and Reformation sources to prove why wives must promise obedience.[36]

The 1928 Book as it finally appeared[37] contains a rewritten exhortation, which keeps the old shape; the second 'reason' deals with sexuality with greater delicacy than Cranmer; the woman does not promise to 'obey' and she *gives* her troth, at long last; when the ring is given the man promises, 'with my body I thee *honour*' (from Cosin, in the Durham Book); the prayers are touched up, and modernized; the biblical exhortation is made optional; and the service can either lead straight into a nuptial Eucharist, which now for the first time has its own collect, epistle, and gospel,[38] or concludes with the 'Comprehension' Collect, and a short blessing. So at last, Cranmer's rite is finally given the surgery which the passage of time and the context of its use demanded; but the book as a whole was too much for the Parliament of the day.

Meanwhile, north of the border, a more thorough-going revision was in progress. In 1912[39] the Scots, who had for long been accustomed to shortening the exhortation, reduced it to include only two 'reasons', deleting the second one (dealing with sexuality), and providing a form of ring-blessing ('Bless this ring, O merciful Lord, that he who giveth it, and she who weareth it may ever be faithful to one another . . .'); the prayers are simplified, and the one for child-bearing is provided with an alternative (the one which appears in 1929 instead); the concluding exhortation may be omitted. In the 1929 book[40] the Scots incorporated much of the English 1928; they had waited until the result of the English débâcle before going to press. The word 'obey' disappears, another alternative portion of the psalter is provided (Ps. 37.3–7, hardly more appropriate than the other two); the blessing before the sermon is expanded to include the archaic phrase, 'who from the beginning hath sanctified and joined together man and woman in marriage'; and a eucharistic proper (different from England) is also available. America had set up a committee to revise their 1892 rite[41] and in 1929 a similar version to the English book appeared, still keeping to the abbreviated form, but including two new prayers at the end, one for children and another for home life.

d. Conclusion

So much for the classical Anglican marriage rite, so beautifully fashioned by Cranmer in 1549/1552, and gently adapted by succeeding generations to suit their needs. In spite of his intentions, later generations see it as a variation of its Sarum predecessor, rather than a reform: as W. S. Gilbert suggests in *Pinafore*, 'a clergyman shall make us one'. The variations in Scotland (in the direction of slight abridgement in certain places and enrichment in others) and America (severe abridgement) are significant, and represent a growing dissatisfaction not just with Cranmer, but with how Cranmer's rite was understood and actually performed, i.e. without a Eucharist, and as an 'Occasional Office', isolated from the regular worshipping community. Thus the Catholic Apostolics were able to restore to the marriage rite what it badly needed, setting it within a proper liturgical context.

For the Anglican tradition, however, Cranmer's rite is a liturgical one whereby the partners contract their marriage, which is witnessed publicly, presided over and blessed by the Church; and (should those partners wish it) their union may be blessed in the celebration of the Eucharist, but this is only done when there are communicants; the semi-private mass has gone for ever. What variation there is shows a dissatisfaction with that 'Occasional Office', either because Cranmer was too explicit about sexuality for the whims of Victorian and post-Victorian society (a sensitivity shared by Anglicans of all persuasions), or because the biblical allusion in his prayers (carefully taken from medieval originals) were no longer comprehensible to an age in which these characters were either remote or meaningless. Moreover, the essential theological difference between Cranmer and the majority of his Anglican clerical successors is enshrined in the typography of the 1928 rite, which distinguishes in bold print three sections of the service as 'introduction', 'the marriage', and (horror of horrors) 'the benediction'. Cranmer's Reformed theology had at last been completely concealed by medieval disguise.[42] We are now well into the era where Anglo-Catholics begin to do meaningful little ceremonies like tying stoles round couples' hands[43] (which probably sent Cranmer into multiple rotations in his grave); and Evangelicals saw little point in walking up to the holy table for a Eucharist which was seldom—if ever—celebrated.

3 Britain: Reformation and Dissent 1555–1940

The strands of Reformed traditions in Britain are multifarious, and become increasingly so in matters liturgical as the centuries progress. In the marriage liturgy this is certainly the case, and the survey in this section will steer a course through an initial period, when Knox's Genevan Service Book (strongly influenced by John Calvin in its liturgical forms) has a dominant role to play until the 1644 Westminster Directory, that low-point in liturgical life. Thereafter, English Dissent lives heavily under the shadow of the Establishment, Browne and Waldegrave leading the Independent tradition in the direction taken by Knox much earlier; and the birth of Methodism sees the Puritan objections to the Prayer Book marriage rite taken seriously, but the Anglican background of Methodists, together with High Church movements in Scottish Presbyterianism in the nineteenth century and subsequent English Congregationalism serve to bring Cranmer's shape into vogue, albeit changed in some respects. But there is opportunity for innovation among churches which do not have to observe the Act of Uniformity, and we shall note the way in which the changing understanding of the role of the partners in marriage begins to show itself.

a. From Knox to Baxter

John Knox's stormy pastorate in Frankfurt is well-known; his main task was to try to keep an 'Anglican' and a more extreme 'Calvinist' group together, and in their short-lived 'Liturgy of Compromise' in 1555 agreement was reached that the marriage service should be a much-simplified version of the 1552 Prayer Book, with the ring-giving and all other references to the ring deleted; similarly, the offensive clause 'with my body I thee worship' was omitted. The most interesting deletion, however, is the prayer immediately following the ring-giving, 'O eternal God', on the grounds that it was associated with the ring; this must either mean that people who had used the service in England from 1549 onwards interpreted the prayer as associated with the ring (unlikely), or else that its critics knew that it was partly based on the old Sarum ring-blessing (more likely).

But the 'Liturgy of Compromise' was short-lived, and Knox soon had to move to Geneva, where a less stormy scene was set, and one which he later observed was the most peaceful time in his whole life. The English Marian exiles there had no difficulty in electing him pastor in 1556, and it was in that year that his first major liturgical project was published, a joint effort, entitled *The Form of Prayers and Ministration of the Sacraments*. The marriage rite is clearly that of Calvin, but recast into English.[1] After directions concerning the banns, the service is described in detail. It must take place 'at the beginning of the sermon', and is therefore set within the context of public worship. The minister reads a long exhortation, the opening sentence of which is taken almost word for word from 1552, but with the words 'to knytte and ioyne' instead of 'to ioyne', obviously an insertion to prevent any priestly notions. After that, Calvin's 1542 rite is followed, with the exception of two short passages from 1552, the first being the Ephesians analogy (but 'the Churche' is quickly defined as 'his electe and faithfull congregation'), the second being an adaptation of the 'procreation reason' for marriage. Unlike 1552, it is heavily didactic. The short address to the couple requesting impediment is also from 1552. The consent (in the interrogative form) is also Calvin, but with the addition of 'forsakyng all other durynge her lyfe' (adapted from 1552); the response is entirely new, and perhaps is the result of English dissatisfaction with the bald Calvin 'Ouy', in preference for something fuller: 'Even so I take her before God and in the presence of his congregation'. No ring is used. The minister then reads some passages of Scripture, similar to the collection in Calvin, and the service concludes with a short blessing: 'The Lorde sanctifie and blesse you, the lorde powre the riches of his grace vppon you, that ye may please hym, and lyue together in holy loue to youre lyues ende. So be it' (another adaptation of 1552). The service ends with Psalm 127 (128), 'or some other', as Calvin. But certain things are missing. The opening verse from Calvin, 'Our help is in the name of the Lord', before the exhortation is absent; the prayer for the couple after the initial agreement to marry, the reading of Matt. 19.3–6, and also the long prayer for the couple afterwards are all lacking. Knox's Genevan order marks a definite step in a more Reformed direction than the Swiss Reformed books themselves, and it influences subsequent Scottish practice, as well as English reaction (and some practice) for a long time to come. When Knox returned to Scotland, his rite appeared in the *Book of Common Order* of 1564;[2] the text is identical to the Genevan book, even including the 1552 material, and continuing to exclude the more liturgical aspects of Calvin's service.

Knox's austere rite is again reproduced in the 1582 Middelburg book of the Separatist Browne, and once more appears in the 1584/1585 Waldegrave book,[3] but at the end of each of these, instead of the psalm, the Minister is 'to proceed to the ordinary exercise', presumably meaning the rest of the (public) service! In the (draft) 1629 Book of Common Prayer[4] (a political move by James VI and I to Anglicanize the Scottish

Church), Knox's rite appears yet again, but with a few significant changes. The rite has become an 'Occasional Office', for the opening directions do not specify any association with normal public worship, but refer to the 'freinds and nighbours'; the exhortation at the beginning is altered, with the explanatory 'electe and faithfull congregation' deleted from the Ephesians analogy, the three Prayer Book 'reasons' included, and the addition of material from the collection of Scripture sentences at the end of the Prayer Book rite (a Calvinist move). The central part of the service is as before, but a longer and fuller prayer is inserted before the short concluding blessing, and it is based on one in the Prayer Book. Evidently, marriages normally took place during main public worship in Scotland at the time, and this, together with the English features, probably helped to doom the book.

Middleburg and Waldegrave perpetuate the Calvin–Knox rite in the English Independent tradition, but the Scottish 1629 book's lack of success in commending itself to the General Assembly merely hardened resolve on the part of authorities in England and the Laudian 'new men' (like Wedderburn) in Scotland to produce another ill-fated book, that of 1637, which we discussed in the previous section. Meanwhile events after 1649 led to the Commonwealth, under Cromwell, and in the 1644 Westminster Directory[5] the extreme Puritan wing had its way. Even barer than Knox's form, the marriage rite contained in it is didactic and defensive throughout, which is hardly surprising, considering the unsympathetic and tactless nature of King Charles I's religious views.

Although marriage be no sacrament, but common to mankind, . . . yet because such as marry are to marry in the Lord, and have special need of instruction, direction, and exhortation from the word of God at their entering into such a new condition, and of the blessing of God upon them therein . . . we judge it expedient that marriage be solemnized by a lawful minister of the word, that he may accordingly counsel them, and pray for a blessing upon them.

From such a description of intentions, we know what we are in for. The marriage must be preceded by banns, the consent of parents, and is to be 'solemnized . . . before a competent number of credible witnesses', but not on Sundays. The service begins with a rhetorical prayer for the couple, and this is followed by a brief biblical exhortation about marriage; the couple then make the marriage vows, in form and language reminiscent of the Prayer Book:

> I N. do take thee N. to be my wedded wife, and do, in the presence of God, and before this congregation, promise and covenant to be a loving and faithful husband unto thee, until God shall separate us by death.

The woman promises similarly, except that she will be 'a loving, faithful, and *obedient* wife ...' The minister then, 'without any further ceremony' (i.e., no rings, or joining of hands), must declare the couple married, and concludes with a prayer for their future married life together. It is indeed a simple rite, but the declaration by the minister has reappeared, probably from the Prayer Book; but the role of the minister, and the explanatory nature of much of the service, will not have made it possible for any priestly theology of bygone days to rear its unacceptable head. Even this reduced form was short-lived, for in 1653 the Long Parliament passed a law which made marriage into a simple vow, between man and woman, using the form of the Directory, but before a justice of the peace, without church, minister, nor congregation, nor prayer, nor blessing.[6]

At the Restoration the hopes raised by Puritans at the Savoy Conference in 1661 were soon dashed by the attitude of the dominant forces of the ecclesiastical establishment. Baxter's 'Savoy' rite[7] reproduces much of the Westminster Directory, but it is filled out. The service (called 'the celebration of matrimony', no doubt taken from Calvin) begins with a sermon on marriage, and the minister asks the couple if they wish to be married (again, similar to Calvin); he asks them, in Knoxian terms, for an impediment, and then prays at great length for their life in the future, ending with a reference to the wedding of the Lamb at the end of time. The woman is then 'given' to the man by someone from her party, and the couple make the same promises as in the Directory, after which the minister declares them man and wife in a form carefully phrased to avoid any priestly overtones:

> These two persons, A and B, being lawfully married according to God's ordinance, I do pronounce them husband and wife. And those whom God hath joined, let no man put asunder.

Another beautiful prayer for them precedes the short concluding blessing. No superstitious ring, no sacramentalizing invocation of the Trinity after the declaration that the couple are married, and no hint of a Eucharist; it was everything a good Puritan would have wanted.

Baxter's rite is an attempt to enrich the Westminster Directory, and shows the fine art of the Puritan prayer-writer; and it bears out Horton Davies' contention that, though the Puritans criticized the ceremonial aspects of the Prayer Book rite, they in fact held a very high view of marriage, since so much of their piety was based around the family. Baxter's refutation of the eucharistic context of the Anglican rite needs to be counterbalanced by the assertion that he and his fellow-Puritans 'were saints who rejoiced in their marriages and their children'.[8]

So ends the story begun with John Knox. It starts the strong Calvinist influence in both Scotland and England, and settles the bare Genevan rite in the Northern Kingdom's Establishment for many years to come. Things were more negotiable in England, and the heavy Puritan objections kept up until the late seventeenth century, to the time of the 'Liturgy of Comprehension', when Dissent was becoming increasingly organized, and the rites of Browne, Waldegrave, and Baxter had a welcome following, but among a minority. The basic features of this development, taken with the corresponding part of our discussion in the preceding section, are that the seventeenth century formed Anglicanism into an alliance of different emphases, which held a more dynamic view of the sacraments and rites of the Church, as compared with the Puritans, whose views on what went on in church were decidedly more static, but were backed up by a strongly moral approach to what went on outside it. Put in liturgical terms, whereas Cranmer's shape dominated Anglicanism, Calvin's shape (suitably reduced by Knox) triumphed in Scottish Presbyterianism, and, with some adaptation by Baxter, in English Dissent.

b. Methodists

If Puritanism was the main revival movement of the seventeenth century, Methodism can surely claim the prize for the following one; John Wesley has been described in many contrasting ways, but as far as his approach to liturgy goes, a 'High Church Puritan' suits most accurately. If Cranmer disguises Swiss theology underneath a medieval dressing, Wesley disguises Baxterian theology underneath a Prayer Book dressing. In his 1784 *Sunday Service of the Methodists in North America*[9] the 'Form of Solemnization of Matrimony' both abridges and purges Prayer Book traditions. Among his alterations the most important are that the giving-away is omitted; the vows end 'and thereto I plight/give thee my *faith*' (instead of troth); all references to the ring are omitted; the walk to the altar and the accompanying psalm are omitted; and the address and reference to communion are also omitted. Thus Cranmer's rite is shortened, and loses the dramatic connection between altar and communion, most probably because the Eucharist was seldom (if ever) celebrated, and because such a walk would not accord with the architecture of North American chapels then being built. But the offending parts of the Prayer Book service as far as the Puritans were concerned were the allusions to the ring, and here Wesley follows in a long-established tradition of liturgical agnosticism; and his implicit championing of female rights puts him well ahead of his time. All these changes were incorporated into subsequent editions of the *Sunday Service* from 1786 onwards, though it is not clear whether the marriage rite was actually used in England, since Lord Hardwicke's Marriage Act of 1753 required all marriages to be held in the buildings of the Established Church. The ring reappears in 1846, but this was perhaps due to popular pressure, and in any case this was after the 1836 Marriage Act, which permitted marriages in nonconformist places of worship, provided a Registrar attended. Wesley's rite reflects lingering Puritanism, and also a popularizing trend, and his abbreviation of the rite is a pointer of things to come; the American Episcopalians followed his lead, as we saw in the previous section.

The most radical Methodist revision was in 1860, with the *Forms for the Administration of Baptism . . . for the use of such Primitive Methodist Ministers as may require them.*[10] But what has happened to Cranmer's rite, even in its truncated Wesleyan form? The exhortation is entirely rewritten, leaving out the three 'reasons'; the 'dreadful day of judgement' is deleted from the final warning to the bride and groom; the legal formulae are recited affirming no impediment; the promises end biblically, 'and *cleave* to her/him . . .'; the vows consist of the legal formulae, and end 'to be my lawful wedded wife/husband', so that the old Sarum contrasts of marital circumstance disappear; the ring-giving remains, and it is at this point that a completely new idea is brought to life, for when the man gives the ring to the woman (it is not placed 'on the book'), he says, 'I give thee this ring as a token of my love and fidelity', and the bride then says, 'I accept it as such, and will wear it as a pledge of our mutual love'; the couple are 'declared' man and wife, but the Matthean pronouncement has disappeared, and there is no reference to the ring; and a new prayer, doubtless based on Primitive Methodist piety, precedes the Cranmerian exhortation (which Wesley had dispensed with altogether), but a sermon may be preached instead; and the service ends with free prayer, and (if the minister wants), the Lord's Prayer, but the 'usual Benediction' at the conclusion is mandatory.

The 'Prims' take Wesley's work much further, and make some drastic liturgical surgery, and they show the way in which the Free Churches flexed their muscles in the light of their numerical growth and their legal freedom; they were not alone. Thus, the United Methodist Free Churches (1867)[11] reduce the opening exhortation right down to the Dunkirk and Catholic Apostolic form, reflecting Bishop Maltby's observations in his 1854 Primary Charge at Chichester. (The couple swear to no impediment, in line with the 1836 Act.) The consent and the giving-away are from the Prayer Book; and the vows are adapted, prefixed by the required formula of the Law; the woman promises obedience. The ring is here, but there is a difference; instead of placing it 'on the book', 'the Man shall now put a ring on the fourth finger of the Woman's left hand, and, holding it there, shall repeat as follows', and the formula is inspired by the Primitive rite of 1860: 'I give thee this ring as a *memorial of our union*, and as a pledge of my love and fidelity'; the Woman *may* then say, 'As such I now receive it'. The rest of the rite is much abridged. The prayer 'O eternal God' which follows is optional; and the Matthean pronouncement comes at the end of the declaration by the minister that the couple are married, following Baxter. The remainder of the service is optional in entirety: a blessing, from the Prayer Book, scriptural material (similar to the Prayer Book, but not addressed to husband, then wife, but both together), another

Prayer Book blessing, adapted, and the Grace, which may be preceded by free prayer. This rite stands midway between Wesley's abbreviation of Cranmer along Puritan lines and the more radical work of the 'Prims': the Baxter formula of declaring the marriage is a neat way of avoiding what the Tractarians were doubtless interpreting as 'priestly', the Matthean pronouncement on its own.

In the Wesleyan *Sunday Service of the Methodists* (1876)[12] a more conservative revision is discernible. The opening exhortation is slightly shortened, with the 'carnal lusts' reason omitted altogether. The ring *is* laid upon the book, again with a new formula: 'with this ring, a token and pledge of the Vow and Covenant now made betwixt me and thee, I wed thee, In the Name . . .', which is reminiscent of the form in the 'Liturgy of Comprehension', but less verbose, and insistent that the couple marry each other, since the ring is only a symbol of the union. The rest of the service is almost word-for-word from the Prayer Book. The Wesleyan *Public Prayers and Services* (1882) reproduces the same form, but the giving-away has been reintroduced, perhaps from popular pressure. In some of these old books, however, the psalm and the *preces* are crossed out, indicating the kind of reduction in the more 'Free' strands of Wesleyan Methodism. Such a development is hardly surprising in that family of Christians which has often been described as having been 'born in song'; hymnody, we may be sure, had its part to play in interpreting and enriching the abridged and adapted Cranmerian rite. The United Methodist Free Churches[15] (*c.* 1880)[13] reproduce their previous service, but with the principle difference that where the Prayer Book rite has the psalm, this order suggests two hymns; the 'free prayer' option at the end is no longer indicated, though from the way in which the service is set out, it would seem that extempore prayer was in current use among this group.

It is in the Bible Christian Church (1903)[14] that we begin to see further signs of a rethink, but still in a reduced Cranmerian framework. The opening exhortation is long, but the first part is expanded with a Genesis quote, and the three reasons have disappeared without trace; instead of 'brute beasts' we have the more delicate 'rashly, thoughtlessly, or lightly'. The giving-away is optional, but when it is used, 'the Father, or Friend taking his place, replies "I do"', which at long last gives some formal liturgical point to the medieval ceremony! In the vows, the woman need not promise to obey the man, and the ring-giving, which uses the United Methodist Free Church form, 'I give thee this ring as a memorial of our union', also has the reply, 'And as such I now receive it'. Immediately, the Matthean pronouncement is said, prefixed by 'The Lord has said', thus further distancing the rite from any priestly notions; and the couple are declared man and wife, still with the invocation of the Trinity, so despised by Puritans of old. The Aaronic blessing comes next, biblical, and also medieval (though this perhaps would not be known to the Bible Christians!), and the scriptural material follows, Eph. 5.22–8. The rest of the service is free in form, and 'may be extended' by hymnody, extempore prayer, or a long intercessory prayer which is based on some of the Prayer Book material, but freely adapted, in terms similar to Baxter's two compositions: 'Teach them to order their household in thy fear; if blessed with children, to train them for thyself; and to regard all that they possess as thy gift, to be employed in thy service.'

The United Methodist Church (1913)[15] (which brought together the Methodist New Connexion, the Bible Christians, and the United Methodist Free Churches in 1907) produces a rite which leans on both the Bible Christians and the United Free Churches. The exhortation is further shortened, with the 'reasons' omitted. The giving-away is optional, but again there is a reply to the question, 'Who giveth this Woman . . .?' The woman does not promise to obey; the ring, of course, is there, with the United Methodist Free Church form of 1867. Then there follows a mixture of the traditions: a long prayer for the couple, with a concluding portion from a Prayer Book prayer; the Prayer Book declaration that they are married; the Matthean pronouncement, with the Aaronic blessing; and a series of optional biblical quotations. A hymn may now be sung, and the final part of the service consists of a sermon, or a longish exhortation (new), and a long prayer, similar to the long prayer of the Bible Christian rite. This service is obviously a compromise of different traditions.

The Book of Offices (1936)[16] was produced after the union of the United Methodists, and the Primitives and the Wesleyans. Hymnody is optional at the start of the service and in the middle. The Prayer Book strain is much stronger. The service begins with a prayer for the couple, and the Lord's Prayer, and the exhortation reproduces the Prayer Book, but with slight abbreviation, and the omission of the 'carnal lusts' reason; but there is an alternative, which is quite short. The giving-away is again optional, and the woman does not promise to obey; and the ring-giving produces the Wesleyan formula, not that of the United Free Churches. After the declaration comes the Matthean pronouncement, followed by a Prayer Book blessing (yet more Calvinist than the Cranmerian order?); and the service continues with the prayer 'O eternal God', a hymn or psalm, a reading, and some concluding prayers; but at the end, there may be a Communion.

Methodism's many groupings were obviously concerned to revise Cranmer's rite, but, more or less, to keep to his shape. The concerns which they all show in different ways are to adapt the exhortation to meet real needs; to express the relationship between man and wife which a changing society was experiencing; to achieve a balance between set and free prayer; to incorporate Scripture into the mainstream of the service (rather than tack it on at the end); to preach a 'living' word at the end of the service, instead of read a dead one; and to allow for liturgical hymn-singing. Their interests were well-founded and fruitful.

c. Presbyterians

Scottish Presbyterian worship was much influenced by the Church Service Society in the nineteenth century, from which it derived a more strongly liturgical tradition, which was firm, if marginal. But the influence of the Society's *Euchologion* is obvious when compared with the later editions of the *Book of Common Order*. The *Euchologion* tradition, starting with the first edition in 1867,[17] tries hard to enrich Knox's rite with prayers from many different Reformed sources, official and unofficial, and by the sixth edition in 1890 has a ponderous exhortation, including biblical material along the lines of the ill-fated 1629 revision. The vows become slightly altered, and the ring appears at last, but only optionally, and it is described as a 'token of fidelity to these vows'. The couple are declared man and wife, with the Matthean pronouncement, as in Baxter, and the United Methodist Free Churches rite of the same year. The last part of the rite is made up of psalmody and prayer, the latter ingredient indirectly influenced by Baxter, in a beautiful composition looking to the Marriage of the Lamb at the end of time.

When it comes to the 1902 *Book of Common Order*,[18] we get a reduced version of the above, but with interesting novelties. The short introduction leads into an epistle (Eph. 5.22–33) and a gospel (Matt. 19.3–6); this is a rationalization of the 1629 solution (putting Cranmer's opening exhortation together with the biblical material at the end) and the Catholic Apostolic version (which puts Gen. 2 near the beginning, but delays the epistle and gospel, because a nuptial Eucharist would usually follow the service). Here at last we see a desire to break away from Cranmer's strait-jacket, and place the Bible readings first. A prayer for the couple follows, and they make their vows more exactly as the Westminster Directory, but without wifely obedience. The ring is treated defensively, even more than in the *Euchologion*: 'What pledge do you give that you will perform these your vows—have you a ring?', barks the minister to the couple. They are declared man and wife, and the Matthean pronouncement follows (as Baxter). The rest of the service consists of the blessings and prayers, the Aaronic blessing as an anthem, and one prayer includes the curious phrase, 'and adorning his doctrine', thus combining serenity and *gravitas*.

The United Free Church of Scotland's *Directory and Forms for Public Worship* (1909)[19] takes a freer form, keeping to a reduced Cranmerian shape, with exhortation at the beginning and word at the end; the couple may make their promises actively or passively, but the woman does not obey; the ring is optional, and again the minister does the talking at this point; and the prayer which follows is a drawn-out intercession for the couple, as in the Bible Christian Methodist rite, but it is mandatory. In the 1940 *Book of Common Order*,[20] designed to seal the union of 1929, the influence of the *Euchologion* tradition is even stronger, particularly in the exhortation and the concluding prayer. The wife still does not promise to obey, though she may promise to be 'dutiful', but the man must do so too, if the option is taken; the minister tells the couple to join their right hands, 'as a *seal* of the vows you are about to make', whereas the ring, which is mandatory, is given 'as a *token* of the covenant into which you have entered'. This is, perhaps, the most thorough rationalization of the symbolism in the central part of the rite. Legalistic Calvinism and a Scottish education have their uses.

The Presbyterian Church of England had existed only as a separate synod of the Church of Scotland until 1843, when it became independent, and until the 1870s its services on the whole copied the Scottish ones. The proposed new Westminster Directory met opposition in 1891[21] because of the proposal to include an invocation of the Trinity when the couple are pledged to be man and wife, on the grounds that this was an objection lodged at the Savoy Conference in 1661. Memories were indeed long, as well as the fear of making marriage into a sacrament through that invocation. The *Directory* of 1921[22] shows strong Prayer Book influence, which was no doubt mediated through the various strands of Methodism as being no longer anathema, but actually adaptable to modern needs. The exhortation is an abbreviated version of the Prayer Book, the 'reasons' being omitted. There is yet another prayer for the couple before the vows, in keeping with Calvin (but not Knox). The bride is given away, and the 'Father, or the Friend' replies to the request. The vows allow wifely obedience to be optional, and the ring is mandatory. The couple are declared man and wife, with the Matthean pronouncement appended (as Scottish Presbyterian rites, and Baxter), and the remainder of the service consists of readings and prayers, one of which is for the family life of all those present. A slightly freer form appears in the 1927 *Sacramental and Other Services*, by the Manchester Minister, Eric Philip.

Presbyterianism enriches Knox's bald rite, and the influence of Baxter is apparent throughout Scottish revision. The Prayer Book is only strongly influential in England, for obvious reasons. We note the desire for mutuality; most significant of all is the restructuring in the 1902 Scottish book; the symbolic precision of the 1940 Scottish book; and the prayer for family life in the 1921 English service. These all show that the service is being adapted to meet obvious concerns and needs.

d. Baptists and Independents

We have little evidence of Baptist practice in the eighteenth century, or before, but Horton Davies[23] quotes a description of Thomas Grantham, the leader of the General Baptists. It is an extreme Puritan's dream. The congregation assembles, the couple, and some clergy; the couple declare their intention, and may seek advice from their friends; they make some vows, which are taken from the Prayer Book; the marriage is registered; an address follows, together with a blessing. The couple are central, and the clergy are representative.

It is not until the end of the nineteenth century that the Independents show much interest in developing their own marriage rites, and once again they rely on the Prayer Book. Congregationalist worship received a considerable boost from the work of John Hunter, whose *Devotional Services for Public Worship* (1882 and 1901)[24] helped to set a high standard for English Free Church worship. But his marriage rite is dull by comparison with others we have discussed, though it has a directness and a simplicity which are engaging. The introductory exhortation is an abbreviated version of the Prayer Book, with the three reasons omitted. There is a prayer for the couple before the vows, which comes in two forms, one for England, another for Scotland (not for legal reasons, but perhaps to reflect Scottish Presbyterian practice). After the ring-giving comes an unusual feature: a longish address by the minister, declaring the couple man and wife, concluding in the Matthean pronouncement and the Aaronic blessing. After a psalm the service ends in an address and a long prayer for the couple. The wife, once more, does not obey. In the 1919 *Divine Service*,[25] however, the Prayer Book is more apparently obvious. The only differences are an abbreviated introduction, a prayer for the couple before the vows, a simple formula at the ring-giving, the declaration and Matthean pronouncement, followed by the Aaronic blessing (these last three in a Methodist order); but the second part looks more Anglican, with Lord's Prayer, *preces*, and a long prayer for the couple. An interesting feature, probably borrowed from proposed revisions in the Establishment, is the use of a concluding collect, 'O Almighty Lord and everlasting God', and short blessing, which was the 'Liturgy of Comprehension's' solution to the problem of bringing Cranmer's rite to a suitable conclusion when (as on most occasions) no Eucharist followed. C. E. Watson's *Rodborough Bede Book* (1930s)[26] does not produce a very interesting marriage rite. It follows a similar structure to the two preceding Congregationalist orders, even including *preces* in the second part of the service; one point of significance is that when the ring is given, *two* may be used; and if only one is used, the woman has to say a full formula, and not just 'And as such I now receive it' (as some of the Methodist rites). Once again, it is

English nonconformity that keeps a watchful eye on marriage as the expression of relationship.

e. Others

The Swedenborgians, Orchard's *Free Church Book of Common Prayer*, and Unitarianism hardly make good bedfellows. None of them produces anything startlingly new. The Swedenborgian rite (1881)[27] begins at great length with an exhortation, and scriptural material. The vows have more interrogatories, but at the ring-giving comes the interesting part, again probably the result of Methodist influence. The man says: 'With this ring I espouse thee to be my Wife, in the Name of the Lord and Saviour Jesus Christ, the Bridegroom and Husband of His church'; and the woman says something similar: 'With this ring, I *accept* thee to be . . .' Only one ring is envisaged, but here are contained medieval ('I *espouse*'), Anglican ('With this ring . . .'), Methodist ('I accept'), and idiosyncratic ('the Bridegroom . . .') features. Orchard's *Free Church* (1929) service[28] reproduces in large measure the 1928 rite of the Church of England, except that there is a reading (and an address may be preached) before the procession 'to the altar' during the psalm, which seems to be a good place to have it. And he even gives a proper for a nuptial Eucharist. Unitarianism, on the other hand, manifests another variant in the adaptation of the Prayer Book. Samuel Clarke's 'Dunkirk' book[29] of 1791 omits the three 'reasons', drops the word 'obey' from the woman's promise and vow, abbreviates the vow, and compresses Cranmer's 'marriage-prayers' into one, and also keeps the biblical exhortation, adapting it along moralising lines. Other Unitarian books take more drastic steps, and tend to omit the Matthean pronouncement, or else to make it into a scriptural quotation, probably to prevent it from being understood as a priestly formula. Anti-Trinitarianism is increasingly apparent in the many local nineteenth-century books, but liturgical features are retained. The structure of the rite in the 1932 *Book of Occasional Services*[30] is adapted Presbyterian; at the ring-giving the Minister says, 'by this token, the ancient and accepted symbol of marriage . . .', as if summarizing in eirenic form the polemics of post-Reformation Britain! But when the couple are declared man and wife, although other Scripture passages are subsequently read in the service, the Matthean pronouncement is not used.

f. Conclusion

From this survey, a number of important factors stand out.

i. The tradition represented by Knox in Scotland and Baxter in England lives on; but in the course of the nineteenth century the Presbyterians in Scotland expand their rite, with some caution on points of doctrine which may be misinterpreted. This expansion, involving Prayer Book material, is mediated through the Church Service Society, producing an enrichment which avoids popish practices but which still leaves a some-what 'preachy' rite.

ii. In England the power of the Prayer Book for a '*rite de passage*' is considerable, but it is carefully adapted by Methodists in ways that denote their own concerns, such as dissatisfaction with the opening exhortation; a desire for both partners to promise the same things, so underlining the concept of mutuality; a reforming zeal in the prayers, so that they are more real and less quaint, but in general these prayers provide inspiration for prolonged *extempore* prayers of intercession for the couple, marking an important euchological development; and unlike the classical forms, which start with creation, these prayers are more accented towards sanctification, reflecting the focus of Western Protestant piety.

iii. Presbyterianism in England stands also in the shadow of the Prayer Book, but not so much as to prevent it from inserting *kosher* Calvinist features, such as prayer for the couple before they make their vows. The Independent tradition synthesizes, allowing for local experiment, notably in the *Rodborough Bede-Book*. Unitarianism's critical theological stance implicitly (and explicitly) questions the use of Scripture in the course of liturgy. Eucharistic links, part of the parent's ideals in 1549, are now so marginal that they appear as an option only, in Orchard's rite, and in the Methodist service of 1936. The bold (but presumably unpopular) experiment of Scotland in 1902 of rethinking the place of the reading of the Word is a sign of things to come.

So the ground is laid for further work, and many of the protests and innovations described in this section are either ironed out or absorbed in an era of much greater change. The 1860 Primitive Methodist experiment of giving the bride a 'receiving-formula' for the ring is repeated in the 1952 Toledo rite,[31] but this is perhaps an example of great minds thinking alike, unless (perchance) Spain boasted of a devout battalion from Yorkshire in the bloodshed of the 1930s.

4   Roman Uniformity?

The sixteenth century was an important one in the history of the Roman rites of marriage, though not, perhaps, for the reasons one would at first expect. Whatever the rights and wrongs of the solution adopted at the Council of Trent over this service, throughout the period from the sixteenth to the early twentieth century, there is a strong development towards *austerity* in the rite, with the notable exception of France (and its immediate environs), where local creativity was the result of taking the Trent *Tametsi* decree rather more literally than elsewhere. Another factor, which can do as much to establish a uniform tradition as it can to dislodge it, is the enormous influence of printing on liturgical life at this time, as we have seen in the previous two sections.

a. France in the sixteenth century

The French rites of the sixteenth century continued—at least in the first half—all the trends of the preceding one.[1] Northern rites worked along the lines of the Anglo-Norman type, with the marriage ceremonies (consent, ring-giving, blessings) at the church door; a procession to the altar and a few blessings; the nuptial mass, with the nuptial blessing after the canon (often with the pall, and usually in the form of a preface); followed (sometimes) by concluding blessings, whether of the couple, or the bedchamber, or of bread and wine. Southern rites had a similar scheme, but with a different form at the beginning of the rite (which takes place inside the church, and not at the door), and with the solemn giving of the bride to the groom by the priest at the end of the mass. But the Norman rites differed from the later English in having the consent in the form of a question, not a vow, and we shall see later how crucial was this influence on Italian rites, thanks to the Norman tradition in

Southern Italy, represented by the Pontifical of Sora, in the thirteenth century. Molin-Mutembe's study reveals the two main 'zones', with the vow ('active') in the South and North-east, and the consent ('passive') in Normandy; but one or two places adopt the 'active' form, before and after Trent.

The role of the priest was described differently, through the variety of formulae given to him to 'pronounce' the marriage. The 'Raguel' prayer, which in England always came after the ring-giving, in France often lacked the 'joining' words,[2] or else came at the end of the mass. Some rites place all the eggs in the sacerdotal basket by giving the priest a strong formula—'I give her to you'; the Normans developed a neater form, 'I join you . . .'[3], which was to become very important, as we shall see. But this was not universally popular, and many Southern dioceses opted for the Matthean pronouncement which was first used in Lyon 1498.[4] Another point of variety was the position of the nuptial blessing, which many French rites started to place at the end of the mass, probably in order to give it some climactic importance, as well as to express the psychology of having a blessing at the end, a practice unknown at the time of the early Sacramentaries. The joker in the pack is the Metz rite of 1543,[5] which, alone among all the others, places the marriage rite at the *offertory* of the mass, thus trying to secure a full liturgical framework for the service; all that precedes the introit is the consent; this means that the vow comes after the liturgy of the Word. (Another peculiarity at Metz is to sing the *Veni Creator* at the end.)

b. The Roman rite and Trent

The thirteenth-century Pontifical of Sora had already established the Norman pre-mass rite in Campania, and it was only a matter of time before this influence got to Rome. In 1523 Castello edited the *Liber Sacerdotalis*,[6] which adopted a brief form of question, 'N. do you want to take N. here present as your lawful wife, according to the rite of holy Mother Church?', and these words are defined as the 'form' of the sacrament, thus paving the way for Trent. There is also a new priestly formula, midway between the German notion of 'presiding' and the Norman one of 'joining': 'by the authority I exercise, I join you . . .'; the stole is also used to bind together the hands. Castello's book had great popularity in Italy and

France. When the Council of Trent eventually discussed marriage liturgy in its penultimate session in November 1563, it made the consent formula of the partners essential, but also insisted on a priestly formula, though the stole-wrapping was not enjoined. Thus medieval insistence on consent as well as legislation concerning the Church's role in marriage were both safeguarded.[7] The Trent marriage rite decree (*Tametsi*) is in many respects the liturgical exception to the whole Council, for whereas in all other services a heavy-handed Romanizing trend is discernible, with authority resting in the Pope, the reverse seems to be encouraged: 'If certain locales traditionally use other praiseworthy customs and ceremonies when celebrating the sacrament of matrimony, this Sacred Synod earnestly desires that these by all means be retained.'[8] The Council Fathers obviously intended that for a *rite de passage* of such liturgical diversity in the Catholic world local peculiarities were to be respected, provided that the consent of the couple and a priestly formula pronouncing the marriage were incorporated into every rite. Moreover, for the first time ever, the presence of a priest at marriage was made legally binding, thus bringing to a supposed final conclusion all the medieval local conciliar decrees on clandestine unions.

The Council did discuss some details in the rite, and one bishop from the South of France proposed that the Matthean pronouncement (Matt. 19.6) which was widely used in the Midi should be an alternative to the priestly 'joining' formula; but this was hardly likely to delight the Fathers, in view of the popularity of the clause in Lutheran and Anglican traditions at the time.

The Council closed, and the Sacred Congregation of Rites was duly set up. Cardinal Santori was charged with the task of producing a *Rituale Romanum*, a new concept in liturgy. In the meantime the Tridentine Missal appeared in 1570,[9] in which the nuptial mass reverted to the old prayers, abolishing the Trinity votive, but with Eph. 5 as the epistle (a very rare occurrence in the Middle Ages), and the nuptial blessing in its traditional position, before communion, without the preface-form, and with a plural ending. Meanwhile, Santori busied himself with a draft version of the *Rituale*, which appeared in 1583 in a *Sacerdotale Romanum*,[10] in several editions. Its marriage rite contains the following items:

—consent in the Norman form, as adapted by Castello: 'N, do you want . . .'
—Matt. 19.6, pronounced by the priest, as in some Southern French books.
—*ego conjungo vos*—as Norman books at the time, but no stole-wrapping.
—sprinkling of the couple.
—blessing of '*arrharum*' (any precious jewels or stone); prayer from *LO*, and in Southern French rites of the time.
—blessing of ring: both traditional prayers.
—ring-giving, with simple invocation of the Trinity.
—*preces*.
—four short blessings.
—Ps. 127.
—three short blessings.
—mass: nuptial blessing in preface-form, plural ending, with the pall.
—before Last Gospel: 'take your spouse, as your wife from this day forward; love her, as Christ loves the Church': adapted from Southern French books of the time.
—warning to abstain for three nights.
—the 'Raguel' prayer, but without the 'joining' clause.
—Last Gospel.

This is an interesting amalgam of different elements. In the Roman Missal of 1474 a short series of blessings appears at the end of the mass, including the 'Raguel' prayer, without the 'joining' words. But this is dropped, no doubt because of the inclusion of the two small groups of short blessings, taken from various French books. The consent is from Castello, the Matthean pronouncement from the Midi, the priestly formula is Norman; and the South of France also gets its hand in with the blessing of precious pieces and the formula of giving-away at the end. It marks a considerable advance for a Roman book, but any loyal Frenchman would have found it paltry in comparison with what he was used to, though it is certainly a good deal more than some German rites included at the time. The most significant aspect of the structure of this rite is that the couple are declared married *before* the ring is given. This is indeed an irony, in the face of Protestants, who either (like Calvin) refuse to use the ring at all, or who (like Luther and

Cranmer) in different ways link the ring-giving loosely with the marriage promise.

The influence of Trent's decree on local Italian books was immediate. Gerona 1579[11] follows this order, but omits the blessing of precious pieces, and the ring-ceremony is optional—not because of Calvin, but because they appear not to have used rings much then. Bologna 1593[12] places the ring-blessing first, then has the consent (giving a vernacular form) and priestly formula. Perugia 1597[13] offers a less austere rite than these two, and follows Trent more exactly, though the preparatory prayer to the nuptial blessing is shifted to the end of the mass, preceding a sermon and a final blessing. Ferrara 1609[14] reproduces the Roman book almost exactly. Verona 1609[15] shifts the blessing of the ring to the end of the mass, although it is put on after the priestly formula at the beginning. The explanation for this curious practice seems to lie in the fact that mass is not always celebrated, so that we appear to have a subtle donkey-carrot for lapsing couples reluctant to participate in the Eucharist: if you do not stay to mass, you will not have your ring blessed! However, in 1614 appeared the *Rituale* of Paul V,[16] which was the official Tridentine book. It has a lengthy preface, referring to the Council, and to Pope Clement VIII. Its marriage rite and subsequent Missals together mark a distinct trend towards austerity. The marriage service allows for local versions at the consent and the priestly formula; but the blessing of precious pieces, Ps. 127, and all but one of the short blessing-prayers disappear. In the mass the nuptial blessing is no longer in preface-form, and the material at the end is cut down to a simple blessing.[17] But the marriage rite does repeat the Council's insistence that local customs should be retained.

c. The Ambrosian rite

Charles Borromeo[18] attended the Council of Trent and wasted no time in convoking a provincial council at Milan in 1565, a mere two years after *Tametsi*. The main alteration was, in fact, contrary to the Roman Missal and previous Ambrosian tradition but the result of Borromeo's anxiety to make the nuptial blessing of the utmost significance by placing it at the *end* of the mass, after communion, as the French rites had been doing for some time. In other respects the 1589 *Sacramentale*

Ambrosianum[19] reproduces Santori's 1583 book, but with the use of the Matthean pronouncement before the priestly formula, thus having the best of both worlds. All in all, the balance of the service is shifted to the end as the climax, for even Ps. 127 is placed there. This is the path taken by the Ambrosian rite in its subsequent editions. Borromeo takes advantage of Trent's broad-mindedness in using Castello's priestly formula, 'By the authority . . . I join . . .', together with the practice of wrapping the priest's stole round the joined hands of the couple.[20]

d. France: Neo-Gallicanism

The influence of Trent on France was also strong, in that everywhere which did not have both consent and a proper formula for the priest adopted them straightaway. But French rites continue to develop in other ways. The Bordeaux 1596 rite[21] is the first French book to have two rings, the result of Spanish influence. On the other hand, some areas where rings were not in use soon introduced them, as, for example, Besançon, and Strasbourg in 1590 even uses the ring-prayer from Castello's 1523 book. But the seventeenth century's great nationalism in France encouraged the many local rites to grow in ways not hitherto known—not that this was originally intended as defiance of Trent, considering its liberal attitude towards marriage rites. Many local French *Ritualia* preface their rites with quotations from *Tametsi*, and most of them also include sample 'exhortations' which should be given at various points in the scheme of things. Migne[22] collected many of these, and they are good reading, although heaven alone knows what precise effect they had on couples and congregations. The French Church was anxious to make Christian marriage and its proper obligations plain to those who came. Some of them even quote Tertullian's famous dictum on marriages that are 'confirmed by the oblation',[23] which is freely translated so that it refers unequivocally to the celebration of the Eucharist. The Paris Ritual of 1839[24] makes special provision for marriages when there is a non-Catholic partner, and Rodez 1733 continues the tradition of its 1513 book[25] in prescribing a most elaborate (and, one suspects, highly Visigothic) rite for the blessing of the bedchamber.

The French rites vary greatly. Some dioceses—a minority—
used the Roman Ritual to the letter, and these included the
Midi (Ajaccio, Alger, Digne), as well as most of the Bordeaux
province, though not Bordeaux itself. Many of them contain a
separate rite of betrothal, consisting of an explanation by the
priest, and a series of questions concerning the intention to
marry in the future, often quite involved, for example the
Rouen 1640 rite,[26] which has no less than eight such questions.
And at the end the priest pronounces the betrothal affirmed, *et
ego affido vos in Nomine* .... Another feature is to bless the ring
before the consent, which had happened sometimes in the
Middle Ages, and is the order taken in Paris 1654.[27] Rouen
1640 elaborates the consent in the wedding proper, so that the
couple swear their contract by *ma foi* (my faith), and in 1771
Rouen[28] substitutes the Matthean pronouncement and the old
'Raguel' prayer (*with* the 'joining' words) for the Tridentine *ego
vos conjungo* which it had had in 1640. Arras 1757[29] places great
emphasis upon the precious pieces, which are blessed and
given with a special psalmic formula, 'Thou wilt bless the
labours of thine hands ...'; and, like Amiens 1784, the couple
make vows ('active') as well as consent ('passive'). An interesting
aspect of these promises and vows is that they tend to be the
same for both, which flies in the face of the medieval English,
Lutheran, Calvinist, and Anglican rites, which invariably
include obedience in some form for the woman. These vows are
only distantly related to any Latin original; Trent's consent
formula is very brief. Amiens 1784 is a fine piece of writing, if
heavy, and seems to be a reworking of Arras 1757. The nuptial
blessing tends to be in its traditional place, usually with the
plural ending (but sometimes, e.g., Reims 1677, in the singular), and the preface-form, which had appeared in Santori's
rite but which had done in the 1614 Rituale, is not unknown
(e.g., Paris 1640 and 1697); often the pall is used (e.g., Paris
1640 and 1697, Toul 1700).[30] The Paris 1786 rite goes so far as
to add an exotic eschatological ending to the nuptial blessing.[31]
It will be seen, however, that these trends represent nothing
very new, but rather show a continuation of medieval
development and enrichment. The tale of the Neo-Gallican
demise in the nineteenth century under the influence of Dom
Prosper Guéranger's scholarly invective is well-known, but
fortunately after Vatican II these local families in their entirety
are getting the credit they deserve; and while the rest of Europe

was being less adventurous, it can at least be said that France took Trent's *Tametsi* decree to its logical conclusion, even if its treatment of other services represents something which the hard minds in Rome found difficulty in accepting.

e. Köln: a case-study

Three Köln rites (1521, 1598, and 1614)[32] tell an interesting tale, and take us from the end of the Middle Ages to the period of the authentic Tridentine *Rituale*. 1521 reproduces and enriches the 1485 rite seen in an earlier chapter; the ring is blessed, and a series of short blessings are said, after Ps. 127; and only then come the vernacular promises (like Schwerin of the same year, seen in a previous section); the priest uses the kind of formula we have seen before, praised by Molin-Mutembe for its avoidance of sacerdotalism, *matrimonium suos contractu ego confirmo in Nomine* . . . ; and the rite concludes with the Last Gospel. The second rite, for 'introducing the bride' after marriage, likewise reproduces the typical German form, Ps. 127 and the blessing of the bride. Time marches on to 1598, well after Trent's *Tametsi* decree, and the same rite reappears, but with a few slight changes in the vernacular. In both books, the title is *Solemnizatio Matrimonii*.

In 1614, there are some changes. First, a form of *betrothal* appears, shorter than some of the later French ones, consisting of two questions, and the priest pronounces a somewhat verbose affirmation, in which he 'accepts and approves, as a minister of the Church', again showing Germany's guarded way of recognizing the priestly function at marriage. The wife can be *led into church*, using the same rite as before. The 'Order for celebrating marriage solemnly' (*sic*) comes last in the series; if there has been no betrothal, the couple are asked if they want to be married, and the ring is blessed and given using the time-honoured form used at the wedding of Charles the Bald many centuries before. Then the old rite is resumed, at the end of which come the promises, which are new, and show signs of French influence, 'mein Herz' is the pledge of loyalty for the future. The marriage is 'confirmed' by the priest, and the Last Gospel concludes the service.

Trent's influence is hardly present at all, presumably because the foundations had already been laid, and the rites in question (though bare) met the essential requirements, consent by the couple and confirmation by the priest. But the peculiarly German rite of 'introducing the wife into church' takes *second* place in 1614; and there is no mention of a nuptial mass.

f. The long road onwards

When Joseph Catalani produced his *Rituale Romanum* of Benedict XIV,[33] he filled out the text (identical to 1614) with copious explanations of marriage procedure, and defended the Roman rite as it then stood. In some ways this is the truth about marriage rites in the intervening centuries down to our era. Many places did continue their own way of doing things: for instance, the Metz Ritual of 1962 persisted in placing the vows and ring-giving ceremonies at the offertory. But for most countries it was a case of taking over the Tridentine form, and adding what little they could, or even wanted. The fact that these centuries involved a considerable degree of missionary work—the age of colonization in Africa and South-America— brings the point home hard that Catholicism took its simplest marriage rite and made little attempt to relate it to the culture of the peoples who were being evangelized.

But the story by no means stops there. The Klausenburg Ritual of 1838[34] was composed for a diverse group of people. Klausenburg is the German name for the city of Cluj (now in Romania, but then part of Hungary). The marriage rite is in Latin, but certain parts are in the vernacular, in four columns; the first is (of course) Latin, then come Hungarian, German, and Ruthenian. The rite is at root 1614, but expanded; the additions include two extra questions at the beginning, 'do you want to marry . . .?' and 'do you love . . .?', before the usual question. The ring is blessed, Ps. 127 is said, and a series of short blessings follow. The priest addresses the couple. Then and only then does he pronounce them married, and he asks them to place their hand on a relic, over which they swear their fidelity to each other, and their prayer for God's help in the future. The mass follows immediately. At some subsequent date the wife is 'introduced' into church; the prayer is new, and asks for the gift of children; the marriage has obviously been consummated.

Klausenburg is an amalgam of different elements, and represents a reordering of Trent, incorporating German and Hungarian features, the latter including the 'oath' rite, which is a charming piece of folk-lore, and probably of considerably greater psychological weight for young couples than the consent, even in the slightly expanded version in which they appear.

Another East European rite is that of Breslau (=Wroclaw) in 1891,[35] in which most of the service, including the prayers, appear in German (first), then Polish. The rite begins with the priest asking the couple if they want to be married; then he blesses the ring, or wedding-wreaths (*serta* in Latin, *Kranz* in German); the couple make their vows ('actively'), the woman promising obedience; the priest makes the Matthean pronouncement, leading straight into the priestly formula; and the rite concludes with the 1614 prayer, still in German; mass follows. Less adventurous in some ways than Klausenburg, yet in others much more radical in its adaptation, Breslau shows a desire to use local customs, and incorporate them into the liturgy.

The Catholic Church at this time was still in a theological frame of mind which was heavily dominated by Trent, and at the First Vatican Council there was even an attempt to define the words of consent as the sacramental form of the rite. Fortunately this was resisted, but Pius X nonetheless pronounced on the unique significance of the consent of the partners in his Decree *Ne Temere* in 1907.[36] But the Modern World was still there, with its need (among other things) for some provision to be made for 'mixed marriages'. With the encouragement now being given to receive communion regularly, the prospect of non-Catholic partners kneeling at the altar while their spouses received the host alone was unthinkable, and in 1914 a special papal indult made provision for two forms of marriage to be used without mass being celebrated.[37] The first is meant for 'mixed marriages', and the second for use during those seasons when marriages were forbidden, e.g., Lent. Both reproduce the 1614 marriage rite, but whereas the former has two prayers at the end, the second of which is a short blessing (the priest extending his hands), the second only has one prayer at the end (and involves no priestly act of blessing). This kind of thinking reflects the conservative attitudes of another era.

g. Conclusion

This section has covered a mixed period, in which the world changed several times over, and the Roman Church became more obviously 'Roman', in the face of the Reformation. Trent clarified medieval thought, and decreed what was the irreducible minimum for a marriage rite. This was badly needed. It is all very well to rejoice in pluriformity, but marriage is still an institution, however organic, however much passing ages may identify certain aspects as 'their own', at the expense of other features, which are left to another age to exaggerate in its own way. But whereas France led the fashion in that vital area of liturgical life—adaptation—the trend was generally towards mediocrity, even given the vivacity of Metz, which the twentieth century takes over in the American Episcopal Church;[38] and even given those areas of Eastern Europe where popular culture brought into church crowns instead of rings (in Wroclaw), and a delightful way of swearing fidelity over a relic (in Cluj). It is these few *exceptions* to the rule that are to point to the future.

5   *Foreground*

1 Adaptation and Rethink: Roman and Anglican

The twentieth century can be divided (for all the main churches) into an initial period (roughly the first half) where the old rites continue, but with some modification, and the era of revision and renewal, dominated by the Second Vatican Council, after which the rites which appear begin to take on a very different aspect. Not that all non-Roman Churches bowed down to the Vatican Council—in some cases they had no need to, as far as marriage rites were concerned—but the work of Roman Catholic liturgical scholars prior to the Council, as well as after, was highly significant. Before the Second World War the German Benedictine, Basilius Binder,[1] had drawn attention to the great variety of local marriage rites in the Middle Ages and he took particular interest in their characteristics. Then after the war appeared the seminal work of another German Benedictine, Korbinian Ritzer,[2] whose name has occurred frequently in our discussion. In his study of marriage during the first millenium, he likewise pointed up local peculiarities, and set them within a legal framework; and his collection of texts is testimony in itself that the Gregorian Sacramentary only masked local differences. We have had occasion to differ from some of his conclusions, notably in the early period before the appearance of texts, but his study is the most important step taken so far in applying a proper liturgical method to marriage rites, and his influence on the Roman revisers and commentators is clear enough from the footnotes of liturgical journals.

Then in 1974 appeared a remarkable joint publication, consisting of a study of French marriage rites from the twelfth to the sixteenth centuries, the result of a doctoral thesis by Protais Mutembe on one hundred and three services from the sixteenth century, and a wider study of French rites by Jean-Baptiste Molin;[3] the foreword was written by Pierre-Marie Gy, director of the Liturgical Institute in Paris, who had been involved with both these laborious researchers, and had also chaired the committee which had produced the new Roman rite in 1969.[4] The specific nature of this study is its fascination, particularly as France knew many differing influences in the late Middle Ages, and the most important fact established by Molin and Mutembe (whom we have dubbed 'Molin-Mutembe' somewhat impersonally) is the strong Visigothic tradition which was firmly built up from the beginning of the period in question in the South of France; some of the theories suggested about marriage promises and vows we have been led to question, but the book is a mine of information, and one always senses in reading it the dual presence of an African who is constantly aware of the social-culture aspects of marriage (Mutembe) and the tireless care of a brilliant medievalist who is thoroughly at home with local service-books (Molin). Binder, Ritzer, and Molin and Mutembe have all, in different ways, helped to fashion the marriage rites which we shall now set about discussing, however indirect that influence is. For once proper studies of a service have appeared, the person assigned the task of drawing up a new rite can see in perspective primary ingredients and secondary elements.

a. Roman Catholic

As we have already seen, Trent encouraged local traditions to be incorporated into the service in the 1614 *Rituale Romanum*; this did happen, but nothing like to the extent known in the Middle Ages, where, of course, there was no central liturgical authority at all. Apart from the Neo-Gallican trends, which were essentially local, the tendency in recent centuries has been for *national* versions of the *Rituale* to be produced, sometimes on a slightly international basis, for instance in the *Manuale Sacerdotum* published in Köln in 1893,[5] where the only national variation is that whereas the German, French, English and Dutch versions of the consent are a translation of the Latin, the Polish is more involved, with three questions, and the bride promises to obey. In this century the tendency has been to translate more and more of the service into the vernacular, and in this respect the German version in 1950[6] was the most radical (trying to set the service in a more liturgical context, with an opening collect, two rings, and most of the rite conducted in the vernacular); Germany clearly paved the way for the 1969 revision. Local survivals continue, however, so that the Metz custom of placing the promises and ring-giving before the offertory of the mass persists, even in the 1962 diocesan Ritual. But you only have to look at the work of Molin and Mutembe in late medieval France to realize that the extent to which Trent's liberties were taken was quite tame by comparison.

The Second Vatican Council opened doors which even the wildest dreams of Binder or Ritzer could not have created. In the Constitution on the Sacred Liturgy the section dealing with marriage is placed after ordination (hitherto Rome generally dealt with marriage after burial), and it is worth quoting in full:

77. The marriage rite now found in the Roman Ritual is to be revised and enriched in a way which more clearly expresses the grace of the sacrament and the duties of the spouses.
'If certain locales traditionally use other praiseworthy customs . . .' [a brief quotation from Trent].
Moreover, the competent territorial ecclesiastical authority mentioned in Article 22, Para 2, of this Constitution is free to draw up its own rite suited to the usages of places and people according to the provision of Article 63. But the rite is always to honour the requirement that the priest assisting at the marriage must ask for and obtain the consent of the contracting parties.

78. Matrimony is normally to be celebrated within the Mass, after the reading of Gospel and the homily, and before the 'prayer of the faithful'. The prayer for the bride, duly amended to remind both spouses of their equal obligation to remain faithful to each other, may be said in the mother tongue. But if the sacrament of matrimony is celebrated apart from Mass, the Epistle and Gospel from the nuptial Mass are to be read at the beginning of the rite, and a blessing should always be given to the spouses.[7]

There is much here. First of all, the principle of local freedom is enunciated in such a way that the consent is focused upon as essential, and in this respect Trent is clearly in the background, although the floodgates opened to local creativity go a sight further. Then in the ensuing paragraph the real changes come to the fore: the marriage rite is now set within a liturgical context, and must follow the readings, and the homily; the nuptial blessing is to be altered so that it refers to both bride and groom; and when a marriage is celebrated without mass (i.e., when one of the partners is not a Catholic, or not a believer), it must still involve liturgical readings, and a proper nuptial blessing (hitherto, neither of these was the case).

Marriage crops up throughout the decrees of the Vatican Council,[8] as well as a general anxiety that Christian marriage is the foundation of Christian life, and is therefore an aspect of the life of faith that needs constant attention, given the many different kinds of pressure to undervalue it, take it for granted, or even distort it. The same undercurrents are apparent in the *Praenotanda* to the *Ordo Celebrandi Matrimonium*, which appeared in 1969,[9] the decree being signed by Cardinal Gut on St Joseph's Day, a happy coincidence. But the real work had begun as early as 1965, when a study-group was set up under the chairmanship of Pierre-Marie Gy, whose scholarship and diplomatic skill suited him admirably to the task ahead. Throughout that year, and until early in 1968, much discussion and consultation took place, and the Council Fathers took every liberty to express their opinions, either in general, or on specific proposals. For instance, Korbinian Ritzer was asked for his comments on many issues, as well as Jean-Baptiste Molin; and Frederick McManus, representing the American Catholics, wrote to Gy in April 1966 to say that there should be a clear distinction in the new rite between the marriage of a Roman Catholic to another Christian, and the marriage of a Roman Catholic to a non-believer. Gy was keen to include a proper 'active' form of consent, as in Sarum, and the Anglican tradition, in order to express in the fullest way possible that the couple marry each other. Drafts were worked out between April 1966 and October 1967, after which the proposed text was submitted to the requisite authorities in Rome and approved in 1968. Among the many points of difficulty was the nuptial blessing, which went through many drafts. A compromise had to be reached between those who wanted to maintain the Roman tradition, as propounded by De Jong's famous article (Johannes Wagner of Trier), and those who wanted to break with it, and follow the rest of Christendom (A. G. Martimort of Toulouse); a compromise involving alternative blessings was found. The major change between the 1967 proposals and the 1969 official texts is the insertion in the latter of an alternative form of the consent, as an interrogative version of the vow; Gy's enthusiasm for the vow (even with the phrase 'for richer for poorer' deleted!) was evidently too radical for Rome.

Comparing the Council's decree and the definitive text, however, we notice some subtle changes: on the one hand, the entire service is to be taken in the mother tongue, and set in the context of the new mass; yet the fine print reproduces some of the old attitudes; for example, the nuptial blessing is still described as the *oratio super sponsam*, even though it expresses *conjugale foedus*; we shall return to this point. But there are many signs of the more positive and dynamic view of marriage which has been a feature of much twentieth-century theology, together with a biblical perspective which is so much the hallmark of the post-Vatican II reforms. The opening paragraph of the *Praenotanda* stresses the nature of marital love and commitment as described in Eph. 5 and 1 Cor. 7. There is much room for local variation: even though the liturgical setting, and the consent of the couple, and the nuptial blessing are the framework of the rite, not even the ring is required, if other more suitable customs are available, and can be adapted to suit the Church's understanding of what it is doing. The hand of the antiquarians is obvious in that crowning or the use of the nuptial veiling (the medieval veil) are permitted, but here the early Roman tradition persists, for the crown and the veil are only for the bride.

What does the rite say? Taking the nuptial mass form first, we notice the great variety of options in the choice of readings; there are eight possible Old Testament lections, ten New Testament, and ten from the Gospels, and these include old favourites as well as new ones, those which are expressly marital (e.g., Jesus on indissolubility) and those which are more generally about the Christian life (e.g., the house built on the rock). The mass-propers are likewise varied: four collects, and three *super oblata* and post-communions. Of these,[10] the first in each series is adapted from the Tridentine book, the second and third are new, and (in the case of the collect) the fourth is adapted from the Fulda Sacramentary (too rich not to include, and yet simple). There are likewise three prefaces, the first being a rewrite of the old, but the other two are new (one picks up a theme from Leo the Great), emphasizing the ideas of creation and future life together. (There is a redrafted version of the old *hanc igitur*: Gy laments that it can only be used with the first eucharistic prayer.) At the end of the mass, following the policy of allowing proper blessings in the Eucharist, provision is made to give a blessing on the lines of the old Visigothic form, in short paragraphs, each with an 'Amen';[11] three are given, the first is adapted from the *Liber Ordinum* (it had appeared in the German 1950 rite), and the other two are new.

The marriage rite itself begins after the homily with a short introduction, which explains the intentions and purpose of the gathering, and this is, of course, only a sample, for the priest can use his own words. Then the priest asks the couple three short preliminary questions—if they want to get married, if they will stay together, and if they will bring up their children in the (Catholic) Church.[12] These seem unnecessary, and the third is obviously contrived to give liturgical expression to that obligation which continues to strain 'inter-Church marriages'; Rome had insisted on this being spelt out in the rite. Then come the real promises, which are either in the form of an interrogative, and inspired by the full Sarum form, or the vow, which is adapted from the Anglican and Sarum traditions. This is a neat way of allowing for a fuller expression of consent than the older Roman Rituals allowed, whilst at the same time doing away with the duplication of consent and vow which is to be found in the English Manuals and the Book of Common Prayer. Unfortunately, the English version of the Roman rite clutters in another way: the couple are asked the preliminary questions, then (because of the state legal requirements) they each have to swear that there is no impediment; the priest asks them each if they want the other, 'according to the rite of our holy Mother, the Church' (which is all that the old Rituals had of consent); and *then* the vows are made, preceded by the legal requirement, 'I call upon these persons present to witness . . .'. The American version is more straightforward altogether.

Now comes the big change. Instead of the formula *ego conjungo vos*,[13] the priest recites a new formula, which (doubtless unintentionally) copies nineteenth-century English Methodism (mediated through Baxter), in combining the declaration that the couple are married as it appears in the Book of Common Prayer with the Matthean pronouncement: 'you have declared your consent before the Church. May the Lord in his goodness strengthen your consent and fill you both with his blessings. What God has joined together, let no man put asunder.' One is left wondering precisely what deliberations were made behind the scenes before this formula was agreed upon, but it appears to be a declaration, and not a prayer, and it occurs in the earliest draft; the German rite of 1950 has a similar formula at this point. The Latin version presupposes two rings, but, of course, the ring is not essential, and in other cultures other signs can be used. Three ring-prayers are provided; only one of them is a 'blessing' in the traditional sense. The first is short and to the point: 'May the Lord bless these rings which you give to each other as the sign of your love and fidelity.' The second one is a rewrite of Trent, and the third is new. The ring-giving is simple and profound, and based on the first ring-prayer: 'Take this ring as a sign of my love and fidelity. In the Name . . .'.

The mass continues with the prayer of the faithful, that timely restoration to the Western rite, and here we have an example of the way in which a modern reintroduction takes the place of a medieval genre of prayer, for the intercession is manifestly the more pastoral aspect of the service, and corresponds with the series of pre-mass blessings which the English rites so cherished in the Middle Ages. (When the rite is celebrated without a mass, the prayer of the faithful *follows* the nuptial blessing.) At the offertory the couple may assist in the presentation of the gifts. Before the Peace, in the traditional position, comes the nuptial blessing, and, once more, we have a choice, from three. The old preparatory prayer has disappeared, and instead there is a short bidding.

The Concilium had some difficulty in the rationale of the nuptial blessing. They knew their remit from the Decree on the Sacred Liturgy—to rewrite the prayer, so that it refers to both. They knew their liturgical history: Ritzer had shown the background of the nuptial blessing, and Jungmann had compared its position before communion with other ancient pre-communion blessings. But they were under pressure from De Jong, who had argued with great force for the retention of the exclusively bridal blessing in an article which we discussed earlier in these pages.[14] The result was a compromise which seems less than satisfactory. The first nuptial blessing is a rewrite of the old Gregorian prayer, keeping much of the argument, but inserting new material, so that the groom is mentioned as well, and no longer by implication at the end. The two new prayers pray for both bride and groom throughout, one concentrating on the Ephesians analogy (written largely by Ligier), the other being a simple and direct composition. Gy expresses the hope that other nuptial blessings will be composed by local Episcopal Conferences; his own country has taken up this option.[15]

The new Roman rite has much to commend it. Its structure and direction are clear, and remarkably uncluttered. The liturgical setting is definitely a bonus, and although an Anglican writer may take exception to the unrealistic nature of the promise to bring up children in the Roman Catholic

Church, the full provision for marriage outside the mass so that it no longer is so manifestly second-class is a distinct advance. Moreover, it is even possible to have a nuptial mass when one of the partners is not a Catholic, and it is to be hoped that the authorities will smile on those parts of the Roman Catholic world where the non-Catholic partner is allowed to receive communion on this occasion. A third form is for use when one of the partners is not baptized; this is in all essentials the same as the form outside mass, except that if the nuptial blessing is recited (and it may be omitted under these circumstances), the third must be used, presumably because its simplicity is seen as giving the least offence to a non-believer. It will be remembered that in the old Order without Mass, *the* nuptial blessing was not given, only a meagre blessing of the couple.

The question-marks are there, of course, and the debate about the nuptial blessing seems one such, where the authorities could have taken the bull by the horns and departed from tradition. But this would have been hard, and perhaps the solution adopted (albeit in a very different situation) over the eucharistic prayer would have been more fortuitous; to keep the old prayer virtually as it was, but allow for the new ones as well. The opening interrogatories seem superfluous, and the theology of 'blessing' (which liturgiologists and others have called into question for some time) seems implicitly thrown into question by the ambiguous provisions of the ring-prayers, and the Visigothic blessing at the end of the rite (they seem to be good drama and good literature, but are they there because the nuptial blessing is insufficient?). Significant, however, are the promises and vows, in which the mutuality is expressed firmly: the word 'obey' does not appear, and the Latin text obviously envisages two rings as the norm (where rings are used); the English version makes the second ring optional.

All in all, it is a considerable improvement on its predecessor. The priest is no longer a quasi-magical figure, but the president of a public act of worship. The symbolism is clear, so clear that the marriage is 'declared' before even the ring is given (just as before, only the priest used the sacerdotal formula, *ego conjungo vos in matrimonium*). Theologically it has stepped away from Trent, and even the Middle Ages, for the sequence of word, consent, prayer, and solemn blessing is maintained starkly, with all the theological and personal genius that this entails. Flexibility is indeed built into the setting, for the rite can even take place at home, if that is the local custom: what would the medieval conciliar pundits have said?

b. Anglican

For some time after 1928/1929 Anglican revision continued to be along the lines there displayed, of keeping the old format, but adapting material within it. The American order of 1953[16] is a slightly modernized version of the 1790, which, as we noted earlier, is a drastic abbreviation of 1662, with the second half of the service virtually left out. The main differences are that the word 'obey' has gone, and that ring *may* be blessed. The Matthean pronouncement still comes after the prayers, and before the declaration that the couple are married. The Canadian book of 1959,[17] however, is more obviously in the 1928/1929 family: the introduction is further rewritten (the three reasons come in a different order, with procreation in second place), the word 'obey' is out, the ring may be blessed (in a somewhat wordy formula), and the prayers in the second half are adapted, and of more even length; there is provision for a nuptial Eucharist, with a collect, epistle, and gospel. India, Pakistan, Burma and Ceylon in 1960[18] give a similar service, except that a *mangalasutra* may be used instead of, or in addition to, a ring (as in the ecumenical South India book of 1962).

Rethinking had to happen, not least because Rome was contemplating such drastic changes; we are in an age of ecumenical co-operation, and much of the work done in Rome was 'watched' by official observers, one of whom was Massey Shepherd, that veteran of the American Episcopal Church. In the meantime the Church of England's *Alternative Services: Series 1* made use of the 1965 Measure and produced the 1928 text virtually as it had been proposed, but with provision to keep the word 'obey', and an option to bless the ring.[19]

In the following years both the English and American Commissions were working on new versions of all the services, and in 1972 the English Commission received its official instructions to draft a new marriage rite.[20] The path of this service in the coming years was notorious, and those responsible for its eventual birth might have refrained from agreeing to work together, had they realized what they were letting themselves in for. Here, of course, there is a difference from the Roman method of revision (where certain things were debated by the scholars, and some public discussion did take place); the Church of England's General Synod by contrast worked out one of the most complicated processes of liturgical revision that Christendom had yet seen, and, indeed, one is left to wonder how the great and good Thomas Cranmer would have reacted, had he been born four hundred years later. That redoubtable figure, Colin Buchanan, kept an increasing liturgical public aware of what was going on,[21] so that by the time the 'Draft' was published in May 1975, all were agog to see its contents.[22]

The shape was still Cranmer's, except that when a nuptial Eucharist was celebrated, the collect and readings followed the introduction, and the service took up again after the sermon, if there was one. This was no doubt because of popular expectation, if not even pressure, that the introduction (in whatever form) must come at the beginning, so embedded in English culture had it become over the years. In this respect the dovetailing was England's Anglican answer to the Roman solution, where there never had been any popular exhortation. Turning to the service itself, the introductory exhortation was quite new, and briefer than the old one, stressing marriage as a means of grace, and putting first on the list the old 'third' reason, thus at last taking up Bucer's suggestion that the companionship aspect of marriage was the most important; Cranmer's 'reasons' are effectively reversed, to advantage; and there was a fairly explicit reference to sexuality, 'that they may know each other with delight and tenderness in acts of love'. The consent and the vows (which may be read, not repeated after the priest, and for which the couple must face each other) are adapted versions of the old, and they *both* appear, again out of pressure from tradition; 'obey' has gone from the text, but is permissible. There is a prayer over the ring (or rings), which is not exactly a blessing; and when it is given, the bride has to 'receive' it, with a formula, if she herself does not give a ring to the groom, here reflecting the experiments that nineteenth-century Methodism had developed: 'I receive this ring as a sign of our marriage . . .' The priest makes a declaration immediately (not after a prayer, as in 1549–1928) but does not 'pronounce' them man and wife, a fact to which the Commission drew attention in its introductory notes. A short blessing-prayer follows the Matthean pronouncement, and a responsorial form of the Jewish *berakoth* comes at the end of the first part of the service: 'Blessed are you, heavenly Father; you give joy to bridegroom and bride . . .'. In the psalmody which follows, there are options, and a hymn may be sung instead, thus at last coming up to date with liturgical music as it had developed since the nineteenth century, for which nineteenth-century Methodism had already provided. In the prayers in the second part of the rite, some are mandatory and there is a collection of options; they are of similar length, and are all unquestionably prayers of intercession, rather than blessing, and they mix new features with old ones (see Appendix I). The Lord's Prayer precedes the final blessing. The provisions for a nuptial Eucharist include the Genesis creation story, the Ephesians analogy (as well as other epistles) and the Johannine farewell discourse on love; a proper preface also appears, leaning heavily on Eph. 5.

The Commission popularized the notion that the couple are the 'ministers of the sacrament', thus extending further a Western theology of marriage, and in the face of Gy's caution-ary remarks that this was not quite an adequate understanding of Christian marriage.[23] They were also anxious to show that their service incorporated many of the insights of the marriage relationship of the present age, in particular the complementar-ity of the sexes. Of the many small improvements from the old service was the provision that the registration of the marriage could be done immediately after the first part of the service, thus bringing to an end the unseemly (and liturgically anti-climactic) custom of registration at the *end* of the rite, which made the bride and groom's procession through church appear to have little to do with the service as a whole.

The Synod was busy with liturgical business and Colin Buchanan wryly observed (before the Synod had even seen it) that 'those who are wanting to get married with it have a lengthy and uncertain engagement ahead'. Some conservative Evan-gelicals objected to the fact that readings were not mandatory when there was no nuptial Eucharist (and at least one objected to the dropping of the word 'obey', thus keeping old Sarum alive). In the November session the Synod finally got round to discussing the 'Draft', and a hot debate ensued, in the course of which much attention focused on the introductory exhortation. A long Revision Committee took up many suggestions in the spring of 1976, and in February 1977 it was at last passed, in spite of strong attacks from Bishop Hugh Montefiore. Although many items were discussed and small points changed, it was over the introduction that the main battle was fought. The final text appeared later in 1977,[24] and this is practically the version in which it came in the 1980 *Alternative Service Book*.[25] The main changes are a new introduction, which is wordy, and more traditional than the 'Draft': the priest does indeed have to 'proclaim' the couple man and wife; and the word 'obey' can be used. Thus the synodical system proved a conservative factor in the process of getting a new service. But the most important change was undoubtedly for the better, namely that the service could begin with a collect, and the readings could either follow straight away (they must do if there is a Eucharist) or come later on. This development is probably the result of Roman and American influence. But it means that (in typography at least) the shape of Cranmer's rite has been altered, in favour of basing the marriage service round the traditional Western synaxis. In spite of disapproval in certain quarters, additional prayers could be written specifically for the occasion, a provision taken up at the marriage of the Prince of Wales and Lady Diana Spencer in St Paul's Cathedral on 29 July 1981.[26]

England got a new rite, even though the political aspects of reform took the 'Draft' in a conservative direction. Its weakness is in the different structures which it can have. When a nuptial Eucharist is celebrated, the consent, ring-giving, declaration, and prayers take place between the gospel and the Peace; this is sound liturgical practice. But when, as (in England) in most cases, there is no Eucharist, the structure can vary a great deal, with the 'Word' before or after the marriage, and thus change the balance of the service considerably. It is ironic that the basic disagreement between the rites of Calvin and Luther over where the readings should occur in marriage should reappear in England four centuries later. But still, there is much advance on the old rite. The arguments about rings, and whether to bless them or not, are gone, at least on paper. Proper mutuality is extended to the vows and the ring-giving, thus continuing Cranmer's euchological principles of the sixteenth century. The symbolism of the prayers varies considerably, from biblical, through traditional, to experiential.

Meanwhile, across the Atlantic Ocean, the American Episcopal Church was hard at work in producing a set of services which were to place them at least neck-and-neck with England in leading future Anglican revision. In 1970 the Standing Liturgical Commission had produced a set of 'Pastoral Offices', which were brought together with other services in the 1971 *Services for Trial Use*.[27] Clearly the result of some Roman influence, the service is uniform in structure, and based round a synaxis. An opening introduction is an abbreviation and rewrite of the Prayer Book, keeping some of the images, but with considerable alterations. The couple are asked for their consent, in language reminiscent of the Prayer Book. The congregation is then asked if they will support the couple, to which they make a reply; this is a feature of many of the American services, which is a welcome innovation, militating against the 'Occasional Office' syndrome. Then a big change; perhaps unconsciously inspired by the Metz rite, the collect, readings, and homily (optional) separate the consent from the vows, which now appear in modernized versions of the Prayer Book, but without 'obey', and the fine concluding word, 'This is my solemn vow', which England took over. The ring is simply blessed, and given, and it is envisaged that two rings will be the norm. The same form of giving is used by England. They are then pronounced man and wife in a declaration which seems adapted from the Prayer Book, and in the first person, and the Matthean pronouncement follows, as part of that declaration, and not as a separate item, as England. The prayers continue, the Lord's prayer coming first, except when there is a Eucharist. They vary according to whether there is a Eucharist, perhaps to add solemnity to them, and the couple kneel (while the congregation remains standing) for one prayer, which the Draft describes as a 'nuptial blessing' (it is a short blessing, based on the Prayer Book). These prayers are fewer in number than England, but the long prayer of intercession in the Eucharist version is particularly fine, consisting of short petitions, each ending with 'Amen'. The Eucharist takes up at the offertory. Additional directions allow for the 'giving-away' to become a 'presentation' by a group of people; and it is made clear that other wedding-tokens may be used in place of the ring. Although America did not have synodical procedures quite like England, the alterations made to the rite before 1977 when the *Draft Proposed Book of Common Prayer* appeared are a similar mixture of conservative and liberal views. Marriage is repeatedly referred to as a 'covenant', taking up Wheatly's phrases.[28] The giving-away is done in silence, if at all. The prayers are altered considerably so that they have a more intercessory role, and they include the addition in the long prayer of such a realistic petition as this:

> Give them grace, when they hurt each other, to recognize and acknowledge their fault, and to seek each other's forgiveness and yours. Amen.

But the most important change, apart from excluding alleged 'sexist' language here and there, is that the consent and the vow are first given and made by the woman; feminists of the Western world will delight in this inverted chauvinism.

Between 1970 and 1977 there was added a second 'Order for Marriage', giving an outline for the service, along the lines of the Rite 3 Eucharist, which had appeared in the 1971 *Services for Trial Use*.[29] It directs that the essentials of the service should be: *i.* the declaration of the teaching of the Church concerning marriage; *ii.* the declaration of consent; *iii.* one or more readings (optional, and one should be from the Bible, i.e., non-biblical readings are allowed); *iv.* the vow, in a set formula; *v.* the declaration of the union; *vi.* prayers for the couple, the community, the world; *vii.* a solemn blessing (only by a priest or bishop); *viii.* appropriate conclusion of the service, whether a Eucharist is celebrated or not. Such an 'agenda' form of service clearly reproduces the essentials of the set rite, and continues to highlight the distinction between consent and vow which we have already seen, as well as the distinction between intercession and 'solemn blessing'. These are important features peculiar to the American rite, and mark a significant adaptation of tradition and contemporaneity.

Comparing the American and English rites is difficult, because they are churches which are markedly different, not least in the way in which marriages are conducted. But it is nonetheless interesting to note the few occasions, e.g., at the vow, where America may have influenced England, as well as the fact that both set the service in a synaxis structure; but the Americans always have the exhortation at the beginning. The deliberate separation of consent and vow by the 'Word' is an adventurous rationalizing of the two forms, which, of course, the Roman rite in the Latin original does not involve. The Standing Commission was anxious to exaggerate 'the far-reaching consequences'[30] of marriage, no doubt with an eye on easy divorce, but its emphasis on the consent is offset by the rather more dramatic presentation of the solemn blessing in the second part of the service. In asking for the congregation's 'support' it is striking out a new path, and recognizing that 'the role of society . . . is often crucial in sustaining or breaking a marriage . . .'. The American revisers were indeed courageous in thus taking their Church so much further from the somewhat paltry rite which it had before.

The English rite seems cleaner and more straightforward. It is ironical that the Roman rite places the ring-giving *after* the declaration (when there never was any debate within its tradition about the liturgical use of a ring), whereas both the modern Anglican rites described place the ring-giving *before* the declaration (even though Anglicanism at least skirted the Puritan debate on whether the ring should be included at all in the service). Apart from the rather tired exhortation, the point which strikes the congregation most forcefully in the English service (as long as it has any corporate memory of the old days) is the bald use of '*That which* God has joined together . . .', which may be more accurate a translation of the Greek, but jars. If there is a liturgical weakness in the English rite, it is the continued repetition of blessings, a hangover from Sarum and Cranmer, and one which some of the drafters (including Donald Gray) attempted to eradicate; but they were unsuccessful.

Other provinces of the Anglican Communion have followed similar paths, sometimes including their own material, sometimes borrowing from other traditions. Australia has two orders, one a touched-up version of Cranmer, the other showing greater signs of innovation, for instance, in the congregational prayer for the couple as they join hands.[31] Similar combinations of new and old exist elsewhere, for example in the American-looking New Zealand rite of 1972.[32]

c. Conclusion

It is no exaggeration to say that the three principal rites described in this section have a great deal in common. Each has travelled a long way in breathing new life into the language and form of the service; and architecture no longer determines choreography. The Roman *Praenotanda*, the English Commission's *Commentary*, and the American 'introduction' in *Prayer Book Studies* repeat the same anxieties: that marriage is serious; that the couple themselves must understand the promises involved, as well as publicly express them; that the whole rite should be set within a proper liturgical context; that the Eucharist is the finest way of 'blessing' the union, though it is not always appropriate or possible; and the woman is no longer seen as 'given away' by her father, like a piece of property.

Anglicans have adapted their language, recovered the eucharistic setting, and have lost some of their Protestant fear of liturgical symbolism. Romans have brought their bare rite into the vernacular, enriched it by setting it more completely within the Eucharist, and deliberately distinguished between the primary and secondary aspects of its symbolism. But above all, and perhaps mostly in the Anglican rites, there is a sense of *joy* in marriage, as it is shared by the couple, and the congregation, and the priest himself.

2 Adaptation and Rethink: Reformed Traditions

We have already seen how the Calvin–Knox and Prayer Book-adapted traditions thrived in Britain in the centuries following the Reformation, the latter reaching a high point in English Methodism in the nineteenth century. These communities adapted what they inherited to meet their own needs, and the needs of the peoples concerned. This means that they had a spirit of adaptation in their blood; they were used to the idea of combining tradition with their own forms of liturgical rhetoric, as witness some of the intercessory prayers composed then. In this present century these tendencies continue to thrive, but they are more in the way of 'adaptation' than 'rethinking', with one or two notable exceptions. The so-called 'Free' Churches do not need an Act of Parliament or an Ecumenical Council to enable them to revise their liturgies; on the other hand, their 'freedom', as is well known, can make for the most rigid forms of worship. Nevertheless, the churches of the Reformed traditions continue to produce interesting marriage rites, but most of them are Cranmerian in shape, style, and even language.

a. Congregationalist

The *Book of Public Worship* which appeared in 1948 was edited by a distinguished team of ministers, and reproduces the rite which had appeared in the 1920 *Book of Congregational Worship*,[1] but with a shorter exhortation, and with alternative prayers before the vows are made, and at the main prayer for the couple in the second part of the service; at the ring-giving, the man says, 'I give thee this ring in token of the loving covenant made this day between us: in the Name. . .'. It is not until the 1959 *Book of Services and Prayers*[2] that a slightly new style of language begins to appear; the exhortation describes marriage as 'a sacred relationship', which probably meant more to couples than the 'covenant' imagery we have seen before. It also begins to meet the needs of folk who are not as well-versed in the Bible as a previous generation: marriage 'is used in the Old Testament to picture the way in which God would join himself to his people, and in the New to portray how Jesus Christ has joined himself to his Church'. The couple swear no impediment, in the statutory way; promises are as in the Prayer Book of 1928. Again there are alternative prayers before the vows and at the end of the service. They are declared man and wife in the Prayer Book manner, which leads into the Matthean pronouncement and the Aaronic blessing.

Two more radical forms have appeared since then. The 'Order for Christian Marriage' in Micklem's *Contemporary Prayers for Public Worship*[3] adopts a deliberately non-hierarchical style, and the book as a whole (as well as the tradition it represented) helped many people in the late sixties and early seventies to rethink their attitudes to the language of prayer. Its use was not (and is not) confined to Congregationalists. It is well laid-out, with headings at the beginning of each section ('the declaration of purpose', 'the declaration that there is no impediment', 'Question', 'Prayer for sincerity in making the Marriage Vows', 'The Vows', 'The Giving of the Ring', 'The Declaration of Marriage', 'The Blessing'). A direct and most pastoral rite, it is still according to the old shape, but is none the worse for it. A modern feature of the exhortation is that 'God is associated with 'present-tense' verbs; the prayer before the vows is blunt, 'make them as conscious of your presence as they are of ours'; and the ring is given 'in God's name as a symbol of all that we shall share', which is language somewhat loftier than the Puritans would ever have allowed, though they would have appreciated greatly the sentiments behind it. A more recent 'Marriage Service',[4] printed as a leaflet, follows Micklem's structure, but is less adventurous in style and language; the giving-away is optional, and, like Scottish 1940, the promises are made passively, to be 'loving, faithful, and dutiful'. The long prayer at the end is another sample of a living rhetorical tradition of extempore prayer.

b. Presbyterian

The Book of Common Order of the Presbyterian Church in Canada (1964)[5] shows a Scottish background, and the language is still Cranmerian. Beginning with the Calvinist 'Our help . . .', and adding, 'except the Lord build the house', the service continues with an elongated exhortation, based on the Prayer Book, but trying to make it more like an old-fashioned sermon than a formal 'declaration'. The usual Presbyterian/Congregational prayer is made before the vows, but these can be either active or passive. The bride is given away, and, like the Scottish books, the minister is the stage-manager at the giving of the ring ('you will now place a ring . . .') and a similar formula appears as in the 1920 English Congregational rite, 'a token and pledge of the covenant'. The long prayers mix realism with sentimentality generously, like the Scottish *Euchologion*; 'may their love never know doubt nor decay, but may common tasks, trials, and joys bind them ever more closely in heart.'

The Presbyterian Service-Book of England and Wales (1968)[6] again begins with 'Except the Lord . . .' and 'Our help . . .' (in that order), but instead of moving on to the exhortation, it experiments with an opening prayer, invoking God's presence on the gathering, and this naturally leads into the Lord's Prayer. The exhortation comes now, reading a little awkwardly after the introductory material preceding it. The giving-away is optional. The most surprising feature, however, is that the ring is blessed ('bless, O Lord, this ring') in words reminiscent of the draft 1928 Church of England form; the bride has to say a new formula when receiving the ring, which links the ring with 'taking' the man as her husband, thus constituting another variant from the experiment initiated in 1860 by the Primitive Methodists, An anthology of Scripture passages precedes a relatively short intercessory prayer and blessing.

The Joint Committee on Worship of the Cumberland Presbyterian Church, the Presbyterian Church in the USA, and the United Presbyterian Church in the USA together produced *The Worship Book* in 1970,[7] where for the first time a truly congregational service appears, which begins (after a short introduction) with a confession (said by all), and continues with proper readings from the Bible. After a 'brief Sermon' the couple make their vows, 'I promise with God's help to be your faithful husband, to love and serve you as Christ commands, as long as we both shall live,' a particularly fortuitous mixture of brevity and tradition. The ring(s) (*sic*) are given 'as a sign of my promise'. The minister reads one of two passages from the Epistles, and leads a short prayer for the couple; and in this latter part of the rite the underlying theme is joy and thanksgiving. Clearly *The Worship Book* leads a section of the Reformed tradition away from what has been familiar, and the rite is based round a synaxis, the minister presiding over an act of public worship. Hymns are recommended to be sung, and a 'hymn of thankgiving' before the final blessing.

Scotland's *Book of Common Order* (1979)[8] is by comparison a dull collection, but it marks considerable advance from 1940, and gives two orders, one a reworking and abbreviation of 1940, the other a new form, along traditional lines, but brief and to the point. One senses an anxiety to preach Christian marriage to a secular age, rather than to 'liturgize' and 'modernize' a Christian community. In both there are shades of Micklem, which may be unconscious. In the first order the lofty reasons for marriage in the *Euchologion* are simplified but omnipresent. In the second form there is an attempt to begin with a prayer, in a fine epiclesis: 'Father eternal, send forth the Spirit and we shall be remade . . .'. The vows can be active or passive; and the prayers in the second part of the service have an engaging lilt and simplicity.

c. Baptist

Baptist marriage rites of this century are a simplified version of the Reformed pattern, and resemble the Congregational and English Presbyterian rites. Their peculiar features are a characteristic directness, and a didactic tone. The traditional *Ministers' Manual*[9] has a familiar sequence: exhortation, swearing of no impediment, consent, giving-away (optional), prayer for the couple's vows, vows, ring-giving, minister's declaration, scriptural anthology, address (optional), Aaronic blessing, and a long prayer of thanksgiving and supplication for the couple. Baptists guard jealously their freedom to use the forms of service they wish, as many other churches of the Reformed tradition, and this is much easier to do in practice when a particular structure is adopted for any given service. The prayers are strongly theocentric as well as personal. The same 'realism' is carried forward and adapted in the 1960 *Orders and Prayers for Church Worship*,[10] where in the exhortation we find the following: 'It was ordained for the welfare of human society, which can be strong and happy only where the marriage bond is held in honour'. The prayer before the vows is one of thanksgiving; the giving-away is optional; the ring is 'a token of the covenant made between us' (cf Scottish *Book of Common Order*, and others). The long prayer concludes:

> Bless all their kindred and friends, and answer the prayers they offer for those whom they love. Keep us all within the fellowship of thy Church, working together for the fulfilment of thy purposes, and bring us at last to our eternal home . . ..

Here we find an insistence on the communal aspect of marriage—that the congregation does not come together just to spectate, but to join in a solemn covenant in which it is essentially involved, and with which it is inseparably connected. Many Baptist congregations use other forms, including the Micklem rite mentioned earlier.

d. Methodist

The Methodist Church's Faith and Order Committee had a sub-committee working on a new marriage service in the late 1960s,[11] and after some considerable work, in the course of which it was increasingly overtaken by the change to 'you' form language, it issued a draft text, in which the rite was set in the framework of a synaxis. They encountered political difficulties from their own authorities, in a similar way to the reaction at the General Synod to the Church of England's original proposals.[12] Hostile reactions also came from the British Joint Liturgical Group in 1968; but this was before the new Roman marriage rite appeared in 1969, after which it took a different attitude. In the end a compromise was reached, so that provision was made for the 'Word' to come *after* the vows had been made, but the typography of the 1975 *Methodist Service Book* leaves the reader in no doubt as to what structure is preferred. Cranmer's shape had clearly as much popularity in Methodism as in the Church of England, where a similar compromise was subsequently reached.

But there are special features too. The introduction makes suggestions about 'inter-faith' marriages, reflecting the development of English society in the industrial areas. The sub-committee suffered most flak concerning the preface-exhortation (again the main battleground in the Anglican sister-church), with the insistence that 'procreation' be included. Although the style is quite different from the Church of England's form, it stresses the 'discovery' aspect of marriage, and is similarly theocentric. After the impediments are denied in the legal form, the Collect for Purity is said, and it may be followed by a confession, which is a new feature, but intended to express penitence if there is to be a Eucharist (it would not fit elsewhere into the rite). The readings come next, and are followed by another prayer, for the vows, which are now made (the giving-away is optional); the vows end roundly, 'and to this I pledge myself'.

The rings are given, but the problem of 'blessing' is beautifully side-tracked by the form, 'bless, Lord, the giving of this ring'; one wonders what Mr Wesley's reaction to this would have been. The couple are declared married, the Matthean pronouncement is made, and the couple are blessed. Then come 'The Intercessions', again following the Roman revision in principle, but they are responsive in form. If there is no Eucharist, the service ends with a thanksgiving based on the Jewish Seven Benedictions (or thanksgiving in the minister's own words). This is indeed a fine piece of work, written by David Tripp, and is reproduced in full in Appendix I. The Methodist rite, like the American *Worship Book*, is an adventurous production. The options allow the service to resemble the structure of the old one. There is a wholesomeness about it which marks it off as one of the most interesting we have seen so far.

e. Others

The list could go on indefinitely. The Swedenborgians in 1972 issued their new form,[13] which reproduces many of the features of their previous books, but the language is simpler. The

Liberal Catholics in 1967 produced a wondrous hotch-potch of Anglican and Roman and idiosyncratic elements, including the *ego vos conjungo* (which was soon to be dropped by Rome), and a nuptial Eucharist.[14] The Moravians in Britain in 1960 and America in 1969 revised their previous rites,[15] on both sides of the Atlantic leaning on the Prayer Book, though somewhat less in America, Britain linking the ring-giving closely with the vows, America producing a form of the *ego vos conjungo*, but quickly adding the Matthean pronouncement, exactly like the Catholic Apostolic rite of the previous century. The Unitarians in 1968 produced an updated version of the kind used before,[16] still avoiding the Matthean pronouncement, but in other ways following the trends already noted, in simplicity of language and directness of imagery; at the ring-giving one of the two forms has a peculiar resonance to it: 'with this ring I thee wed, with my body I thee honour, and with my whole mind I make covenant with thee this day'.

As an example of how things can change over the years, the two ecumenical rites of the Church of South India (1952)[17] and the English United Reformed Church (1977)[18] are quite a contrast. South India uses the Primitive Methodist (1860) formula 'cleave to her alone' in the consent; the word 'obey' still appears; the *mangalasutra* may be used instead of (or in addition to) the ring; and in the arrangement of the prayers one has a gentle impression of fusing together the Presbyterian and more up-dated Anglican traditions. The English United Reformed rite, however, betrays the influence of Micklem, as well as the Methodist and Church of England rites. The typography makes the direction of the service clear, with an opening prayer, a new exhortation and simple vows. In the exhortation God provides marriage *inter alia* 'for the enrichment of society, so that husband and wife being joined together may enter into the life of the community as a new creation', a happy blend of experiential and biblical concepts; the ring is blessed Methodist-style, 'bless the giving and receiving of the wedding ring (s)' (*sic*); and at the vows yet another ending appears, 'and to this end I pledge my word', appropriate in an age which trusts them less and less. The Jewish blessings from the Church of England rite ('Blessed be God the Father . . .') follow the Aaronic blessing.

f. Conclusion

Bold attempts to adapt and rethink—that is the tale of some of the Reformed traditions. We find ourselves increasingly distant from the sixteenth century, with its culture of wifely obedience, and its euchology of the Authorized Version and Cranmer's prose, as well as all the theological and liturgical battlegrounds that find expression in so many of the agreed forms of that era, as much as in the strong disagreements caused by a particular text in a particular community. Rites tend either to plod on with some cautious recognition of changes in society and revision in other churches; or else they strike out in order to reach new territory, risking suspicion from their own back-woodsmen. But then that is so often the tale of liturgical development in any age. If the prizes go to any one rite, it is to the British Methodists, who took the latter course, to great advantage, following the example of their nineteenth century predecessors, even if the pathway is so obviously different. It is an ecumenical age, as well as one of liturgical borrowing, and the kind of provision made by the British Joint Liturgical Group's *The Daily Office Revised* (1978)[19] perhaps shows the way different traditions can bring their euchological riches together for a rite which is increasingly celebrated between people who are not as conscious of their denominational roots as they once were, and who can come together in agreement about what is being celebrated before God and his people. More interesting still is the synthetic rite suggested in Ottfried Jordahn's collection of German ecumenical services,[20] boldly put forward for use between Roman Catholics and others; we are into an age when the differences are more between those of no faith and those who have faith, rather than between rival versions of traditionally opposing Christianities.

Epilogue

'Many lands, many customs, says the proverb . . .'. Such were Luther's apt words when he began to write about the marriage liturgy. We have indeed travelled far, from the supposed customs of the Jewish devout about the time of Christ, to the certain procedure of a Genevan burgher in Calvin's time. It has been a varied story, and one which involved so often the need to defend marriage against those who would take it lightly, or ignore its proper obligations because the heart has grown cold. There have been many solutions, but even to elevate the state of matrimony to number among the sacraments of the Church, as Catholicism achieved in 1439, after much theological debate, does not solve the continuing problems faced by a continuously changing society which has different perceptions of marriage. These changing perceptions often become expressed in the liturgy, which at least ensures that peoples' ideas become part of the praying life of the Church, and are not left elsewhere, whether that is the lecture-room, the theological tract, or the other person's bedroom. What are these perceptions? And how are they expressed in the liturgy?

The main turning-points in the history of the Church each left its mark on the rite, though in the case of the first one (the Bible) we cannot be sure precisely what that mark was, except that we can be certain it was thoroughly based on the John 2.1–11 pericope, that Christ (according to John) performed his first miracle at a wedding, and that marriage is therefore one of the founding relationships of the new covenant. Marriage is also practised by other religions, so that when the Christian world meets the pagan one, it has to do some hard thinking; thus, Athenagoras uses all his powers to persuade the Emperor that Christians understand marriage in Stoic-like terms and are not casual about it. Roman Law had insisted on the need for consent in marriage, and this the early Christians could take for granted, particularly as it approximated to the Jewish practice of betrothal before marriage, which was a necessity in an agricultural community, where many preparations had to be made, not least a feast of some expense lasting seven days. But the Fathers soon begin to emphasize the need for the marriage rite to be focused in the Christian community, however that was done; so that from the time of Tertullian, and certainly from Ambrose (in the West) and the Cappadocians (in the East), the church's blessing is defended, and its roots seen in the book of Genesis.

After the fourth century the Church settles down to a more ordered liturgical life, though the same problems recur: different strands within the household of faith have differing views, tending either to be more rigorist or more lenient, the former represented by Augustine in the West, who is the formative figure on subsequent theological (and pastoral) thinking. The Church manages, in different ways, to assert the need for a Church marriage service, at least for some of its adherents, whether this is done in the building, or at home; but the rite of betrothal, with its roots in folk-lore, is less easy to make into a liturgy, except in the East, where the liturgy is much more adventurous. So the need is felt for some expression of consent in marriage, to replace (or to duplicate) betrothal, as well as to bring home to people (whether they are Frankish royalty or English peasants) that marriage involves commitment and choice. The theologians help along this process, in discussing both the need for this consent, and also the sacramentality of the rite; and Peter Lombard and Thomas Aquinas figure heavily here. The result is that by the time of the Council of Trent the way had been laid open for consent to be isolated from among the other ingredients of the rite; but even here we discern a slight scepticism with the isolation, and the priestly formula is therefore also indicated (even though its actual life-span in the liturgy was considerably shorter than many other ingredients). Nevertheless, as David Tripp once wrote of the official Tridentine theological view of the marriage liturgy, 'the one advantage of working against the background of a scholastic theology is that the intention is what matters: state the intention adequately, and the rest of the rite will look after itself'.[1]

Meanwhile the Reformers had hotly debated not only the sacramentality of marriage, but also the setting and the form of the service, with Luther content with the 'Occasional Office' (as the medieval rite had become in practice), but insisting on the need for the service in relation to its role in society, and its binding nature; and Calvin working along similar theological lines, but giving more stress to the need for divine grace in the relationship, and (ideally) inserting the service into Sunday worship. But each in his own way builds on the medieval theological foundations: they may not like a nuptial mass, but they certainly make much of consent. When we get to England in 1549, Cranmer had only to glance across the Channel and see what was going on in Germany and Switzerland to realize that he had it made for him in the Sarum Manual, with its lengthy vernacular pre-mass rite, and its heavy emphasis on consent. And whatever the nature of the rites of these three traditions, whether Lutheran, Calvinist, or Anglican, each maintains the centrality of consent, but demotes the blessing ingredient, so that it becomes a form of intercession, however 'strong' in its liturgical style; to this, and other aspects, we shall return later on.

The twentieth century has seen an unprecedented degree of rapprochement in the churches of the West, and in the midst of an increasingly secular society, Christian values are under question. So yet again is the relationship of marriage. As Christopher Brooke once put it, the modern theologian 'has to grapple both with the harsh realities and sublime idealism of recent generations',[2] and this makes him wary of looking to the twelfth century for much help. Such contradictory trends as easy divorce and marriage enrichment speak volumes; it is hard to instil in a modern generation, to which contraceptives are easily available, the need for marriage as a stabilizing effect on society, still less as one of the most spiritually fulfilling of all human relationships. Perhaps, like earlier ages, we have to learn by old mistakes in new dress. Certainly the writings of social scientists and moral theologians have begun to converge, in that they all approach marriage as something which is to be lived, rather than codified. Laurence Stone's study of family life in recent centuries easily complements Edward Schillebeeckx's theological survey, principally because they are covering similar ground, with sensitive critique, but no axe to grind other than the quest for truth.[3]

But we must return to the liturgy, for that is where we began and that is where we must end. Looking back on the centuries of Christian marriage rites, we can see five specific ingredients which play an important part in making (or breaking) the service:

i. *Consent.* We have seen how this slowly emerged in the Middle Ages, either as a question asked by priest (either to the man alone, or else to both partners), or as a vow made by both partners; or, as in England, both forms, and the vow in particular as part of a living vernacular tradition. Consent also infected Eastern rites, whether as a result of Latin influence, or because it was thought a good idea in principle. But a twentieth-century person really does find it amazing that it is not until the Middle Ages were well on their way that this ingredient makes its first appearance, and then gains more and more prominence, so much are we the products of post-medieval theology, and the modern Western cult of choice as the means to fulfilment. Without doubt consent properly belongs in marriage liturgy, in the same way that it was in the Middle Ages that ordinands were publicly questioned, and we today could not think of an ordination rite without this ingredient. The danger, however, is that the formulae express the marriage relationship in a way that a subsequent age finds difficult, as witness the long trek from Cranmer to 1928 when the word 'obey' was to be dropped, and the adoption of wifely obedience in many other Reformation services. What is radical and meaningful and relevant in fourteenth-century England becomes the social heresy of a succeeding generation. Thus contemporary rites tend to revert to the more primitive (and Eastern) tradition of not differentiating between the roles of the partners in liturgical formulae.

ii. Euchology. We have seen how this developed at an early stage, whether from the Seven Benedictions, or from such wandering rites as the Apocryphal *Acts of Thomas*; but undoubtedly from well before the time of the classical formulae of the Western Sacramentaries and Barberini 336 in the Byzantine rite. The content and the styles vary enormously. In the Sacramentaries the solemn blessing follows the logic of the ancient Roman rite, thanksgiving in the preface, supplication in *hanc igitur*, and pre-communion extended collect, all for the bride. But this proved inadequate for the rest of Europe, so that Spain composes its own style of blessing, declaratory rather than precatory, punctuated by 'Amens', and short and to the point; and, like the Anglo-Norman tradition, invents short blessings, sometimes in the form of a 'strong collect', later as a direct 'blessing'; and these are spread out over an extended rite, before, during, and after the mass. At the Reformation the tendency is to go for long collect-type prayers, and short blessings (whether soundly biblical and Aaronic or mildly medieval and liturgical); and in the sixteenth century local Lutheran orders and in nineteenth/twentieth-century Methodist and Presbyterian rites these tendencies are to be seen in evidence as the result of an active tradition of *extempore* forms, in much the same way as the *ad libitum* techniques of prayer-writing which lay behind the Sacramentary and Visigothic traditions. The East knows the same kind of variety, in the 'strong collect' and the 'blessing', but the context of each rite is so closely connected with what is going on (whether clothes-blessing in Armenia or crowning in Byzantium) that there is less chance of confusion through complexity. In sum, our story here has been a history of the development of the theology of blessing, with all the problems inherent in Western duplication and accumulation (e.g. both a nuptial blessing *and* an intercession before it *and* a Visigothic blessing at the end, as in the new Roman rite).

iii. Symbolism. Symbols are two-a-penny in some rites (e.g., the Chaldean), and practically non-existent in others (e.g., Knox's rite), and certainly the West experienced too much of a pendulum-swing in the sixteenth century. The era of origins is crucial. The ring starts life as a sign of betrothal, and soon gets into the marriage rite in both East and West, the original use becoming duplicated in the recent custom of the 'engagement ring'. The crown is universally used in the East, because it is biblical and Jewish. The veil is used in both East and West, but the West makes much of it because the central part of the Eucharist is traditionally a bridal blessing associated with the veiling, as we saw in the Sacramentaries. And yet it takes until the veiling is incorporated into the Visigothic rites for this veiling to be mentioned in the prayers themselves, as witness *LO* B and *Vich*; that speaks volumes about an inner scepticism with regard to bringing symbolism into prayer-writing at Rome, a scepticism which becomes iconoclastic when we get to the Reformation. Then in the Middle Ages and after we sometimes see the use of the 'pall' or canopy during the nuptial blessing, surely a piece of drama to distinguish this blessing from all the others which had recently invaded the rite. Different parts of the church building play a major role in distinguishing parts of the rite, whether male-female (as in the Coptic service), or the conditional nature of the consent for the ensuing mass (as in the Anglo-Norman tradition); when this latter is taken over by Cranmer, the 'walk to the altar' comes under fire in the Wesleyan tradition because it is architecturally meaningless as much as because the Eucharist is not celebrated. In the East symbolism seems to be an easy feature of the various rites, where we do not see any tendency to rationalize or define, and so the semi-ecstatic enters the liturgy of the Byzantine rite in the 'dance of Isaiah' in a circle to symbolize the union of love; and the crowns themselves receive many biblical and experiential associations after the bald defence by John Chrysostom that they are a reward for continence.

iv. Liturgical Setting. The wedding in Cana of Galilee probably lasted seven days, and it was a Jewish folk-festival, probably within a liturgical setting; the same atmosphere exudes from the *Acts of Thomas.* The feast becomes the Eucharist in Tertullian, and is probably the foundation of the Roman rite from the fourth century as well as the various Eastern rites, from a similar time. But throughout the post-Constantinian era the conflict between the marriage as a 'family occasion' and the marriage as a celebration of the local Christian community is obvious, and it is to be seen in the medieval attempts to make it festive (the Votive Mass of the Trinity), as well as the ritual first kiss at the altar after the nuptial blessing, at the Peace. The debate about the place of the Eucharist in Anglicanism betrays the same problems. And even if we exclude the question of the Eucharist, the role of the Bible readings in the rite is also unclear; should they come *before* the marriage (as in the East and modern Roman), as the corporate reading among the assembly of the faithful, or should they come *after* the marriage (as Luther and Cranmer), as an exhortation to the couple? There are arguments on both sides, the former being the 'purer' view, based on an ideal notion of the Christian assembly, the latter being the 'pastoral' view, based on a pragmatic view of the assembly. The 'ideal' notion is undoubtedly the one most popular in the twentieth century; as Bryan Spinks has wryly put it, 'The Western Protestant satisfaction with an "Occasional Office" is alarming'.[4] The problem is exacerbated for clergy who have to preside at marriage rites where the partners show little interest in the Christian community; Eugêne Bersier's presentation of the Bible to the couple is indeed a '*cri de coeur*'.

v. Who does it? Ever since the fourth century the Christian East has been launched firmly in the direction of seeing the climax of the rite as the Church's blessing, expressed by the priest. The West, however, started putting the eggs in the 'consent' basket from the time of the scholastic theologians onwards, and this was enshrined in the *Tametsi* decree of the Council of Trent, even though the Visigothic practice of the priest 'giving' the girl to the man persisted. The Reformers, as we have seen, built upon the medieval foundations, but because they (usually) held no sacramental theory of marriage, nor a magical notion of blessing, they were able to hold a more balanced view: the couple consent, the faithful are there, the service is led by the minister. Luther's descriptions of how marriages were *understood* by ordinary people in the young Lutheran congregations betrays the same sort of idea. Indeed, it is the medieval German priestly formula, whereby the priest is the *president* of the service (and not the 'tier of the knot', as in the late medieval Norman tradition), that Père Gy singled out for praise when he wrote about the new Roman rite soon after it was promulgated. The question remains, however—is it the consent? Or is it the priest? And if the latter, in what way? History does not opt for any one to the exclusion of the other until the ninth century in the East, when the crowning by the priest became mandatory for a valid Byzantine wedding, and until the sixteenth century in the West, when the consent is defined as what makes the marriage. Those are indeed long passages of time, and the two legislations were both the product of particular theological traditions, and arising out of the need to enforce marriage in church. An Anglican will be allowed to react somewhat pragmatically to these contradictory view-points by affirming the need for *both*, and by entertaining some suspicion of the scholastic preoccupation with sacramental 'magic words'. Whether or not, however, marriage is a sacrament, the scholastics were right in fighting for its importance, as a thoroughly biblical and traditional quest; Cromwell's radical experiment in the Long Parliament was a disaster; and modern theologians generally agree that marriage is a sacramental rite, even if they differ on details; yesterday's theological battles have partially disappeared.[5]

So much for history; what of the rites of today? They have much in common. Language has been updated; the corporate features of the service have been emphasized; the Eucharist figures more prominently; the Bible is read from properly, rather than in short snatches taken out of context; and in euchology there is a tendency to distinguish between solemn blessing and intercession, which is brought out most clearly in the American Episcopal rite. However, it is likely that for many centuries to come the same tensions we noted earlier will continue to be apparent—between the 'ideal' and the 'actual', between the shining white bride of the perfect Christian community, and the murky fragmented community which comes together somewhat reluctantly, unable to face up to its family quarrels. The secret of new rites will not lie in *technique* and *slickness* so much as *identification* and *adaptation*. When discussing Luther's rite, I could not help noticing the absence of 'joy and a congregation'. It is these two dimensions of Christian living which are going to be the most important, a point made with some force by Achille Triacca.[6] Not that these qualities can be forcibly 'injected' into the service, but as any parish priest will know, the festive atmosphere of a wedding depends greatly on the attitude of the couple, the nature of the congregation, and, in the liturgy, in the way it is conducted, and the style of such seemingly mundane aspects as the music and hymnody.[7] It is this festive 'style' of marriage which is such a prominent part of the Eastern rites; from there the Christian West has still much to learn. It was not for nothing that the Archbishop of Canterbury reached out to the East in his sermon at the Royal Wedding of 1981, when he said, 'There is an ancient Christian tradition that *every* bride and groom on their wedding day are regarded as a royal couple. To this day in the marriage ceremonies of the Eastern Orthodox Church crowns are held over the man and the woman to express the conviction that as husband and wife they are Kings and Queens of Creation.'[8] The modern Western rites may like to think of adaptation as a good idea, but they still wear the heavy cloak of a legalized and cerebral Christian tradition. The new Roman nuptial blessings, the British Methodist Jewish-inspired thanksgiving, and the Church of England's long alternative prayer of blessing and supplication for the couple, point the way to further developments in euchology which are built on themes at once contemporary and timeless.

In one regard, however, some further work may have to be done: the question of divorce and marriage. It is not our purpose here to argue either way, which would be out of place in a study of this sort. But various alternatives have been exercised by Christians in the past, and are in practice today or are under consideration. In the Byzantine rite,[9] marriage after divorce was permitted at an early stage, and a special rite was drawn up, basically the same as the full form, but including a penitential prayer; since then, it has largely ceased to be performed, and most couples who come to church for marriage under these circumstances generally get the full service. In the Roman Church the procedure of annulments allows for a full-blown nuptial mass, since the first marriage is taken to be non-existent. More recently within Anglicanism services of 'blessing' have been conducted, either using diocesan or unofficial forms, these latter often reproducing the services of blessing a civil marriage which have usually been appended to the marriage rite in twentieth century service-books. Within Reformed and Lutheran Churches the normal practice is to have a full service, but since their rites are usually simpler, and do not normally involve a Eucharist, they may be easier to adjust. Theologically, the Anglican practice of 'blessing' the couple in these circumstances cannot be defended on any grounds, even the slenderest. If you are going to ask for God's blessing on a couple who come either straight from the Registry Office or after an interval in which they arrive at a mature Christian faith (perhaps for the first time, and therefore without a 'lapse'), you are, theologically, performing exactly the same thing as a full wedding service. Those who defend the 'blessing' are relying, in part, on a warped scholasticism, which abrogates responsibility for the vows, and separates vows and blessing in a way which is not part of a wholesome view of the marriage liturgy itself;[10] vows and blessing are *distinct*, but they belong together, the one is the consequence of the other, the two flow into each other as expressing not just the inner meaning of the *rite* but the inner meaning of the relationship under God. When the churches consider the issue of divorce and marriage, they may find that an adapted form of the earlier Byzantine practice (some kind of penitence, perhaps optional, but one that may well be wanted by the couple), together with the Visigothic and later medieval tradition (writing new blessing-prayers for new circumstances) answers the need,[11] without having recourse to the pretence that the first marriage never existed, as in the Roman procedure, or the double-think of some Anglicans.

Another serious contemporary pastoral issue is related to the problem of divorce, and it concerns those occasions when couples are married at a civil ceremony, for the first time, and for whom the church rite is an appendage, carried out immediately, or else something which they ask for at a subsequent date, when they become part of the worshipping community. Von Allmen[12] alludes to the difficulties which face the various churches in such circumstances; even when the promises made before a civil official are different from those required at the local church, the problem remains of how to give the church service sufficient impact, whether the couple are serious about their faith or not. One solution may be to opt for another style of expressing the consent at the marriage, for example for the partners to make a short speech or a dialogue together; there is no reason why formulae for consent should be tied to the styles offered in the official books. But the problems of adaptation envisaged in Roman, American Episcopal, and Methodist rites for 'inter-faith' marriages will certainly test the liturgy much more, and reveal just how far it is able to christianize pagan/secular customs, as well as be prepared to look at those customs and the teaching behind them to see what there is of common ground, and opportunities for fresh discovery. So will Christian liturgy carry on a tradition that it has known before, albeit in a different context.[13] The repertoire of marriage spirituality is by no means exhausted.

Marriage rites in Christianity are a rich tapestry, woven with care and love and creativity. They speak of the things of the Kingdom of God in the differing ways in which the central relationship of humanity has been, is, and will continue to be experienced within the Body of Christ. It is a story of mankind restored and forgiven, lost and loved, resolute to undertake a commitment to live together, 'in sickness and in health', as prophetic signs of the new creation which Christ 'adorned and beautified' at Cana, the same creation glimpsed at from the very beginning in the story of Adam. For those who look to the rite as imparting the acceptance of society, it may (and should) speak of higher and deeper things. For those who hope that it will 'join together' and mark the end of any further perception in experience of the deep mysteries of God, it may (and should) challenge them to see their future life together as an adventure, of which the wedding is a focus, an imparting of grace for strength in the years ahead. For those who even think for one moment that it will deflect the difficulties of the future, it may (and should) convince them that these can only properly be met and faced and transcended by the help which comes from the source of all love. As we saw in the Eastern Fathers, any theology of marriage must arise from reflected experience, mediated through the liturgy; for if it simply starts in church and ends there, it runs the risk of being a theology of a wedding service, and no more.

These are the convictions which have underlined the great rites of the Christian past, and by their very uncertainty of what to call the service (whether 'veiling', 'solemnizing', 'blessing', or 'celebrating') they bear testimony to the truth that every marriage is the same and every marriage is different. Marriage rites, and in particular marriage prayers, tell us of the different ways in which tradition and experience have been brought together; whether it is the creating God of Israel, as in the time-honoured Jewish blessings; the fidelity of Sarah, as in Rome at the time of Gregory the Great; the merciful goodness of God in helping the couple to stay together, as in Luther; the protecting power of angels, as Visigothic Spain; the strength of the Holy Spirit, as in Calvin; the procreation of children, as in Cranmer; the joys of sexuality, as in contemporary rites; or the ever-new and ever-creative love of eternity, as in the Catholic Apostolics. For Christians the story starts at Cana, with Jesus coming to bless an unknown couple.

Notes

1 Background

1. Biblical and Jewish Models

1. M. H. Pope, *El in Ugaritic Texts* (Leiden 1955), pp. 37–9.

2. C. H. Gordon, *Ugaritic Literature* (Rome 1949), pp. 63–5; see also A. Van Selms, *Marriage and Family Life in Ugaritic Literature* (London 1954), pp. 35–44.

3. E. A. Speiser, in J. B. Pritchard, *Ancient Near Eastern Texts Relating to the Old Testament* (Princeton 1955), pp. 106–9.

4. *Midrash Rabbah,* Gen. 8.9; 17.2; Babylonian Talmud, *Yeb.* 63a.

5. See P. Grelot, *Le couple humain dans l'écriture* (Paris 1962), p. 34; 'si le mariage n'a plus d'archétype divin, il a donc un prototype humain, créé par Dieu à l'origine, qui reste à jamais le modèle à reproduire'.

6. H. H. Rowley, *The Servant of the Lord and Other Essays* (London 1952), pp. 187–234; cf. J. Daniélou, *Bible et Liturgie* (Paris 1958), pp. 259ff.

7. K. W. Stevenson, 'The Origins of Nuptial Blessing', *Heythrop Journal*, 21.4 (October 1980), p. 413 (hereafter referred to as 'The Origins'); for the discussion of Tobit, see O. Eissfeldt, *The Old Testament* (Oxford 1966), p. 585.

8. See pp. 51, 55ff.

9. The blessing 'through' Tobias reappears only in the Pontifical of Egbert, a domestic rite reflecting late eighth-century practice in England (see Stevenson, 'The Origins', p. 413), which is discussed later (pp. 63ff), as are the short blessings which use angelic-protection themes.

10. K. W. Stevenson, 'Benedictio Nuptialis; reflections on the blessing of bride and groom in some Western Mediaeval rites', *Ephemerides Liturgicae*, 93.6 (November–December 1979), pp. 464ff (hereafter referred to as 'Benedictio').

11. *Encyclopoedia Judaica* (Jerusalem), 11, coll. 1032ff; cf. *The Mishnah,* tr. Herbert Danby (Oxford 1933), *Keth.* 1.1 (pp. 245ff); *Meg.* 4.3 (p. 206, n. 11, where the marriage-blessings are alluded to).

12. Maimonides, *Hilchoth Isuth* iii.

13. For full discussion of these blessings, see Rabbi Epstein (ed.), *The Babylonian Talmud; Kethuboth I* (London 1936), pp. 31–3; cf. J. H. Hertz, *The Authorized Daily Prayer Book* (New York 1946), p. 1013; British Reform Judaism keeps these blessings, but adds three optional prayers of intercession which are more personalized, see *Forms of Prayers* (1977), pp. 276–83; the same sentimentalizing tendencies are discernible in later Christian practice, particularly in the later Middle Ages, and in Reformed traditions.

14. J. Heinemann, *Prayer in the Talmud* (Berlin–New York 1977), p. 47.

15. *Encyclopoedia Judaica*, 11, coll. 1036ff; the *huppah* was originally the tent in which the man and wife came together, and different customs arose among Jews in the Middle Ages in various countries. The medieval Christian canopy is discussed in Chapter 2.2 and thereafter.

16. Heinemann, op. cit., pp. 37ff.

17. Ibid., p. 74.

18. Josephus, *Jewish War*, 2.21; cf. 'The Damascus Rule V', in G. Vermes, *The Dead Sea Scrolls in English* (London 1970), p. 101.

19. See 'The New Testament Evidence', Appendix 4 of *Marriage and the Church's Task* (London 1978), a report of the Church of England; the Appendix referred to was written by Professor Barnabas Lindars, and the writer owes much of the discussion here to him.

20. See pp. 100ff on the Eastern rites; for a discussion of this passage, cf. Barnabas Lindars, 'Two Parables in John', *New Testament Studies* 16 (1969), pp. 318–24.

21. *Marriage and the Church's Task*, p. 153.

22. Stevenson, 'Benedictio', p. 476; this point is discussed in later chapters.

23. See D. R. Catchpole, 'The Synoptic Divorce Material as a Traditio-Historical Problem', *Bulletin of the John Rylands University Library of Manchester* 57.1 (Autumn 1974), pp. 92–127, for a recent summary of the discussion, in addition to the Appendix 4 cited in n. 19.

24. E.g. P. F. Bradshaw, *Daily Prayer in the Early Church* (London 1981), pp. 1ff.

25. The legendary marriage of Joseph and Asenath, whose precise origin is unknown, depicts Pharaoh as the celebrant; the bridal pair are betrothed and they come before him for crowning and blessing, and the long feast follows immediately. This curious rite seems to have elements from late-Jewish practice, and echoes later Greek and Syrian ones; see E. W. Brooks, *Joseph and Asenath* (London 1918), especially pp. 61f.

2   *Literary Evidence: the First Three Centuries*

1. Ignatius, *Ad Polycarpum* 5.2; see *The Epistles of St Clement of Rome and St Ignatius of Antioch*, tr. James A. Kleist (London 1945), p. 98.

2. K. Ritzer, *Le Mariage dans les Eglises chrétiennes de 1er au XIè siècle* (Paris 1970), pp. 81–4 (hereafter referred to as Ritzer).

3. *Athenagoras: Legatio and De Resurrectione*, tr. William R. Schoedel (Oxford 1972), *Legatio* 33, p. 81.

4. See p. 30.

5. Op. cit., p. 81, n. 1.

6. L. Barnard, *Athenagoras: A Study in Second Century Christian Apologetic* (Paris 1972), p. 63; cf. p. 74.

7. Athenagoras, *Ep. ad. Diognetam* 5.

8. Quoted by Eusebius, *Ecclesiastical History* IV.23.7.

9. J.-P. Broudéhoux, *Mariage et Famille chez Clément d'Alexandrie*, Paris 1970.

10. Clement of Alexandria, *Stromateis* II.23; discussed by Broudéhoux, op. cit., p. 74.

11. *Stromateis* II.140.1.

12. *Pedagogiae* II.83.1; *Stromateis* III.84.2.

13. *Stromateis* III.74.2; cf. Broudéhoux, op. cit., p. 75.

14. *Pedagogiae* III.63.1; cf. Broudéhoux, op. cit., p. 96.

15. *Stromateis* IV.126.1.

16. *Tertullian: Treatises on Penance, on Purity,* tr. Le Saint (London 1959), *On Purity* 5, pp. 100ff.; see also p. 196, n. 32.

17. *De Oratione* 22.9–10.

18. *De Corona* 13.14–14.2; *De virginibus velandis* 8.3; 11.3; cf. G. De Plinval, 'Tertullien et le scandale de la couronne', *Mélanges J. de Ghellinck* (Gembloux 1951), I, pp. 183–8.

19. *De virginibus velandis* 11.2; cf. 17.1: 'disciplina velaminis'.

20. *De Corona* 14.2; *De virginibus velandis* 11.2.

21. *De Oratione* 22.10; *De virginibus velandis* 11.3.

22. *Ex. cast.* 5.2.

23. *Adv. Marcionem* 1.29; here Tertullian links procreation with the word '*benedixit*' in a similar way to Augustine; see pp. 29–30.

24. *De idolatria* 7.2; *Apologia* 6.4.

25. *Tertullian: Treatises on Marriage and Remarriage, To his Wife, Exhortation to Chastity, Monogamy,* tr. Le Saint (London 1951), *Monogamy* 11, pp. 93f.

26. Ibid., *To his Wife* 2.8.6–9, pp. 35f.; quoted, e.g., by Lowther Clarke (ed.), *Liturgy and Worship* (London 1932), p. 460, n. 5.

27. Ritzer, pp. 110–20.

28. E.g. Broudéhoux, op. cit., p. 96; Gy seems a little sceptical of Ritzer; cf. P.-M. Gy, 'le rite sacramental du mariage et la tradition liturgique', *Revue des Sciences Philosophiques et Théologiques* 38 (1954), pp. 258f.

29. H. Crouzel, 'Deux textes de Tertullien concernant la procedure et les rites du mariage chrétien', *Bulletin de Littérature Ecclésiastique* (1973) 1, pp. 3–13.

30. *De pudicitia* 4.4.

31. *Tertullian: Treatises on Marriage,* pp. 132f., nn. 142–5.

32. The most recent (and exhaustive) summary of the discussion about Tertullian and marriage is by Renato Uglione, 'Il matrimonio in Tertulliano tra Esaltazione e Disprezzo', *Ephemerides Liturgicae* 93 (1979), pp. 479–94; but it lacks a specifically liturgical perspective.

33. Ritzer, pp. 108ff.; text also in E. Lodi, *Enchiridion euchologicum fontium liturgicorum* (Rome 1979), pp. 179–80.

34. Ritzer, p. 109; cf. Stevenson, 'The Origins', p. 414; cf. also Georg Kretschmar's correct (in our opinion) assessment that the *Acts* 'are in the style of Greek travel stories and not ritual texts' (Lecture given at 25th Aniversary of the Institut Supérieur de Liturgie, Paris, 21 August, 1981). See also 'La liturgie ancienne dans les recherches historiques actuelles', *Maison-Dieu* 149 (1982), p. 65.

35. *Philosophoumena* 9.12.24.

36. *Theophilus of Antioch: Ad Autolychum,* tr. Robert M. Grant (Oxford 1970), 3.13, p. 117.

37. *Ad Caecilium* 12.28.

38. *Cyprian: De Lapsis and De Ecclesiae Catholicae Unitate,* tr. Maurice Bevenot, S.J. (Oxford 1971), *De Eccl.* 5, p. 65.

39. *De habitu virginum* 18.

40. Ritzer, pp. 81–123; the early centuries clearly had much liturgical pluriformity, and this would hold good of marriage procedure, but the evidence examined in this chapter points to a gradual tightening of the Church's grip on the marriages of its members; cf. P.-M. Gy, 'Problèmes de theologie sacramentaire', *Maison-Dieu* 110 (1972), p. 139.

1. *The Symposium*, Logos 2.1; cf. Musrillo's introductory remark on Methodius' theology: 'It is a dull, humorless world that he paints. True, this drabness is relieved by the profound meaning he attaches to marriage, as well as to virginity ...'; *St Methodius: The Symposium; a Treatise on Chastity*, tr. Musrillo (London 1958), p. 21.

2. *De Spiritu Sancto* 19.

3. *Hexaemeron* 7.5.

4. *Ep. ad Amphilochum* 188; 199.

5. *Oratio* 40, *In Sanctum Baptisma* 18.

6. *Ep.* 193, *Ad Procopium*.

7. On '*epithamalia*', see below on Paulinus of Nola, p. 28.

8. *Ep.* 231, *Ad Eusebium*.

9. *Ep.* 230, *Ad Theodosium/Theodorum*.

10. *Ep.* 222, *Ad Dioclem*.

11. Gregory of Nyssa, *De Oratione* 1; Evagrius Ponticus, *Historiae* 1.42.

12. *In Mat. Hom.* 51/52; *Spur. in Mat.* 32.

13. *Hom. in Col.* 12.4; *Hom. in Ep. ad Eph.* 5.20.

14. *Bapt. Inst.* 6.24; *De res. dom.* 50.

15. *De verba propter fornicationes, passim*.

16. *Hom. in I Tim.* 9.

17. *Hom. de Capto Eutropio et de divitiarum vanitate*, 13.

18. *In Gen. Hom.* 48.6.

19. Cf. Stevenson, 'The Origins', p. 414.

20. *Commentary on the Gospel* 2.26; cf. Giuseppe Baldanza, 'Il rito del Matrimonio nell'Euchologio Barberini 336. Analisi della sua visione teologica', *Ephemerides Liturgicae* 93.4–5 (1979), p. 344, n. 112.

21. *Cat.* 17, *De Sp. Sancto* 2; *Cat.* 6, *De Uno Deo* 35.

22. *Ep.* 52.16.

23. *In Ps. 138* 7–10.

24. *Palladius: The Lausiac History*, tr. R. Meyer (London 1965), pp. 41f.

25. *Resp.* 11.

26. J. D. Mansi, *Sacrorum conciliorum nova et amplissima Collectio* (Florence–Venice 1757–98), (hereafter referred to as Mansi), II, pp. 518 (Ancyra), 541 (Neo-Caesarea), 564, 569, 573 (Laodicea).

27. *Liber quaestionum* 50.400; *In. Ep. I. ad Cor.* 7.40; *In Ep. I. ad Tim.* 3.12.

28. *Ep. I.* 4, *Ad Himerium*.

29. E.g. *De Abraham* 288.19; 311.91; *De Viduis* 2.188.10; 15.210.88; *Exp. in Lucam* 1.1276.30; 1280.43; *in Cor.* 7.5 133.

30. E.g. *Hexaemeron* 86.18; *In Ps 118* 1004.32; *De Virg.* 6.221.33; *De Viduis* 11.204.69; *Exhort. Virg.* 4.283.21; cf. Zeno of Verona, *Tract.* 1.4.8; 1.14.4; for a discussion of these (and other) issues regarding Ambrose and marriage, cf. E. Cattaneo, 'La celebrazione delle nozze a Milano', *Archivio Ambrosiano* 29 (1976), pp. 145–8, especially p. 146.

31. *Hexaemeron* 86.18; see above n. 3, from Basil's *Hexaemeron*. The coincidence seems too great; Ambrose must be quoting the great Cappadocian master; cf. Ritzer, p. 224, n. 27.

32. *Exp. in Lucam* 8.1470.2f.

33. *De Insitut. Virginis* 17.273.108.

34. *Exp. in Lucam* 7.231; *De poenitentia* 2.3.18; *De Isaac et anima* 1.8; *Ep.* 41.18; 60.7; *In Ps.* 39.17.

35. *De Abraham* 1.312.93; *De laps. virg.*5.

36. *Ep.* 19 (65).844.7.

37. *Ep.* 59 (92).1018.1.

38. *In I Cor.* 7.40.138.

39. *Exp. in Lucam* 6.1386.9.

40. *Ep.* 2.6.

41. *Statuta Ecclesiae Antiquae*, Canon 101; a favourite passage in subsequent conciliar documents, it also mentions three nights of continence.

42. *Carmen* 25, lines 199–232; for a discussion of this piece, see Stevenson, 'The Origins', pp. 414–5.

43. *Tractatus vel Sermones* 8.2.35ff; 9.38ff.

44. *Regula Pastoralis* 3.27, *Admonitio* 28.

45. *Ep.* 7.2.7.

46. *Sermo* 42 (288).4; *Sermo* 43 (289).3, 5.

47. *Vita S. Caesarii* 1.59.

48. Pedro Langa, 'Equilibrio Augustiniano entre Matrimonio y Virginidad', *Revista Agostiniana* 21 (1980), pp. 73–134; the classical study of Agustine's ethical views is still J. Mausbach, *Die Ethik des hl. Augustinus* (2nd ed., Freiburg-i-Br. 1929), I, pp. 318ff.

49. *Ep.* 253 (1069), *ad Benenatum*.

50. E.g. *De fide et operibus* 7.10; *De bono conjugio* 7.13.18; *In Johannem* 9.2.

51. E.g. *De bono conjugio* 3.11; *De concupiscentia* 10.11; *De nuptiis et concupiscentia* I.13.15.

52. E.g. *De bono conjugio* 26; *De nuptiis et concupiscentia*, 11.13; 17.19; *De Genesi* 9.7; *De pecc. orig.* 34.39; 37.42 (though in this last instance he substitutes '*pudicitia*' for '*fides*').

53. *De Symbolo* 13.13; *Sermones* 332.4.

54. E.g. *Ennaratio in Ps 80*, n.21; *Sermones* 9.11.18; 51.13.22; 51.14.23; 278.9.9; *De nuptiis et concupiscentia* I.4.5.

55. E.g. *De bono conjugio* 2; *De Genesi* 3.5; *De Civitate Dei* 14.10; 21, 22; *De nuptiis et concupiscentia* 21.23; *De pecc. orig.* 35.40; 37.42.

56. See pp. 50ff.

57. For a summary of the debate about Augustine's views on marriage in general, cf. *Augustine: The First Catechetical Instructions*, tr. J. Christopher (London 1946), p. 125, n. 183; see also *de Genesi* 9.7.

58. *De pecc. orig.* 36.41; *De Civitate Dei* 14.18.

59. *De haeresibus* 1.87.

6q. *Vita S. Augustini* 24; 27.4–5.

61. *Ep. Ad Probam* 3.14.

62. cf. R. Metz, *La consécration des vièrges* (Paris 1949), pp. 366ff.

63. cf. L. Anné, 'La conclusion du mariage dans la tradition et le droit de l'Eglise latine jusqu'au VIè siècle', *Ephemerides Theologicae Lovanienses* 12 (1935), pp. 513–50, esp. pp. 536t., on the veiling, where Anné (rightly) dismisses any connection between the Jewish *huppah* and the Roman bridal veil; cf. the pagan para-liturgical features of Catullus in his *Carmina* 61 and 62.

64. Mansi, II, pp. 7, 8, 14 (Elvira), p. 472 (Arles), and p. 330 (Milevis).

65. Cabrol/Leclerq, *Dictionnaire d'Archéologie Chrétienne et Liturgie*, Vol. x, pt. ii (Paris 1932), 1843–1981; the ring was used in pagan Rome as a sign of betrothal.

1   The Roman Sacramentaries

1. E.g. D. M. Hope, *The Leonine Sacramentary* (London 1971), esp. pp. 107ff.
2. L. C. Mohlberg, L. Eizenhöfer, P. Siffrin, *Sacramentarium Veronense* (Rome 1956), 1105–10.
3. cf. Gelasian and Gregorian *secreta*.
4. Hope leaves this question open (op. cit., p. 34), but Ritzer assumes that the prayer is meant to take place between the canon and communion (Ritzer, pp. 239ff.).
5. cf. Paulinus' *Carmen*, see p. 28.
6. See pp. 26ff.
7. cf. *LO* 439, 'tegatur propria castitate, pudoris sui *velamen* . . .', the only one (of two) direct references to veiling in a western prayer, in E.-E. Moeller, *Corpus Benedictionum Pontificalium* (Turnholti-Brepols, 1971), II, 473 (hereafter referred to as Moeller); on this question, see p. 50. cf. Byzantine reticence on crown language in euchology.
8. A. Chavasse, *Le Sacramentaire Gélasien* (Tournai 1959), esp. pp. 1–xxxiii.
9. L. Eizenhöfer, P. Siffrin, L. C. Mohlberg, *Liber Sacramentorum* (Rome 1960), 52.1–10.
10. The preface is strong in the early English books (e.g. Leofric, Magdalen); on the sources, cf. E.-E. Moeller, *Corpus Praefationum* (Turnholti-Brepols 1980), 967.
11. Ritzer, p. 244, n. 95a; cf. Chavasse, op. cit., p. 485, n. 36.
12. *Liber Sacramentorum*, 52.9.
13. Chavasse, op. cit., p. 486: '. . . le gélasien du VIIIè siècle, qui les recopie scrupuleusement . . .'; cf. *Konkordanztabellen zu den römischen Sakramentarien*, II (Rome 1959), pp. 185f; cf. also A. Dumas, *Liber Sacramentorum Gellonensis*, (Turnholti-Brepols 1981), 406 (see table, ibid p. 119).
14. Moeller, I, pp. i-lxvi.
15. See Stevenson, 'Benedictio', pp. 462–4, & p. 465, nn. 62–3 (with comparative table of texts).
16. J.-A. Jungmann, *Missarum Sollemnia*, III (Fr. tr. Paris 1953), pp. 182–5.
17. *Liber Sacramentorum*, 52.6: 'ut pariter bene et pacifice senescant et videant filios filiorum suorum usque in tertiam et quartam progeniem'; this bears a striking resemblance to some of the 'plural-ending' versions of the Gregorian nuptial blessing; see Stevenson, 'Benedictio', pp. 460ff.
18. Gr. Richter, A. Schönfelder, *Sacramentarium Fuldense* (Fulda, 1912), 2612; there are some variants; this rite is discussed on pp. 57f.
19. Chavasse, op. cit., p. 485.
20. J. Deshusses, *Le sacramentaire grégorien* I (Fribourg 1971), 833–8b; on the authorship of Benedict of Aniane, see Deshusses' case (argued successfully, in our opinion), pp. 29ff.
21. 'hanc igitur oblationem famulorum tuorum quam tibi offerunt pro famula tua illa, quam . . .', Deshusses, op. cit., 836; cf. Ritzer, p. 246.
22. H. Lietzmann, *Das Sacramentarium Gregorianum nach dem Aachener Urexemplar* (Münster, 1921), p. 111.
23. Deshusses, op. cit., p. 36 (= his manuscript 'A').
24. See Deshusses, op. cit., 838b, with 'table des sigles' and *apparatus criticus*.

25. Stevenson, 'Benedictio', pp. 46of.

26. A. Olivar, *El Sacramentario de Vich* (Barcelona 1953), 1422; Josep Romà Barriga Planas, *El Sacramentari, ritual i pontifical de Roda* (Barcelona 1975), pp. 334–5 (but here there are some manuscript variants in the Roman direction); see p. 55.

27. G. Dix, *The Shape of the Liturgy* (London 1945), pp. 581ff.; T. Klauser, *A Short History of the Western Liturgy* (London 1969), pp. 45ff.

28. Text in Ritzer, p. 446; discussed in Stevenson, 'Benedictio', pp. 46of.

29. W. G. Henderson, U. Lindelöf, *The Durham Collectar* (2nd ed., Durham 1927), pp. 106–11; on the dating, see pp. xlivff.

30. Each component of the rite has its title (including '*benedictio*' for the nuptial blessing), but the sequence gets a little confused at the end; the first blessing of the bedchamber appears to be said during the mass, as it is only before the second blessing of the chamber that we find the title '*in thalamo*', ibid., p. 111.

31. G. Morin, 'le plus ancien Comes ou Lectionnaire de l'Eglise Romain', *Revue Benedictine* 27 (1910), p. 66; see also H. A. P. Schmidt, *Hebdomada Sancta*, II (Rome 1957), p. 321.

32. Ritzer, p. 251.

33. A. Martini, *Il cosidetto Pontificale di Poitiers* (Rome 1979), p. 336; the gospel pericope (Jn. 3.27–9) is also unusual, and the nuptial blessing has plural ending.

34. Ritzer, p. 252, n. 126b.

35. R. Amiet, 'un "Comes" carolingien de la Haute-Italie', *Ephemerides Liturgicae* 73 (1959), p. 361; on the gospel readings in the early Roman rite, see W. H. Frere, *Studies in Early Roman Liturgy: II The Roman Gospel-Lectionary* (London 1934), pp. 26, 57.

36. Text in Ritzer, pp. 429f.

37. Texts in Enzo Lodi, *Enchiridion euchologicum fontium liturgicorum*, pp. 1079f.

38. E.g. Bernard Moreton, *The Eighth-Century Gelasian Sacramentary* (London 1976), pp. 20–4.

39. cf. Stevenson, 'The Origins', p. 416.

40. J.-P. De Jong, 'Brautsegen und Jungfrauenweihe', *Zeitschrift für katholische Theologie* 84 (1962), pp. 300–22.

41. P.-M. Gy, 'le nouveau rituel romain du mariage', *Maison-Dieu* 99 (1970), p. 127. n. 11; there were difficulties in this. See pp. 184, 187.

42. R. Metz, *La consécration des vierges*, pp. 366ff.

2 Visigothic Creativity

1. M. Férotin, *Liber Ordinum* (Paris 1904), pp. 433–41.

2. P. F. Bradshaw, *Daily Prayer in the Early Church*, pp. 115–23, 126f.

3. T. C. Akeley, *Christian Initiation in Spain* (London 1967).

4. J. Pinell, *De Liturgiis Occidentalibus* (pro manuscripto) (Rome 1967).

5. L. Brou, *The Psalter-Collects* (London 1949).

6. Barriga Planas, *El Sacramentari, Ritual i Pontifical de Roda*, pp. 329–40 (cf. pp. 134–6); A. Olivar, *El Sacramentario de Vich*, pp. 208–15; these editions will be referred to hereafter as *Roda* and *Vich*, respectively.

7. Isidore of Seville, *De Ecclesiasticis Officiis* II.20, *De Conjugatis* 5–10; text in Ritzer, pp. 432–4.

8. Ritzer, p. 299: 'Le rite mozarabe présente un développement particulièrement riche de la liturgie nuptiale'.

9. Férotin, op. cit., pp. xvii–xxiv; the two manuscripts are preserved in the monastery of Santo Domingo de Silos, in Old Castile.

10. See p. 43.

11. The text is as follows:
'May almighty God fill this marriage-shelter with his abundant blessing, and bless those who come together in it with perpetual sanctification. Amen.
May every invasion of evil spirits flee away from this place, and the visitation of the angels come forward here. Amen.
May the celebration of marriage be held here by the gift of God so that honesty of husband and wife be not warped. Amen.
May all activity and conversation among those who come to this celebration be so good that it does not turn to shipwreck through lust and greed. Amen.
May honesty and shame come upon those who are married now, and may eternal peace sustain those who come together for the joys of this marriage. Amen.' (*LO* 433).

12. Férotin gives some added material on the background of this rite from the Spanish *Carta de Arras* (*LO*, 545–7).

13. If the prayer antedates ring-giving, then it is earlier than even Isidore (see below); it is not until much later that the Visigothic marriage rites sort out the precise difference between tokens and rings.

14. 'B' seems to come after the priest's communion, but before the communion of the couple: cf. 'before the deacon gives the dismissal, they come forward to the priest' (*LO* 436) and (after the blessings and the giving of the girl) 'and so they communicate' (*LO* 439); 'A' has a communion chant inserted in a later hand after the blessings, and then 'he communicates them' (*LO* 437).

15. E. A. Lowe, *The Bobbio Missal* (London 1920), no. 550; this puts the prayer back as far as possibly the seventh century; see below, p. 56.

16. The other prayer which concentrates on the bride is only used when she marries a widower, and it appears in the text after the nuptial rite (*LO* 440); Roman influence is more obvious here; see Stevenson, 'Benedictio', p. 463, nn. 62, 63.

17. *LO* 436–7.

18. Stevenson, 'The Origins', p. 413; see p. 6.

19. If the long domestic blessing (text in n.11) was specially written after the domestic rite was replaced by the full service in church, this throws the precise use of the order of pledges in the present rite into further confusion; Roda and Vich reverse the domestic rite and the order of pledges, but the mass still comes at the end (see below).

20. See p. 220 n. 14.

21. That is, apart from the special blessing for a bride marrying a widower.

22. Even the last paragraphs seem artificially broken up by the 'Amens', particularly the last section immediately before the Lord's Prayer (*LO* 437).

23. This office can be filled out with material from the (tenth-century) Antiphonary of Léon: see L. Serrano, *Antiphonarium Mozarabicum de la*

Cathedral de Léon editado por los PP. Benedictinos de Silos (Léon 1928), pp. 216ff; Ritzer, pp. 434f.

24. See pp. 44f.

25. See p. 222 n. 7.

26. 'Marriages are blessed in the rite of joining together, for this was done by God in the very first condition of man, for so it is written' (*De Conjugatis* 5).

27. cf. The 'Blessing of the girl only' in *LO* 'B' which mentions both the veil and Rebecca; is he quoting the liturgy?

28. See pp. 29f; Augustine's influence on a writer like Isidore is likely.

29. See p. 16 on the pagan Roman garlands, so disliked by Tertullian.

30. See p. 221 n. 6.

31. *Vich*, p. xcvi.

32. Stevenson, 'Benedictio', pp. 474f.

33. But not Olivar's ms 'E', which is early-twelfth century, though it does appear in 'M', which is later, *Vich*, p. xcvi; if this is an eccentric addition to the original rite (as I suggest), the textual instability at this point gives support to this supposition; cf. *Roda*, xxxiii, 10, p. 336; see above, n. 16.

34. *Roda*, xxxiii, 12, p. 338.

35. *Vich* 1424; a later hand puts this prayer after communion.

36. *LO* 439 and *Vich*, 1429; see above n.16.

37. E. A. Lowe, *The Bobbio Missal*, pp. 167f.

38. Gr. Richter, A. Schönfelder, *Sacramentarium Fuldense*, 2605–17.

39. Ibid., 2610; it might be based on an older (lost) *super oblata*, or even a Mozarabic *illatio* (preface).

40. Ibid., 2613; 'pure and immaculate' mankind, propagation of children 'by the mystery of love', 'go above the flesh', and other similar expressions.

41. Ibid., 2616, 2617; *LO* places them at the beginning of the blessing section at the end of mass, Vich places the first at the beginning of the blessing, and the second *after* the Gregorian nuptial blessing; Roda places both immediately before the nuptial blessing, separated only by the Gregorian preparatory prayer.

42. What we now call 'French Catalonia' was not part of France itself until the sixteenth century.

43. Text in J.-B. Molin, P. Mutembe, *Le rituel du Mariage en France du XIIè au XVIè siècle* (Paris 1974), pp. 291–2, (hereafter referred to as Molin-Mutembe); on the Midi's consent on love (not will), see pp. 64ff.

44. It also appears in the Arles Pontifical (see below), but it does not survive in France, cf. below on the Gerona rite.

45. Text in Molin-Mutembe, pp. 292–3.

46. Martène, *De Antiquis Ecclesiae Ritibus* (Antwerp, 1763), II, Cap. IX, Art. V, Ordo V (pp. 130–1).

47. D. Codina, 'El ritual de Matrimoni del MS. 142 del seminari de Girona', *Il Congrés Litúrgic de Montserrat* (Montserrat 1967), pp. 225–8; I am indebted to Dom Alexander Olivar, OSB, of Montserrat, for drawing my attention to this important little study.

48. J.-B. Molin, 'Le mariage au diocèse d'Elne avant le Concile de Trente', *Revista Catalana de Teologia* 4 (1979), pp. 117–22.

49. Molin-Mutembe, pp. 310–12.

50. E. Allain, 'un *ordo ad sponsalium* bordelais du XVè siècle', *Bulletin historique et philologique* (1894), p. 116.

51. *Enchiridion ecclesiae Pallantine* (1508), f. xxvii (v)–xxxix (v).

52. *Manuale secundum consuetudinem almae ecclesiae Salmanticensis* (1532), f. xvi (v)–xxix (v).

53. *Manuale sacramentorum secundum usum almae ecclesiae Toletanae* (1554), f. xxvi (r)–xxxvi (v).

54. *Manipulus sive Manuale secundum almae ecclesiae Conctiensis* (1560), f. 48 (v)–74 (v).

55. *Ordinarium de ministrandorum sacramentorum secundum consuetudines almae metropolitanae sedis Valenciensis* (1514), f. lvi (v)–lxxvi (v).

56. *Ordinarium sacramentorum secundum ritum et consuetudinem sanctae metropolitanae ecclesiae Tarraconensis* (1530), f. xl (r)–xlx (v).

57. On the Visigothic features of the Tarragona rite, cf. Adalberto Franqesa, 'Elementos visigoticos en el ritual Tarraconense', *Hispania Sacra* II (1958), pp. 6–11, where Catalan pride rides high.

3 The Anglo-Norman Synthesis

1. W. Greenwell (ed.), *The Pontifical of Egbert* (Durham 1853), p. xi, for discussion of date and origin; marriage rites on pp. 125f., and 132; hereafter referred to as *Egbert*.

2. Ritzer, p. 281, n. 224, citing Lüdtke, 'Ordo ad facienda sponsalia', in *Festschrift für R. Haupt* (Kiel 1922), pp. 99, 106, 118, 124–7.

3. See pp. 42f.

4. W. G. Henderson (ed.), *The York Manual* (Durham 1875), p. 158* (hereafter referred to as *York*).

5. *Egbert*, p. 132.

6. *Statuta Capitularia* IV: 'in primo conjugio debet presbyter missam agere, benedicere ambos' ('at first marriages the priest must celebrate mass, and bless both'); see Ritzer, pp. 323f., and nn.

7. Molin-Mutembe, pp. 320–1, nos. 7, 8, 9, 10; the *Egbert* text (which Molin-Mutembe fail to note, instead attributing to Durham) runs as follows: 'creator and preserver of the human race, giver of spiritual grace, Eternal God, send The Holy Spirit, the Paraclete, on this ring.'

8. G. H. Doble, *Pontificale Lanaletense* (London 1937), 65a; comparative text with citations in Moeller, p. 735 (no. 1798), where Moeller omits to mention that the first three paragraphs appear in the sixteenth-century Pontifical of Christopher Bainbridge, Archbishop of York 1508–14; cf. W. G. Henderson (ed.), *The Pontifical of Christopher Bainbridge* (Durham 1875), p. 182.

9. See p. 30.

10. See Moeller, no. 1978.

11. Molin-Mutembe, pp. 323f, no. 23; the first appearance of the short version appears to be in the twelfth-century so-called Pontifical of Lyre (= Martène's Ordo III, Molin-Mutembe's Ordo III).

12. R. M. Woolley (ed.), *The Canterbury Benedictional* (London 1917), p. 126; Woolley notes (p. 163) of this prayer, 'I cannot find it elsewhere'; nor can Moeller, p. 416, no. 1020.

13. Woolley, op. cit., p. xxv.

14. H. A. Wilson (ed.), *The Benedictional of Archbishop Robert* (London 1903), pp. xiv–xvii (discussion of origin), pp. 149–51 (marriage rite).

15. cf. Molin-Mutembe, pp. 137–8, for this curious compilation, which we shall hereafter refer to as 'the psalmic verses'.

16. Text in *York*, p. 159* (Ordo III); Molin-Mutembe, p. 30.

17. Molin-Mutembe, Ordo V, pp. 289–91.

18. cf. Molin-Mutembe, p. 50, and n. on Aquinas; see also Jean Dauvillier, *Le Mariage dans le droit classique de l'Eglise* (Paris 1933), *passim*.

19. See Ritzer, p. 256, n. 144; on the origin and use of the Trinity mass, see Jean Deshusses, 'Les messes d'Alcuin', *Archiv für Liturgiewissenschaft* 14 (1972), pp. 1–41; the Trinity mass was festive in tone.

20. We only come across this prayer again in Scandinavia; see pp. 86ff.

21. Molin-Mutembe, Ordo IV, pp. 288–9; Martène, Ordo IV; on the dating, cf. A.-G. Martimort, *La Documentation Liturgique de Dom Edmond Martène* (Vatican City 1978), p. 359 (no. 693), p. 143 (no. 177).

22. One is from a monastic Missal from Normandy, the other can be traced to Bayeux (texts in Ritzer, pp. 456–60).

23. F. E. Warren (ed.), *The MSS Irish Missal* (London 1879), pp. 81–4; Warren dates it 1152–7 (p. 49).

24. H. A. Wilson (ed.), *The Pontifical of Magdalen College* (London 1910), pp. 221–5.

25. Text in *York*, pp. 161–2* (Ordo V).

26. Text in Mansi, 22, Col. 1038; cf. also Dauvillier, op. cit., esp. Part 2.

27. Molin-Mutembe, Ordo VIII, pp. 294–5.

28. Ibid., p. 78.

29. Ibid., Ordo IX, pp. 295–7.

30. Stevenson, 'Benedictio', pp. 474f.

31. Molin-Mutembe, Ordo X, pp. 297–8.

32. Ibid., Ordo XI, pp. 298–300.

33. Ibid., Ordo XVII, pp. 311–14; Ordo XV, pp. 305–8.

34. Martène, Ordo VI; on the dating, cf. Martimort, op. cit., p. 359 (no. 696), p. 56 (no. 38).

35. Martène, Ordo VIII.

36. Molin-Mutembe, p. 327, no. 38.

37. Ibid., p. 17; but cf. Martimort, op. cit., p. 360 (no. 698), pp. 139–40 (no. 171).

38. For Amiens, see Martène, Ordo IX; cf. Martimort, op. cit., p. 360 (no. 699), p. 38 (no. 2); for Barbeau, see Molin-Mutembe, p. 106 (see also discussion of subsequent French use of vow).

39. Molin-Mutembe, Ordo XIV, pp. 303–5; Ordo XVIII, pp. 315–16.

40. Gy thinks that *'ego conjungo vos'* appeared earlier, and that its general thrust is the priest's resumption of the parental role, in 'handing over' the girl, and he cites Duns Scotus, 'Le nouveau rituel . . .', p. 133, n. 22; I would myself see it as an instance of the unresolved question of whether the priest 'joins' the couple, or the couple themselves.

41. Text in *York*, pp. 162–3* (Ordo VI).

42. Text in *York*, pp. 163–4* (Ordo VII).

43. H. A. Wilson (ed.), *Liber Evesham* (London 1893), pp. 35–46; on the dating and origin, see discussion, pp. ix–xv.

44. See Stevenson, 'Benedictio', p. 467, n. 91.

45. J. Wickham Legg (ed.), *The Westminster Missal* (London 1891), III, coll. 1233–43.

46. Duncan McGregor (ed.), *The Rathen Manual* (Aberdeen 1905), pp. 1/2–5/2.

47. See pp. 79f, 82.

48. Text in *York*, pp. 167–9* (Ordo X).

49. A. Jeffries Collins (ed.), *The Sarum Manual* (London 1960), pp. 44–59 (hereafter referred to as *Sarum*); the marraige rite probably goes back to 1330–40, if not before: see pp. ixff; York text in *York* pp. 24–39 (the marriage rite probably goes back to fourteenth century also); cf. W. G. Henderson (ed), *The York Missal* (Durham 1872), II, pp. 190–3, where one MS ('G') gives the full Manual rite; for Hereford, see ibid., pp. 115*–120*.

50. Ironically enough, Cranmer's adoption of 'worship' (instead of the older 'honour') was the subject of much controversy: see pp. 136, 144f, 150, 153.

51. MS 'D', the Douai version, 1610–11, *Sarum*, p. 48, n. 28; this proves how conservative the living vernacular tradition can become in time!

52. Cf. 'hafa nu ond geheald/husa selest' ('Have now and hold the best of houses') in *Beowulf*, an Anglo-Saxon poem known to have roots in the eighth century; and also 'habban and healdan' in *The Battle of Maldon*, from the tenth or early eleventh century; texts are to be found in G. P. Krapp and E. V. K. Dobbie (eds), *The Anglo-Saxon Poetic Records, A Collective Edition* (London/ New York), iv (1953), p. 22; vi (1942), p. 13. The liturgical (preaching) use in the tenth century is to be found in R. Morris (ed.), *The Blicking Homilies* (London 1874), p. 55. I am indebted to Dr. Gale Owen, Lecturer in English Language, University of Manchester, for drawing my attention to this, as a result of preaching at her wedding.

53. Stevenson, 'Benedictio', pp. 473–4; Rathen has it also. Evidence from English inventories suggests that the 'care-cloth' (as it was often called) was white in the thirteenth century, and gradually became red, the usual colour of the mass vestments; see W. St. John Hope and E. G. Cuthbert Atchley, *English Liturgical Colours* (London 1918), pp. 158f.

54. Collins dates this restriction to the second part of the fourteenth century, before 1370, see *Sarum*, pp. 54–6.

55. Molin-Mutembe, pp. 384ff.

56. See pp. 84ff.

57. See H. S. Kingsford, *Illustrations of the Occasional Offices* (London 1921), figures 19–24; some of these describe a rite which begins at the church door, whereas others have the preliminary part of the rite before the altar. Cf. J. B. Molin, 'L'iconographie des rites nuptiaux', *102è Congrès national des Sociétés savantes* (Limoges 1977) archéologie, pp. 353–66, esp. pp. 359–61 for discussion of the veil and 'iugale'.

4   Scandinavia, Germany, Italy

1. See pp. 61f.

2. Basilius Binder, *Geschichte des feierlichen Ehesegens* (Abtei Metten 1938), pt. 1, *passim*.

3. Helge Faehn, *Manuale Norvegicum* (Oslo 1962), pp. 24–6 (MS. 'B'), pp. 19–24 (MS. 'O').

4. The vernacular material appears in *Manuale Norvegicum*, pp. 19–20; it even looks like an insertion in the manuscript. I am grateful to Helen Maclean, Lecturer in English Language, University of Manchester, for examining the Old Norse here.

5. These prayers, and a third, are *directed* to be used with older couples in Bury: see p. 69; cf. Stevenson, 'Benedictio', pp. 467f.; it is tempting to suggest that in *Manuale Norvegicum* they were also intended for older couples, even though the specific direction is lacking.

6. The Ephesians analogy in the nuptial blessing is restricted to virgins, as in Sarum; cf. Stevenson, 'Benedictio', pp. 461f.

7. Knud Ottosen, *The Manual from Notmark*, Copenhagen 1970; for origin and dating, see pp. 17ff.; peculiar features of the nuptial rite assist him in identifying Notmark with the Diocese of Odense, rather than Slesvig; the marriage service is on pp. 69–74.

8. The nuptial pall also appears in the fragment of the 1483 Missal of Odense: see Ottosen, op. cit., p. 21, n. 2.

9. Isak Collijn, *Manuale Upsalense* (Uppsala 1918), pp. 25–32; Bengt Strömberg, *Den Pontifikala Liturgin i Lund och Roskilde under Medeltiden* (Lund 1955), pp. 187–90; Ottosen spots other French features, op. cit., p. 22; for the Reims text, see Molin-Mutembe, p. 217. Strömberg does not comment on this marriage rite, but these observations support his argument about other features in the Lund book originating from Reims in the twelfth century.

10. J. Freisen, *Manuale Lincopense, Breviarium Scarense, Manuale Aboense* (Paderborn 1904), pp. 131–6 (Skara); Hilding Johansson, *Hemsjömanualet, en Liturgi-historisk Studie* (Stockholm 1950), pp. 171–5 (Hemsjö).

11. J. Freisen, *Liber Agendarum Ecclesie et Diocesis Slesvicensis* (Paderborn 1898), pp. 61–8 (Slesvig); J. Freisen, *Manuale Roschildense* (Paderborn 1898), pp. 15–22 (Roskilde).

12. J. Freisen, *Manuale Lincopense, Breviarium Scarense, Manuale Aboense*, pp. 172–7 (Åbo), pp. 31–53 (Linköping).

13. C. Vogel, R. Elze, *Le Pontifical Romano–Germanique du Xè siècle*, II (Vatican City 1963), pp. 414–19; see *apparatus criticus* and notes.

14. Text in Ritzer, pp. 455–6; for the discussion, cf. W. Lüdtke, 'Ordines ad facienda sponsalia', *Festschrift T. Haupt* (Kiel 1922), pp. 95–128.

15. A. Franz, *Das Rituale des Bischofs Heinrich des Ersten von Breslau* (Freiburg-i-Breisgau 1912), pp. 21–3.

16. A. Schönfelder, *Liturgische Bibliothek*, I (Paderhorn 1904), pp. 97–8; a similar non-eucharistic rite appears in Mainz, 1480; see Ernst Kelchner (ed.), *Der Pergamentdruck der Agende Ecclesiae Moguntinensis von 1480* (Frankfurt 1885), p. 6.

17. Binder, op. cit., pp. 33f. We take up the Köln story again on pp. 175f.

18. Since the prayer is unique, it is worth quoting in full: 'Almighty and everlasting God, who guards each faithful person; deem worthy of blessing this your handmaid who stands outside the doors of your church seeking entry to the house of prayer; that she may be able to enter the home of your blessing and persevere in the honour of your name; so that free from the taint of the sins of each (partner) she may with your help deserve to keep the quality of your goodness'; text in Schönfelder, op. cit., p. 98.

19. I am indebted to The Revd. Bryan Spinks for photo-copies of this part of the Magdeburg Agenda; references are: folio lxxi (r)–f. xxii (v).

20. Schönfelder, op. cit., pp. 26–7.

21. The Constance rite of 1482 also describes the 'enthroning', distinguishes it from 'blessing', and lays down that 'enthroning' should only take place after confession; text in Alban Dold, *Die Konstanzer Ritualientexte in ihrer Entwicklung von 1482–1721* (Erzabtei Beuron 1923), p. 98.

22. Schönfelder, op. cit., pp. 62–3.

23. A. Schönfelder, *Liturgische Bibliothek*, II (Paderborn 1906), pp. 22–3.

24. Ibid., pp. 23–4.

25. Binder, op. cit., pp. 116–18.

26. M. Magistretti, *Pontificale in usum Ecclesiae Mediolanensis* (Milan 1897), pp. 65ff.

27. E. Cattaneo, 'La celebrazione delle nozze a Milano', *Archiva Ambrosiano* 29 (1976), pp. 142–80; our discussion here is based on his findings, pp. 154–74.

28. E.g. the Irish Missal and the Magdalen Pontifical, but these are both twelfth century; see Stevenson, 'Benedictio', p. 461.

29. See p. 38.

30. See p. 72.

31. See p. 172.

32. R. Lippe (ed.), *Missale Romanum, 1474* (London 1907), pp. 287f., 319ff.

33. Robert Amiet, 'Le rituel et la messe du Mariage selon le rit valdotain', in *Recherches sur l'ancienne liturgie d'Aoste*, VI (Aoste 1976), pp. 213–62, esp. pp. 218–19, for a list of the MSS used; the blessing of the ring does not appear until the early fifteenth century, though this may be because of lack of manuscripts available.

3 The East

1 The Byzantine and Armenian Rites

1. J. Goar, *Euchologion* (Venice 1730), pp. 310–26, giving the Byzantine text, together with some textual notes, and the Barberini 336 text; A. Dmitrievski, *Opisanie liturgiceskich rukopisej chranjascichsja v bibliotekach pravoslavnago vostoka*, II, *Euchologhia* (Kiev 1901), gives many unedited early texts; the nearest to a critical edition is P. Trembelas, *Mikron Euchologion*, I (Athens 1950), pp. 28–75; A. Raes, *Le Mariage dans les Eglises d'Orient* (Chevetogne 1958), pp. 49–68, gives a brief introduction, together with a French translation; cf. also *Mariage*, tr. Dennis Guillaume (Rome 1979), for the modern Uniate rite. Detailed studies are confined to A. Raes, *Introductio in Liturgiam Orientalem* (Rome 1947), pp. 156–60; and two important articles, G. Baldanza, 'Il rito de Matrimonio nel 'Euchologio Barberini 336', *Ephemerides Liturgicae* 93 (1979), pp. 316–51, and G. I. Passarelli, 'La cerimonia dello Stefanoma (Incoronazione) nei riti matrimoniali bizantini secondo il Codice Cryptense G.b. VII (X sec.)', *ibid.*, pp. 381–91; these last two articles give excellent documentation, though some of the theological speculation in them needs to be treated with caution.

2. See the comparative chart in Passarelli, art. cit., pp. 389–91.

3. See p. 24: but the ring may have been in use in the liturgy at the time, and not actually mentioned, because of the nature of the Barberini 336 text (i.e. for the use of priest and deacon).

4. See Stevenson, 'The Origins', p. 416, n. 32.

5. Cf. pp. 21ff on Basil, Gregory of Nazianzus, and Chrysostom.

6. Goar, op. cit., p. 318.

7. The text of the prayer is as follows: 'God, who made all things in your power, who established the world, who adorned all your creation as a crown; bless now this drink with spiritual benediction, and provide a yoke for those joined in marriage' (Goar, op. cit., p. 319); the symbolism here suggests that the prayer was written after the crowning was established as a custom, and in order to link the crowning with the common cup.

8. Thus even Ritzer, pp. 202–6, who suggests that the common cup in Barberini 336 is to be regarded as eucharistic; Passarelli thinks otherwise, art. cit., pp. 386f.; if the custom is much earlier than Barberini 336, it cannot be a eucharistic substitute; Eastern liturgies should not be studied through Western spectacles.

9. Baldanza, art. cit., esp. pp. 329ff.

10. Theodore the Studite, *Ep.* I.22, 31; see Baldanza, art. cit., pp. 324ff.

11. Theodore the Studite, *Ep.* I.50; the word 'crowning' appears several times, and means 'marriage', without any explanation.

12. See n. 1 for the texts and studies used; see Appendix II for chart; cf. G. Baldanza, 'Il rito matrimoniale dell'Eucologio Sinaitico greco 958', *Ephemerides Liturgicae* 95 (1981), pp. 289–315.

13. The absence of epistle and gospel from earlier manuscripts need not be taken to imply that they were not used; indeed, I would suggest that the Ephesians and Johannine readings go right back to the fourth century, and earlier.

14. Cf. J. Mateos, *La célébration de la parôle dans la Liturgie Byzantine*, Rome 1971; G. Bertonière, *The Historical Development of the Easter Vigil and related Services in the Greek Church*, Rome 1972; R. Taft, *The Great Entrance*, Rome 1975.

15. J. Meyendorff, *Marriage: An Orthodox Perspective* (St Vladimir's Seminary, 1975), p. 30.

16. E.g. A. Raes, *Introductio in Liturgiam Orientalem*, p. 158, n.i.; cf. also his series of articles, 'Le consentement dans les rites orientaux', *Ephemerides Liturgicae* 47 (1932), pp. 34–47, 126–40, 249–59, 431–45; 48 (1933), pp. 80–94, 310–18; cf. also Ritzer, pp. 211–13.

17. A. Raes, *Introductio in Liturgiam Orientalem*, pp. 159f.; cf. *The Greek Marriage Office* (Manchester 1894), p. 3; see also n. 16 above.

18. A. Baumstark, *Liturgie Comparée* (Chevetogne 1955), p. 72, n. 3; cf. Stevenson, 'The Origins', p. 412.

19. See below; on the use of the 'blessed' prayer of Jewish origin, see C. Kucharek, *The Byzantine-Slav Liturgy of St John Chrysostom* (1971), pp. 337ff.; the introduction of this liturgical form on its own at the beginning of rites (or sections of rites) may be related to its use at the beginning of prayers.

20. Goar, op. cit., pp. 315f.

21. Ibid., pp. 311f.

22. Cf. remarks in a similar vein made by O. Rousseau, of the Eastern rites of marriage in general, in his 'introduction' to Raes' *Le mariage dans les Eglises d'Orient*, p. 19.

23. E.g. the importance attached to the Armenian eucharistic rite at the transfer of the gifts, Taft, op. cit., *passim*, and (e.g.), pp. 102ff.

24. Ritzer, pp. 146–8.

25. Ritzer, p. 146; this is not to underestimate the importance of the fifth-century regulations in Armenia concerning marriage as an institution, and the Church's role in blessing it: cf. E. Herman, 'De benedictione nuptiali quid statuerit ius byzantinum sive eclesiasticum sive civile', *Orientalia Christiana Periodica* 4 (1938), esp. p. 190, n. 3.

26. F. C. Conybeare, *Rituale Armenorum* (Oxford 1905), pp. 108–14, see notes.

27. The first two texts in H. Denzinger, *Ritus Orientalium*, II (Würzburg 1864), pp. 451–67, 467–77; the third text is taken from A. Raes, *Le Mariage dans les Eglises d'Orient*, pp. 77–101.

28. Cf. Raes, *Introductio in Liturgiam Orientalem*, pp. 160–3; cf. charts, pp. 174–7.

29. Ibid., p. 162.

30. Text in Denzinger, op. cit., pp. 458, 471; see p. 27.

31. The Vienna 1905 order terms this part of the rite 'the blessing of the crown of a young girl'; this is probably Latin influence, of a recent date; the earlier manuscripts reflect nothing like such an understanding of the service.

32. It has long since disappeared from popular usage, as a result of the introduction of the ring.

2   Other Eastern Rites

1. The apocryphal 'arabic' canons of Nicea: see Ritzer, p. 160.

2. E. Lanne (ed.), 'Le Grand Euchologue du Monastère Blanc', *Patrologia Orientalis* XXVIII/2 (Paris 1958), pp. 392–9, and nn.

3. Quoted in full by Ritzer, pp. 160f.

4. Denzinger, op. cit., pp. 364–7; cf. 1763 text, pp. 367–81; 1619 text, pp. 383–4 (shorter, but few differences); Raes' text in *Le Mariage dans les Eglises d'Orient*, pp. 27–45 (based on contemporary Coptic usage); discussion of the history of the rite in Raes' *Introductio in Liturgiam Orientalem*, pp. 168–71, together with texts given on p. 155. The discussion which follows is based on these works.

5. Raes, *Le Mariage dans les Eglises d'Orient*, p. 24.

6. Text in Denzinger, op. cit., p. 369; is this ancient, too?

7. Raes, *Introductio in Liturgiam Orientalem*, p. 170; but the anointing appears to be an infrequent option, O. H. E. Burmester, *The Egyptian or Coptic Church* (Cairo 1967), p. 138, n. 1.

8. On the stability of this prayer, see E. Segelberg, 'The Benedictio Olei in the Apostolic Tradition of Hippolytus', *Oriens Christianus* 48 (1964), pp. 268–81, esp. p. 269, where he discusses the Eastern versions.

9. Denzinger, op. cit., pp. 375–6 (same text in both versions); 'priests and kings and prophets' provide the rationale (cf. Segelberg, art. cit., for discussion of this theme), but the prayer then takes off, and asks that the oil may fill the couple with all kinds of virtues, each group punctuated by 'Amen'; this kind of sequence is very similar to the prayer for blessing the crowns, which we quote, pp. 111–12.

10. Raes, *Introductio in Liturgiam Orientalem*, pp. 169f.; C. Kopp, *Glaube und Sakramente der Koptischen Kirche* (Rome 1932), pp. 192–203; cf. Raes' article in *Ephemerides Liturgicae* 48 (1933), pp. 310–13, referred to above, p. 229, n. 16.

11. Denzinger, op. cit., p. 378.

12. For this discussion, cf. Raes, *Introductio in Liturgiam Orientalem*, pp. 171–2.

13. Cf. discussion in J. Dauvillier, *Le Mariage dans le droit classique* (Paris 1933), p. 432.

14. Texts in Denzinger, op. cit., pp. 386–402; and Raes, *Le Mariage dans les Eglises d'Orient*, pp. 109–33; historical notes, Raes, *Introductio in Liturgiam Orientalem*, pp. 163–5.

15. See p. 100.

16. Texts in Denzinger, op. cit., pp. 402–18; and Raes, *Le Mariage dans les Eglises d'Orient*, pp. 139–52; historical notes, Raes, *Introductio in Liturgiam Orientalem*, pp. 165–7.

17. Text in Denzinger, op. cit., pp. 407–8.

18. Text in Denzinger, op. cit., pp. 403f; cf. the theme of forgiveness in the second oil-prayer from White Monastery, cited in n. 2 above.

19. Text in Raes, *Le Mariage dans les Eglises d'Orient*, p. 144; Denzinger only alludes to hymn-singing at this point.

20. Cf. Dauvillier, op. cit., pp. 429–31, for this and subsequent literary evidence; cf. also Ritzer, pp. 150ff.

21. Texts in Denzinger, op. cit., pp. 419–49; and Raes, *Le Mariage dans les Eglises d'Orient*, pp. 157–97; historical notes, Raes, *Introductio in Liturgiam Orientalem*, pp. 167–8. I am also indebted to the Revd. Dr. Gianfranco Tellini of Edinburgh, for allowing me to use his dissertation for Master in Theology, Rome, 1963, entitled *De Ordine Coronationis in ritu matrimoniali chaldaico*; the sixteenth-century text (the earliest dealt with) describes a marriage rite identical in structure to the later ones, but less cluttered. Cf. other (slightly differing) texts in G. P. Badger, *The Nestorians and their Rituals* (London 1852), pp. 244–76; Metropolitan Athanasius Yeshue Samuel (ed.), *The Order of the Sacrament of Matrimony According to the Ancient Rite of the Syrian Orthodox Church of Antioch* (Lebanon 1974); see Bryan Spinks, 'The Marriage Service in the Church of England: some Considerations', *Liturgical Review* 11 (1981), pp. 90–112.

22. Text in Denzinger, op. cit., p. 427.

23. Cf. J. Vellian, 'The Church as Bride in the East Syrian Liturgy', *Studia Liturgica* 11 (1976), pp. 59–64, for a survey of this theme, though not referring to the marriage liturgy.

24. See p. 99.

25. The one instance of *'velatio'* in the Byzantine tradition, which is Italo-Greek, and in any case, we consider to be a freak; see p. 100.

26. See P.-M. Gy, 'Le nouveau rituel romain du mariage', *Maison-Dieu* 98 (1969), p. 134; and also his earlier article, 'Le rite sacramental du mariage', *Revue des Sciences philosophiques et théologiques* 38 (1954), pp. 261f., where he sets the matter in a wider context.

27. Cf. in general the article by Gianfranco Tellini, 'Marriage and the Oriental Churches', *Liturgical Review* 6.1 (1976), pp. 22–30; we shall return to the importance of the Eastern Churches in the final chapter. A. M. Allchin blows the Oriental trumpet in 'The Sacrament of Marriage in Eastern Christianity', in *Marriage, Divorce, and the Church* (London 1971), pp. 113ff. I have been much helped by Robert Murray's discussion of marriage imagery, *Symbols of Church and Kingdom* (Cambridge 1975), pp. 131–42, 150–7 (esp. pp. 154ff., where Murray suggests that the Chaldean rite was well-established by the fourth century).

4 Reformulations

1 Luther and Calvin

1. For text see F. Hubert, *Die Strassburger liturgischen Ordnungen* (Göttingen 1900), pp. 1–24; its basic conservatism is a parallel with Cranmer, if not an indirect source.

2. For Zürich, see H. A. Daniel, *Codex Liturgicus Ecclesiae Lutheranae* (Leipzig 1847–9), III, pp. 202–5; for Farel's rite, see below, n. 12, for text, in Barth/Niesel, op. cit., where Farel's service is set out with Calvin's.

3. Ulrich Leupold (ed.), *Luther's Works, 53, Liturgy and Hymns* (Philadelphia 1965), p. 111; the quotations which follow are from pp. 111–15; for an excellent discussion of this rite, see Bryan Spinks, 'Luther's Other Major Liturgical Reforms: 3. The Traubüchlein', *Liturgical Review* 10 (1980), pp. 33–8.

4. Leupold notes that 'the entry into the church marks the beginning of the religious ceremony' (op. cit., p. 114, n. 1); this is a mistaken remark, in our opinion; Luther is following traditional liturgical practice, and makes no distinction between the two parts of the rite in the way Leupold suggests.

5. Spinks, art. cit., p. 34.

6. Cf. the Lyon rite of 1498, Molin-Mutembe, p. 315; Spinks observes that Luther did not interpret this text as implying 'that all marriages were therefore *a priori* joined by God' (art. cit., p. 38, n. 10).

7. For the local German Agendas, see E. Sehling, *Die Evangelischen Kirchenordnungen des XVI. Jahrhunderts*, Leipzig, in its various fascicles, from Ii, 1903; the collection is still incomplete; for Mansfeld 1580, vol. Ii (1903), pp. 224–6; Prussian 1568, vol. IV (1911), pp. 93–5; Frederick II 1563, Frederick IV 1601, vol. XIV (1969), pp. 398–401, 575–6; the 'conservative' revision of 1540 is to be found in Daniel, op. cit., II, pp. 320–5. (A similar progress from conservative revision to radical adaptation is to be seen in the early Strasbourg Agendas, cf. the 1524/1525 orders with the later ones, culminating in the 1561, texts in F. Hubert, op. cit., pp. 1–24.) On the subsequent development of the German Lutheran orders, cf. G. Rietschel, *Lehrbuch der Liturgik*, II (Berlin 1909), pp. 251ff; for the early Lutheran orders, see F. E. Brightman, *The English Rite* (London 1915), I, pp. xxxixff.

8. See *Den Danske Kirkeordinants af 1539*, ed. Max Olsen (København 1936), pp. 82f. (on Bugenhagen); *Peder Palladius: Visitatsbog*, ed. Helge Haar (København 1940), pp. 107f. (on Palladius); text of Palladius' rite, corresponding broadly with the Visitation articles, in *Alterbogen*, København 1681 (no page nos); the Norwegian text is in *Den Forordenede Alterbog* (Christiania 1862), pp. 223–8; the Icelandic in *Handbok* (Reykjavik 1869), pp. 152–6. I am indebted to my father, The Revd. Dr. Eric Stevenson, for assistance with these questions.

9. For discussion of the 1890 rite, see Frederik Nielsen, *Ritualet for Brudevielse*, København 1890, which gives the old text (pp. 3–7), notes and points of discussion, including favourable reference to Bersier's rite in Paris (pp. 8–11), and the draft rite (pp. 12–14); the 1897 and 1912 texts are to be found in *Gudstjenesteordning* (København 1955), pp. 87–96; in none of these rites is there any distinction in the promises made by bride and groom. Nielsen was Professor of Church History at Copenhagen at the time, a 'Grundtvigian', and much interested in liturgiology.

10. See E. Yelverton, *The Manual of Olavus Petri, 1529* (London 1953), pp. 33–41; text on pp. 69–75, which involves a form of the nuptial blessing, bridal throughout; the first part is clearly influential on the more reformed subsequent Lutheran rite; cf. *Den Svenska Evangelieboken* (Stockholm 1943), pp. 590–4, where Petri's ring-giving and some of his prayers persist.

11. For a summary, see Brightman, op. cit., I, pp. xlvff.; for the full text, see the anonymous English translation, *Deliberatio, A Simple and Religious Consultation* (London 1548), pp. 391–406; the *Consultation* rite is an endurance-test of didacticism.

12. The text used and discussed is from Peter Barth and Wilhelm Niesel (ed.), *Joannis Calvini: Opera Selecta*, II (Munich 1952), pp. 50–6.

13. Cf. 'ordonnances', 1561, ibid., p. 349; the 1541 'ordonnances' give a clue—marriage should not be celebrated when there is a Eucharist 'pour l'honneur du Sacrement'; see B. J. Kidd (ed.), *Documents Illustrative of the Continental Reformation* (Oxford 1911), p. 598.

14. The 'Pseudo-Romana 1542' book; cf. ibid., pp. 6–7; in a number of points this rite is briefer than Farel's, and Calvin follows Farel in preference. Farel could conceivably be following Luther in his brevity.

15. Not *just* Matthew 19.6, as in Luther's rite.

16. See pp. 148, 154, 156, 163, 165, 167.

17. The title 'liturgie' seems to be an eighteenth-century development; cf. *La Forme des Prières*, Geneva 1703 and 1712; it appears in books which refer to the Eucharist as 'la liturgie eucharistique' rather than 'la Cène'.

18. See J.-J. Von Allmen, 'Bénédiction nuptiale et Mariage d'après quelques liturgies de l'Eglise Réformée', in *Mélanges Botte* (Louvain 1972), pp. 9, 15; the same features are to be found in the Palatinate rite of 1684. The modern rites to which he refers are the French Reformed Church (1955), Geneva (1945), and Berne (1963); cf. also the 1963 French Reformed rite: *Liturgie des Églises Réformées de France* (Paris 1963), pp. 287–99; cf. also R. Paquier, *Traité de Liturgique* (Neuchâtel/Paris 1954), pp. 196–9.

19. Von Allmen, op. cit., p. 16, n. 69, for modern examples; he goes the whole hog and calls this feature an 'epiclesis', with justification.

20. E. Bersier, *Liturgie à L'usage des Églises Réformées* (Paris 1876), pp. 297–313; cf. his *Projet de revision de la Liturgie des Églises Réformées* (Paris 1888), pp. 211–20; the '76 rite places a biblical catechesis at the beginning (resembling the 1549 Prayer Book *catena* of biblical material, which comes at the *end* of the rite), and like 1549, there are separate addresses to bride and groom; but by '88 these addresses were moved to the end of the rite. Bersier had an English mother.

21. Cf. the very Lutheran-looking rite in the Hungarian Reformed Church, in Geza Szabo, 'The History of the Protestant Liturgy in the Danube Area', *Studia Liturgica* 9 (1973), p. 194; for a modern German rite, see *Agende für evang-luther. Kirchen und Gemeinden*, III (Berlin 1963), pp. 115–27.

2   The Anglican Prayer Book Traditions, 1549–1929

1. W. Perry, *The Scottish Prayer Book: its Value and History* (Cambridge 1929), p. 117.

2. For this and the 1552 and 1662 services as well as sources, see Brightman, op. cit., II, pp. 800–17; comparisons are also made with sources

mentioned in the preceding section in the discussion which follows; cf. J. Dowden, *The Workmanship of the Prayer Book* (London 1902), pp. 37–9, 259–61.

3. J. Wickham Legg, *Ecclesiological Essays* (London 1905), pp. 200ff.

4. G. J. Cuming, *A History of Anglican Liturgy* (London 1982), p. 63; for the pre-1549 English sources of the exhortation, see *Formularies of Faith put forth by authority during the Reign of King Henry VIII*, ed. C. Lloyd (Oxford 1825), pp. 82–92 (*The Bishops' Book*, 1537); and T. A. Lacey (ed.), *The King's Book*, (London 1932), pp. 57–65; it is interesting that these sources relate to what becomes the *didactic* feature of the rite; but Matt. 19.6 is quoted in *The Bishops' Book* (p. 88). Wickham Legg even finds two of the 'reasons' in John de Burgo's *Pupilla Oculi*, a copy of which Cranmer had in his library: op. cit., p. 203, n.2.

5. See also Brightman, op.cit., II, pp. 810ff.; Cranmer may have known two similar such adaptations of the old nuptial blessing in the 1524/1525 Strasbourg orders, and also in the 1540 Brandenburg Agenda (see p. 232, n. 7; if not, they mark an important instance of parallel development, even though the German experiments are swept aside by later rites, in the name of reform.

6. See p. 65.

7. Wickham Legg, op.cit., pp. 206ff.; medieval practice was not uniform, but Cranmer's change does seem deliberate, and for no apparent reason.

8. Cf. Perry, op.cit., p. 118: 'the otherwise meaningless act of laying the ring on the priest's book'.

9. Gregory Dix, *The Shape of the Liturgy* (London 1945), p. 656; for a discussion of this cf. K. W. Stevenson, *Gregory Dix—25 Years On* (Bramcote 1977), pp. 31ff.

10. E. C. Whitaker, *Martin Bucer and the Book of Common Prayer* (London 1974), pp. 120–5, for the section dealing with the marriage rite.

11. Brightman, op.cit., II, 800–17; liturgical influence from John à Lasco does not seem to be present, see his *Forma ac Ratio* (Paris 1556, but reflecting earlier usage), pp. 258–80, where the euchological ingredient is very small, though 'three reasons' appear.

12. *Queen Elizabeth's Prayer Book, 1559* (Edinburgh 1909), pp. 122–8.

13. An English version, 'approved by Calvin' for the use of English exiles under John Knox (entitled *The Form of Prayers and Ministration of the Sacraments*), had been published in Geneva in 1556; the marriage service appears on pp. 81–7; see pp. 153f.

14. Cuming, op.cit., pp. 102ff.

15. Gordon Donaldson, *The Making of the Scottish Prayer Book of 1637* (Edinburgh 1954), pp. 14, 78; text, pp. 223–9.

16. Itself the result of much discussion, among those proposals which were not included are: altering 'till death us depart' to 'till death us do part' in the 'Haddington Book'; reintroducing gold and silver pieces in the 'Dalmeny Book'; querying 'with my body I thee worship' and the insistence on communion in the 'Egerton Book'; see Donaldson, op.cit., pp. 338f. On the changes actually made and agreed upon in the marriage rite, see James Cooper (ed.), *The Book of Common Prayer 1637* (Edinburgh 1904), pp. 289–93 (though some of his treatment is out of date, in the light of Donaldson).

17. *The Works of that Learned and Judicious Divine, Mr Richard Hooker*, II (Oxford 1845), pp. 145–51 (*Laws of Ecclesiastical Polity*, V, lxxiii, 1–8).

18. In this respect, he is in the good company of Gaudentius of Brescia: see above, p. 28.

19. H. L'Estrange, *The Alliance of Divine Offices* (London 1690; reprinted in *Library of Anglo-Catholic Theology*, Oxford 1846), pp. 438–46; on the relation of L'Estrange's work with subsequent events in general, see Cuming, op.cit., pp. 112ff.

20. G. J. Cuming, *The Durham Book* (London 1961), pp. 230–41; cf. E. Cardwell, *A History of Conferences and other proceedings connected with the Book of Common Prayer* (Oxford 1840), pp. 240, 276, 330f., 360, 363, 392.

21. For 'do parte' cf. 'The Haddington Book' in n. 16 above. Cosin suggested a somewhat periphrastic alternative to the ring-giving, involving the verb 'honour'; this is how the matter is ultimately resolved in 1928; see below.

22. Cf. 'The Dalmeny Book' in n. 16 above.

23. See Brightman, op.cit., II, pp. 800–17.

24. It takes until 1928 for the Old Testament characters to disappear altogether, and this link with the medieval Church finally to be broken: see below.

25. Text in T. J. Fawcett, *The Liturgy of Comprehension* (London 1973), pp. 137–141 (notes, pp. 258–60); on the question of nuptial Eucharists, Increase Mather ranted about frivolous weddings, affirming that if all had to come to communion, they 'will eat and drink Damnation to themselves' (p. 260); the Church is already divided into those who 'come' and those who are 'indifferent', and the clergy are divided about how to deal with them.

26. Charles Wheatly, *Rational Illustration of the Book of Common Prayer* (London 1720), pp. 385–418.

27. Cf. F. C. Eeles, *Traditional Ceremonial and Customs Connected with the Scottish Liturgy* (London 1910), pp. 124–36.

28. For the texts, see W. McGarvey, *Liturgiae Americanae* (Philadelphia 1895), pp. 312–23; cf. John Suter, *The American Book of Common Prayer* (New York 1949), pp. 62 ff.; I disagree with Marion Hatchett's distinction of the two parts of the rite into 'civil' and 'sacramental', in connection with the American abridgement from 1786; see his *Commentary on the American Prayer Book* (Seabury 1980), p. 430.

29. R. C. D. Jasper, *Prayer Book Revision in England, 1800–1900* (London 1954), pp. 14 f.

30. Ibid., p. 22.

31. 'Liturgical Revision', a privately-printed sheet; cf. *The Book of Common Prayer of the Reformed Episcopal Church* (1888), pp. 145–6, where provision is also made for hymns.

32. Jasper, op. cit., pp. 85, 89.

33. *Liturgy and Other Divine Offices of the Church* (London 1880), pp. 370–9; the service is called 'Solemnization of *Marriage*' (*sic*); the definitive rite is contained in their *Book of Occasional Services*, 1847; on the history and development of this Church and its liturgy, see K. W. Stevenson, 'The Catholic Apostolic Church—its History and its Eucharist', *Studia Liturgica* 13 (1979), pp. 21–45.

34. *Royal Letter of Business, First Report of the Committee* (London 1909), nos. 96–103.

35. *A Suggested Prayer-Book, being the text of the English Rite, altered and enlarged in accordance with the Prayer-Book Revision Proposals made by the English Church Union* (Oxford 1923), pp. 412–25: *A New Prayer-Book: Proposals for the Revision of the Book of Common Prayer, and for additional services and prayers, drawn*

up by a Group of Clergy (London 1923), pp. 156–61; A Survey of the Proposals for the Alternative Prayer Book, II, The Occasional Offices (London 1924), pp. 43–59.

36. R. C. D. Jasper (ed.), Walter Howard Frere: Correspondence on Liturgical Revision and Construction (London 1954), pp. 111–14: 'subordination . . . is something utterly different from inferiority' (p. 111); Gore, on the other hand, wrote, 'I desire fuller evidence as to the liturgical authority for "the restoration in the Marriage Service of equal vows for man and woman"', A Prayer-Book Revised (London 1913), p. viii (the word 'obey' does not appear in the marriage service of this unofficial book, pp. 140f.); J. Wickham Legg, On the Retention of the Word 'Obey' in the Marriage Service, London 1915; it was addressed to Gore!

37. See above, n. 34, and also Jasper, Walter Howard Frere: Correspondence . . ., p. 106; for the 'final' book, see The Prayer Book as Proposed in 1928, pp. 399–406; the draft version is contained in the National Assembly report, Book Proposed to be Annexed to the Prayer Book Measure 19— (London, February 7th, 1927), pp. 287–92.

38. The first Anglo-Catholic provision for a nuptial mass appeared in Votive Masses for the Use of the Church of England (London 1902), p. 24, which reproduces the Tridentine form, but the English Missal (London 1912), adds the 'Marriage Prayers' from the second part of the Prayer Book rite after the Lord's Prayer, i.e. in an analogous position to the Roman nuptial blessing; the 'Sarum' branch of the movement opted for a slightly different variation: The English Liturgy (London 1903) gives the Trinity Sunday collect, and the Trent readings, but prescribes the 'O God of Abraham, God of Isaac' prayer before the blessing (pp. 309–10); but An Altar Book . . . with additions from the Sarum Missal (London 1930), pp. 135–6, has the Trinity and nuptial collects, secrets, and post-communions (like medieval English books), but no special directions about a quasi-nuptial blessing before communion. Clearly, the High Church groups were reluctant to tamper with a 'rite de passage', with all its legal and popular conservatism, until a new Prayer Book was really envisaged. I am indebted to the Revd. Dr. Mark Dalby for drawing my attention to this.

39. The Scottish Book of Common Prayer (Edinburgh 1912), pp. 373–84; cf. Cooper, op.cit., p. 289.

40. The Scottish Book of Common Prayer (Edinburgh 1929), pp. 405–14; cf. Perry, op. cit., pp. 117–19; of the change in the woman's promise and vow he writes wittily, 'here the word "obey" is omitted from the woman's troth, a change which at least improves the balance of the sentence, though, as everyone knows, that is not the reason for its omission' (p. 118).

41. Cf. Suter, op. cit., pp. 64ff.

42. William Shakespeare was no liturgiologist, but the Priest expresses such a view perfectly in Twelfth Night, act V, Scene 1, lines 160ff.:

> A contract of eternal bond of love,
> Confirm'd by mutual joinder of your hands,
> Attested by the holy close of lips
> Strengthen'd by interchangement of your rings
> And all the ceremony of this compact
> Seal'd in my function, by my testimony.

Wickham Legg wrongly suggests that the rite of betrothal is here described, Ecclesiological Essays, p. 182, n. 3 (and he gives lines 150ff, incorrectly). I am indebted to Professor David Palmer, Department of English Language and Literature, Manchester University, for help with this matter.

43. The custom is absent from the first edition of *Ritual Notes* (London 1898), but by the time of the tenth edition (1956) it is described as a practice performed 'in many places in accordance with ancient precedent' (p. 215), which scarcely accords with the facts, since it is a sixteenth century French ceremony, adopted in Italy (see pp. 169f. and p. 239 n. 6); it is not found commented upon in Catalani (except of Milan), nor does Martinucci describe it, *Manuale Sacrarum Caeremoniarum* III (Rome 1879), p. 176; although it does appear in many local rites in the past hundred years (including the 1950 German rite), it is not universally popular, either in practice, or among liturgists.

3   Britain: Reformation and Dissent, 1555–1940

1. W. Maxwell, *The Liturgical Portions of the Genevan Service Book* (Edinburgh 1931), pp. 144–59, for text and notes; pp. 3ff., on Knox in Frankfurt and Geneva.

2. *The Liturgy of John Knox Received by the Church of Scotland in 1564* (Glasgow 1886), pp. 147–52.

3. Middelburg liturgy in P. Hall (ed.), *Reliquiae Liturgicae* (Bath 1847), I, pp. 62–70.

4. G. W. Sprott (ed.), *Scottish Liturgies of the Reign of James VI* (Edinburgh 1871), pp. 76–83.

5. I. Breward (ed.), *The Westminster Directory* (Bramcote 1980), pp. 24–6; the Scottish Church Service Society loyally reprinted it, with Knox's rite, in *The Book of Common Order and the Directory of the Church of Scotland* (Edinburgh 1868), pp. 129–34, 312–15; see nn., pp. 247, 358–61.

6. H. Boone Porter, *Jeremy Taylor—Liturgist* (London 1979), pp. 90ff., where Porter is baffled by Taylor's lack of provision of a marriage liturgy, even though Taylor's view of marriage is a high one; Cromwell's strictures must not be taken as anything other than the logical conclusion of the Christian Commonwealth performing public functions, but it could hardly have been popular.

7. In P. Hall (ed.), *Reliquiae Liturgicae*, IV, pp. 97–101. The ring was not high on the list of Baxter's *bêtes-noires*: 'The ring in marriage I made no scruple about' (*Richard Baxter: Autobiography*, Everyman edn, p. 17).

8. Horton Davies, *Worship and Theology in England*, I (Princeton/London 1970), p. 429.

9. *The Sunday Service of the Methodists in North America. With other Occasional Services* (London 1784), pp. 149–55; cf. Nolan B. Harman, Jnr, *The Rites and Ritual of Episcopal Methodism* (Nashville, Tennessee 1926), pp. 248–61; cf. also *The Sunday Service of the Methodists* (London 1786), pp. 152–8; later editions: 1817, pp. 145–51; 1825, pp. 158–64; I am indebted to the Revd Raymond George for help in this matter, and for generously allowing me to use his (rare) xerox-copy of the 1784 American book. It is interesting to note that whereas some Puritans objected to 'the excellent state of matrimony' at Savoy, Wesley retained the phrase.

10. *Forms for the Administration of Baptism . . . for the use of such Primitive Methodist Ministers as may require them* (London 1860), pp. 15–23.

11. *Book of Services for the use of the United Methodist Free Churches* (London 1867), pp. 19–29.

12. *The Sunday Service of the Methodists* (London 1876), pp. 71–6; *Public Prayers and Services* (London 1882), pp. 30–7.

13. *Book of Services for the use of the United Methodist Free Churches* (London c. 1880), pp. 75–85.

14. *Book of Services for the use of the Bible Christian Church* (London 1903), pp. 43–50.

15. *Book of Services for the use of the United Methodist Church* (London 1913), pp. 78–93.

16. *Book of Offices* (London 1936), pp. 83–6.

17. *Euchologion—A Book of Common Order* (1st edn., Edinburgh 1867), pp. 62–74, 75–9; cf. 4th edn. (1890), pp. 328–36.

18. *Book of Common Order* (Edinburgh 1902), pp. 186–95.

19. *Directory and Forms for Public Worship* (Edinburgh 1909), pp. 144–50.

20. *Book of Common Order* (Edinburgh 1940), pp. 154–60.

21. *Liturgical Proposals to Presbyterians of England Tried by History, Experience, and Scripture* (London 1891), p. 8; the Directory was eventually authorized in 1898, but the marriage proposals remained substantially the same: Horton Davies, op. cit., IV, pp. 108ff.

22. *Directory for Public Worship* (London 1921), pp. 67–71; cf. *Sacramental and Other Services* (Manchester 1927), pp. 23–9.

23. Horton Davies, op. cit., III, p. 137.

24. *Devotional Services for Public Worship* (London 1903), pp. 167–75.

25. *Divine Service* (London 1919), pp. 181–5; on the use of the concluding collect, see above, pp. 146, 150.

26. Privately printed; Watson's experiment at vernacular 'rustic' liturgical forms, couched in traditional language, deserves more attention than it has received; each service is called a 'bede' of some sort, the marriage rite being called, charmingly enough, 'the bridal bede'; on his place in the development of Congregational worship, see Horton Davies, op. cit., V, pp. 369f.; it was reprinted, in 'modern' English, in 1972, but a marriage rite does not appear.

27. *Liturgy for the New Church* (London 1882), pp. 167–74; earlier editions give a similar rite.

28. *A Free Church Book of Common Prayer* (London 1929), pp. 271–8.

29. In P. Hall (ed.), *Fragmenta Liturgica* (Bath 1848), VII, pp. 71–80.

30. *A Book of Occasional Services* (London 1932), pp. 27–35; omission of the Matthean pronouncement can be traced back to the preceding century in *Forms of Prayer* (Manchester, n.d., but after 1836 Act), pp. 92–9; the formula *does* appear, however, in the guise of a quotation from Jesus, 'the law-giver', in the (Unitarian) *Book of Common Prayer Revised* (London 1846), p. 66.

31. Cf. Pierre Jounel, 'La liturgie romaine du mariage. Étapes de son élaboration', *Maison-Dieu* 50 (1957), pp. 54f.; see also *Appendix ad rituale romanum ex Manuali Toletano* (Toledo 1953), quoted in Jounel, art. cit., p. 45, n. 22.

4 Roman Uniformity?

1. For this discussion, see Molin-Mutembe, *passim*.

2. Cf. Roda and Vich: see p. 55.

3. Molin-Mutembe, p. 127, for list of dioceses using this form before Trent.

4. See p. 76.

5. Full text in Molin-Mutembe, pp. 316–18; no manuscripts have been discovered indicating Metz usage prior to this date (conversation with Père Molin).

6. F. 30–42; Castello's marriage rite is closely followed by Samarini, *Sacerdotale* (1593), I, f. 3v ff. and 116v ff.; cf. Cyrille Vogel, 'Introduction aux sources de l'histoire du culte chrétien au moyen âge', *Studi Medievali* (1963), pp. 556f. Molin-Mutembe mention other instances of the use of the stole, either in leading the couple to the altar (cf. the Byzantine 'dance of Isaiah'), as at Trier 1574 (p. 200), or at the consent, as here; cf. Reims 16th century, Cambrai 1503 (pp. 99, 100); Charles Borromeo introduces the practice at Milan after Trent, although Santori's rite and the official rite of 1614 do not.

7. For an excellent summary of the discussion at Trent, and its subsequent influence, see André Duval, 'Contract et sacrement de mariage au Concile de Trente', *Maison-Dieu* 127 (1976), pp. 64–105.

8. Council of Trent, Session 24, November 11th, 1563, *On Reform*, c.1: *Concilium Tridentinum*, ed. cit. IX, Actorum pars VI (Freiburg-im-Breisgau 1924), p. 969.

9. *Missale Romanum ex decreto Sacrosancto Concilii Tridentini restitutum* (Antwerp 1682), pp. xcvi–xcviii.

10. *Rituale Sacramentorum* (Rome 1583), pp. 501–24; the whole story of the production of the 1614 Ritual is told by B. Löwenberg, *Das Rituale des Kardinalis Julius Antonius Sanctorius: Ein Beitrage zur Entstehungsgeschichte das Rituale Romanum*, Munich 1937.

11. *Sacramentorum libellus secundum Romanam Ecclesiam* (Venice 1579), pp. 89–91.

12. *Rituale Sacramentorum ad Institutum Sanctae Romanae Ecclesiae* (Bologna 1593), pp. 84–7; pp. 67ff. contain 'Avertimenti per celebrare il sacramento de matrimonio', loyally quoting Trent at length.

13. *Liber Ritualis pro recta Sacramentorum et Sacramentalium Administratione* (Perugia 1597), ff. 30v–32v; the change in position of the preparatory prayer to the nuptial blessing serves to make a special point of the sermon and the final blessing because the bride removes her veil before leaving church with the groom.

14. *Sacramentale Sanctae Ferrariensis Ecclesiae* (Ferrara 1609), pp. 102–4.

15. *Rituale Ecclesiae Veronensis* (Verona 1609), pp. 163–5; Trent is loyally quoted in the introduction, pp. 154ff.

16. *Rituale Romanum* (Antwerp 1824), pp. 222–35.

17. *Missale Romanum* (Antwerp 1682), pp. xcvi-xcix.

18. E. Cattaneo, 'La celebrazione delle nozze a Milano', *Archiva Ambrosiana* 29 (1976), pp. 174ff.

19. *Sacramentale Ambrosianum* (Milan 1589), pp. 258–64; another feature is that the rite is divided into 'ordo celebrandi matrimonium' (everything up to the mass), and 'ordo benedicendi sponsum et sponsam' (*sic*) (after the mass).

20. E.g. *Rituale Sacramentorum ad usum Mediolanensis Ecclesiae olim a Sancto Carolo* (Milan 1645), pp. 262–9 (=Martène's Ordo XV); *Rituale Sacramentorum* (Milan 1885) pp. 261–9; the resemblance of the text almost goes as far as the pagination; Cattaneo does not comment on this.

21. Again see Molin-Mutembe, *passim*.

22. Migne, *Le Rituel des Rituels*, I (Paris 1866), coll. 1219–1337; these clerical addresses come at different points, e.g. after betrothal, before marriage, after marriage. Their overall style is heavy, but thoroughly biblical, liturgical, and pastoral.

23. E.g. Chartres 1832 (ibid., coll. 1238f); Versailles 1854 (ibid., col. 1248).

24. Ibid., coll. 1234f.

25. Ibid., coll. 1259f; cf. 1513 rite in Molin-Mutembe, pp. 310f.; the later rite is a revision, in which some of the old prayers have gone.

26. *Sacerdotale seu Manuale Ecclesiae Rothomagensis* (Rouen 1640), pp. 121f.

27. *Rituale Parisiense* (Paris 1654), pp. 316ff.

28. *Sacerdotale seu Manuale Ecclesiae Rothomagensis* (Rouen 1771), p. 219 (a misprint calls this p. 229, and adds ten to the preceding and following pages).

29. *Rituale ad usum Ecclesiae Arrebatensis* (Arras 1757), pp. 219f.

30. See Stevenson, 'Benedictio', pp. 474f.

31. *Rituale Parisiense* (Paris 1786), pp. 283ff.

32. Texts in *Agenda Ecclesiastica* (Köln 1521), f. iii-r. ff; (1598), pp. 72–81; (1614), pp. 151–80; on the 1485 rite, and other medieval German rites, see pp. 89ff.

33. J. Catalani, *Rituale Romanum*, I (Rome 1757), pp. 427–53; he gives a well-documented discussion of the priestly formula, *ego conjungo vos*, pp. 447–8.

34. *Rituale Romano-Colocense* (Budapest 1838), pp. 186–204.

35. *Rituale Wratislaviense* (Breslau 1891), pp. 259–69.

36. Cf. P.-M. Gy, 'Le nouveau rituel romain du mariage', *Maison-Dieu* 98 (1969), pp. 131ff.; Gy goes as far as questioning the theory that the couple are 'ministers of the sacrament'; see below, pp. 206f.

37. *Rituale Romanum* (Ratisbon 1935), pp. 478–80, see notes; these orders are printed in an Appendix.

38. See pp. 193f; but in 1962 pressure from Rome and the onward movement of liturgical renewal caused the Metz rite to place the entire marriage rite (i.e., consent as well as vow) before the offertory, and the Veni Creator was shifted from before the nuptial blessing to the beginning of the mass, after the introductory bidding; see *Rituale Matrimonii ad usum diocesis Metensis*, Metz 1962.

5 Foreground

1 Adaptation and Rethink: Roman and Anglican

1. B. Binder, *Geschichte des feierlichen Ehesegens*, Abtei Metten 1938.

2. K. Ritzer, *Formen, Riten und religiöses Brauchtum der Eheschliessung in den christlichen Kirchen des ersten Jahrtausends*, Münster 1962; French translation, *Le Mariage dans les Églises chrétiennes du Ier au XIè siècle*, Paris 1972 (used in this study).

3. J. B. Molin/P. Mutembe, *Le rituel du mariage en France du XIIè au XVIè siècle*, Paris 1974.

4. P.-M. Gy, 'Le nouveau rituel romain du mariage', *Maison-Dieu* 98 (1969), pp. 124ff.: Gy's own output on the subject of marriage has been

wide-ranging: 'Le rite sacramentel du mariage et la tradition liturgique', *Revue des Sciences Philosophiques et théologiques* 38 (1954), pp. 258–63; 'Le sacrement de mariage—exige-t-il la foi?', ibid. 61 (1977), pp. 437–42; as well as others.

5. *Manuale Sacerdotum*, ed. J. Schneider (Köln 1893), II, pp. 423ff.

6. Cf. J. Wagner, 'Zum neuen deutschen Trauungritus', *Festschrift für Bischof Dr Albert Stohr* (Mainz 1960), I, pp. 422–9; for the text, see *Collectio Rituum . . . pro omnibus Germaniae Dioecesibus* (Ratisbon 1950), pp. 88–99.

7. *The Documents of Vatican II*, ed. Walter Abbott (London 1967), pp. 161–2; cf. text of Liturgy Constitution, with notes by Gy, in *Maison-Dieu* 76 (1963), pp. 101–3.

8. Cf. discussion by J. D. Crichton, *Christian Celebration: the Sacraments* (London 1974), pp. 114ff.: Crichton notes the change of tone from hierarchical language to a more moderated style as the Council grew in its self-understanding and approach to current problems.

9. *Ordo Celebrandi Matrimonium*, Vatican City 1969; see also *The Rites*, I (New York 1976), pp. 529–70; and the official English version, *The Marriage Rite* (for use in the dioceses of England and Wales), London 1970; cf. also *Manual of Celebration* (Washington 1970), pp. 11–22; I am much indebted to Père Gy for making available to me his files concerning the preparation of this rite. Cf. also C. Braga, 'La genesi dell' "Ordo Matrimonii"', *Ephemerides Liturgicae* 93 (1979), pp. 247–57.

10. Sources are discussed by Gy, 'Le nouveau rituel ...', p. 130, n. 6, and Braga, art. cit., p. 256; on the prefaces, see Moeller, *Corpus Praefationum*, 967 (the old one), and 1317 and 989 (the new ones); cf. also A. Dumas, 'Les Préfaces du nouveau Missel', *Ephemerides Liturgicae* 85 (1971), p. 27, no. 74.

11. Moeller laments that these prayers are insufficiently Visigothic in their style and cursus: 'Benedictions solennelles', *Questions Liturgiques* (1971), 4, pp. 324f.; he suggests how one of them could be improved.

12. The Latin text does not actually define which Church it is referring to, but the English translation makes it clear by implication; in 'inter-Church marriages' the word 'Catholic' needs close definition, preferably inclusively.

13. Cf. A. Duval, 'La formule "Ego vos in matrimonium conjungo" au concile de Trente', *Maison-Dieu* 99 (1969), pp. 144–53; this number of *Maison-Dieu* was given over to a discussion of the new rite.

14. A problem alluded to by Gy, 'Le nouveau rituel...', pp. 136ff.; De Jong's article was 'Brautsegen und Jungfauenweihe', *Zeitschrift für Katolische Theologie* 84 (1962), pp. 300–22; we have already discussed this controversial article, and questioned some of its assumptions on pp. 46f.

15. See *Rituel pour la célébration du mariage* (Paris 1969), pp. 55f., where two fine additional nuptial blessings appear, referring to both partners throughout, and in the 'strong collect' genre of prayer; cf. the German rite, *Die Feier der Trauung*, Einsiedeln/Köln, 1975, which gives the three official nuptial blessings only, but is more experimental in the vows, where it is possible to link them closely with the ring-giving; the declaration and Matthean pronouncement are taken from the 1950 Ritual.

16. *The Book of Common Prayer, according to the use of the Protestant Episcopal Church of the USA* (New York 1953), pp. 300–4; cf. the South African rite of 1954, which omits 'obey', blesses the ring, and, in the case of a nuptial Eucharist, dovetails the entire second part of the service (with abbreviation)

with the conclusion of the mass: *A Book of Common Prayer for use in the Church of the Province of South Africa* (London 1954), pp. 440–50.

17. *The Book of Common Prayer, according to the use of the Anglican Church of Canada* (Cambridge 1959), pp. 563–72.

18. *The Book of Common Prayer, according to the use of the Church of India, Pakistan, Burma, and Ceylon* (London 1960), pp. 637–46; more 'indigenisation' had been tried much earlier, without success: see T. S. Garrett, *Christian Worship* (2nd edn, London 1966), p. 173.

19. *Alternative Services: First Series* (London 1966), pp. 80–4; the ring blessing disappeared in the official version, under Evangelical pressure.

20. Cf. C. Hutchins, *Liturgy for Marriage*, Bramcote 1976; the 'Root' Report had paid some attention to the need for reform of the liturgy, but mainly concerned with language: *Marriage, Divorce, and the Church* (London 1971), pp. 54ff.

21. The narrative of events is based on Colin Buchanan's monthly *News of Liturgy*, which had begun in 1975 as part of Grove Books.

22. *Alternative Services Series 3—The Wedding Service*, General Synod Report 228, London 1975; N.B. the title 'wedding'.

23. Gy, 'Le nouveau rituel . . .', p. 134.

24. *Alternative Services Series 3—The Marriage Service*, London 1977; N.B. the title 'marriage'.

25. *The Alternative Service Book 1980*, pp. 287–304.

26. The prayer was written by Fr Harry Williams, CR, in consultation with the couple, and combined traditional and experiential allusions.

27. *Prayer Book Studies 24: The Pastoral Offices* (New York 1971), pp. 3–8 (notes), 25–36 (text); *Services for Trial Use* (New York 1971), pp. 310–22; cf. Marion Hatchett, *Commentary on the New American Prayer Book*, pp. 431–40, for a useful discussion of the service in retrospect, and in relation to the sources; the Metz tradition is not mentioned (Hatchett would have done so if the imitation were conscious), but it is the same form, reappearing in a new way.

28. This is the word used repeatedly by Charles Wheatly, *Rational Illustration of the Book of Common Prayer*, pp. 385ff.; a case could be argued for Wheatly's influence on the American rite as a whole, in that in the draft version, as well as the final version, the consent and the vow are separated by the ministry of the Word, thus reflecting Wheatly's conviction that the consent is the 'espousal' (i.e., betrothal), and the vows are the marriage, op. cit., pp. 399ff.

29. *The Draft Proposed Book of Common Prayer* (New York 1977), pp. 435–6.

30. See *Prayer Book Studies 24: The Pastoral Offices*, p. 5.

31. Church of England in Australia, *An Australian Prayer Book, 1978*, pp. 548–59 (First Order), pp. 560–7 (Second Order).

32. *An Order of Christian Marriage and Marriage Service, 1972*, Provincial Commission on Prayer Book Revision, 1972.

2   Adaptation and Rethink: Reformed Traditions

1. *Book of Congregational Worship* (London 1920), pp. 52–5; *Book of Public Worship* (London 1948), pp. 172–7.

2. *Book of Services and Prayers* (London 1959), pp. 65–71.

3. *Contemporary Prayers for Public Worship* (London 1967), pp. 100–2: cf. the Scottish equivalent, *Worship Now*, referred to in n. 8 below.

4. *A Marriage Service*, Independent Press, pp. 1–5.

5. *The Book of Common Order*, Presbyterian Church in Canada (Toronto 1964), pp. 139–48.

6. *The Presbyterian Service-Book of England and Wales* (London 1968), pp. 85–91.

7. *The Worship Book* (Philadelphia 1970), pp. 65–70.

8. *The Book of Common Order* (Edinburgh 1979), pp. 73–8 (First Order), pp. 79–86 (Second Order); a list of suggested hymns for marriages is appended, pp. 86–7. These rites show the influence of the (unofficial) Scottish *Worship Now* (Edinburgh 1972), pp. 70–85.

9. *Ministers' Manual* (n.d.), pp. 7–17.

10. *Orders and Prayers for Church Worship* (London 1960), pp. 161–9.

11. I am indebted to the Revd David Tripp for supplying me with documents related to the British Methodist rite; for the final text, see *The Methodist Service Book* (London 1975), pp. E 1–13.

12. See pp. 189ff.

13. *Worship* (London 1972), pp. 180–5.

14. *Liturgy according to the Liberal Catholic Church* (1967), pp. 281–9.

15. *The Moravian Liturgy* (1960), pp. 80–5; *Hymnal and Liturgies of the Moravian Church* (1969), pp. 116–17.

16. *In Life and Death* (London 1968), pp. 19–25; the ring is no longer called 'the ancient and accepted symbol', as in previous books; see above, pp. 166f, and p. 238 n. 30.

17. *The Book of Common Worship* (London 1963), pp. 139–47; this is the same service as had appeared in 1960; a Eucharist after the marriage is optional.

18. *Order for a Wedding Service* (1977), pp. 3–9; N.B. the use of 'wedding' when 'marriage' was in vogue elsewhere.

19. *The Daily Office Revised*, ed. Ronald C. D. Jasper (London 1978), pp. 142–9; the sources for these prayers are given at the back of the publication.

20. Ottfried Jordahn (ed.), *Oekumenische Gottesdienste* (Hamburg 1981), pp. 51–5.

2 Epilogue

1. Correspondence with the present writer.

2. Christopher Brooke, *Marriage in Christian History* (Cambridge 1978), p. 33; see also the useful bibliography, pp. 34–6.

3. Laurence Stone, *The Family, Sex, and Marriage in England, 1500–1800*, London 1977; Edward Schillebeeckx, *Marriage, Secular Reality and Saving Mystery*, New York 1966; I found both these books very valuable, but I have been led to question Schillebeeckx's theory that there was no primitive Christian marriage rite.

4. Bryan Spinks, 'Symbolism in the Sacraments', in Kenneth Stevenson (ed.), *Symbolism in the Liturgy*, II (Bramcote 1981), p. 32.

5. See Geoffrey Wainwright, *Doxology* (London 1980), pp. 77f., for a helpful and biblical analysis of the debate; I myself have no difficulty in seeing marriage as a sacrament; the Anglican tradition has generally veered on this side of the Reformation dispute. Cf. two other excellent and eirenical studies; Hermann Schmidt. 'Rituel et sacramentalité du mariage chrétien', *Questions Liturgiques* (1975), pp. 3–39; and the articles in *Maison-Dieu* 127 (1976), esp. Raymond Didier, 'Sacrement de mariage, baptême et foi', pp.

106–38. On 'magic words', cf. Richard F. Buxton, *Eucharist and Institution Narrative* (London 1976), *passim*; although the Western theological tradition can (just) trace isolation of the institution narrative back to Ambrose, it cannot claim the same liturgical pedigree for consent.

6. Achille Triacca, '"Celebrare": Il Matrimonio Cristiano. Suo Significato Teologico-Liturgico', *Ephemerides Liturgicae* 93 (1979) pp. 407–56, where he gives a full discussion of these themes in Western euchology, ancient and modern; cf. the somewhat critical remarks of J.-J. Von Allmen, 'The Celebration of Christian Marriage', *Liturgical Studies (Liturgical Review)* 1.1 (1971), pp. 1–17.

7. Marriage hymns seem only to have flourished in the West in the Dane, Grundtvig, whom we have mentioned before; when I helped the Royal School of Church Music to edit *The Marriage Service with Music*, Croydon 1981, we were hard put to it to include many such hymns; one recent excellent composition is by Ian Fraser, and borrows from the Byzantine 'crown' image: see *More Hymns for Today* (1980), No. 117.

8. Quoted from *The Times*, Thursday, 30 July, 1981, p. 3; reproduced by permission of the Archbishop of Canterbury.

9. On the Byzantine rite, see A. Nelidow, 'Caractère pénitentiel du rite des deuxièmes noces', *Liturgie et Rémission des Péchés* (Rome 1975), pp. 163–77. The 1954 South African Prayer Book (pp. 450f.) was the first in Anglicanism to allow for a 'service of blessing' for such circumstances; it begins with an 'acknowledgement' that the marriage has taken place according to law, and proceeds with the marriage prayers from the second part of the normal rite.

10. Cf. Clifford Longley, 'Implications of the marriage vows', *The Times*, Monday, 13 July 1981, where he writes, 'But the vows themselves do not have some magical gift of immortality, and if their object is insuperably and undeniably frustrated, they cease to bind, and therefore cease to exist'.

11. The 1978 Report, *Marriage and the Church's Task* (referred to in chapter 1.1), urged that the services of blessing should cease, and that the existing marriage service should be used in certain cases, 'with the addition of an appropriate and invariable preface' (p. 100); such a course as this has the advantage of not seeming to demote the rest of the service into a second class wedding (which may be desirable), but it runs the severe risk of failing to ritualize what the service as a whole would have to carry, i.e. the reality of the divorce/divorces. A more liturgical proposal, involving both a confession and special prayer, appears in David Silk's *Prayers for use at the Alternative Services* (London 1981), pp. 136–8; cf. his excellent order for 'Renewal of Marriage Vows', pp. 134–5, which allows for further blessing of rings.

12. See above, p. 233, n. 18; but he alludes to a problem shared by many of the Western Churches.

13. Cf. the French publication, *Célébrer le Mariage*, ed. Béraudy, Leprêtre, and Lionnet (Paris 1981), which contains the 1969 Roman rite, in French, but with new additional prayers, and copious notes on the marriage customs of other faiths. On the liturgical adaptation of pagan rites, see Adrian Hastings, *Christian Marriage in Africa* (London 1973), pp. 71–2 and 110–13.

Appendices

1 A Procession of Nuptial Blessing-Prayers

1. The Jewish Seven Benedictions (Talmudic, perhaps earlier)

Blessed art thou, O Lord our God, King of the universe, who createst the fruit of the vine.

Blessed are thou, O Lord our God, King of the universe, who hast created all things to thy glory.

Blessed art thou. O Lord our God, King of the universe, Creator of man.

Blessed art thou, O Lord our God, King of the universe, who hast made man in thine image, after thy likeness, and hast prepared unto him, out of his very self, a perpetual fabric. Blessed art thou, O Lord, Creator of man.
May she who was barren (Zion) be exceeding glad and exult, when her children are gathered within her in joy. Blessed art thou, O Lord, who makes Zion joyful through her children.

O make these loved companions greatly to rejoice, even as of old thou didst gladden thy creature in the garden of Eden. Blessed art thou, O Lord, who makest bridegroom and bride to rejoice.

Blessed art thou, O Lord our God, King of the universe, who hast created joy and gladness, bridegroom and bride, mirth and exultation, pleasure and delight , love, brotherhood, peace and fellowship. Soon may there be heard in the cities of Judah, and in the streets of Jerusalem, the voice of joy and gladness, the voice of the bridegroom and the voice of the bride, the jubilant voice of bridegrooms from their canopies, and of youths from their feasts of song. Blessed art thou, O Lord, who makest the bridegroom to rejoice with the bride.

Text: Joseph Hertz (ed.), *The Authorized Daily Prayer-Book* (New York, 1946), p. 1013; discussed above, pp. 7ff.

2. The Gregorian Sacramentary (sixth century + +)

O God, by your mighty power you have made all things out of nothing, and having set in order the elements of the universe and made man to your image, appointed woman to be his inseparable helpmate, so that the woman's body took its origin in the flesh of man, thereby teaching that what you have been pleased to institute from one principle, might never lawfully be separated;

O God, you have hallowed marriage by a mystery so excellent that in the marriage bond you prefigured the union of Christ with the Church;

O God, by whom woman is joined to man, and that union which you ordered from the beginning is endowed with a blessing which was not taken away, either by the punishment for original sin or by the sentence of the flood;

Look in your mercy on this your handmaid who is to be joined in wedlock and implores protection and strength from you. May the yoke of love and of peace be upon her. Faithful and chaste may she wed in Christ; and may she ever follow the pattern of holy women; may she be dear to her husband like Rachel, wise like Rebecca, long-lived and faithful like Sara. May the author of deceit work none of his evil deeds within her, may she ever be firm in faith and in keeping the commandments. May she be true to one husband, and fly from unlawful companionship. May she fortify her weakness by firm discipline. May she be graceful in demeanour and honoured for her modesty. May she be well taught in heavenly lore. May she be fruitful in offspring. May her life be good and sinless. May she attain in the end to the peace of the blessed and the kingdom of heaven. May *they both* see *their* children's children to the third and fourth generation, and reach that old age which *they* desire. Through . . ..

Text: *The Saint Andrew Daily Missal* (Bruges 1962), pp. 1806–7; NB plural ending; discussed above, pp. 40ff.

3. *The Byzantine Rite* (Barberini 336, eighth century)

Holy God, who made mankind out of chaos and from his rib provided woman, and yoked her as a help to him, because it pleased your great goodness that he should not be the only man on the earth; even now, Lord, stretch forth your hand from your holy dwelling-place, and fit together this your servant and this hand-maid, that the woman may be fitted by you to the man. Yoke them together in unity of mind; crown them in love; unite them to be one flesh; graciously bestow on them the fruit of the womb, the enjoyment of children; for yours . . ..

Text: J. Goar, *Euchologion* (Venice 1730), p. 317 (and other sources); discussed above, pp. 98f.

4. *The Pontifical of Roda* (eleventh century, Catalonia)

May the Lord bless you, who granted Eve to first-man Adam as a help like himself, lest he should live alone on the earth, and ordered them to multiply, to bless, to grow, and increase. Amen.

And may he who has deigned to join these young people in their youthful age, send on them the tear and the love of his holy name, and bring to life in them sons and daughters born from them, so that they may grow in offspring, and see their children's children to the third and fourth generation. Amen.

That rejoicing together they may be able to pass through this present age, so that they may be worthy of enjoying the heavenly kingdom with the choirs of angels. Amen.

Text: Josep Roma Barriga Planas, *El Sacramentari. Ritual i Pontifical de Roda* (Barcelona 1975), p. 338; discussed above, p. 55.

5. Martin Luther—Traubüchlein (1529)

O God, who hast created man and woman and hast ordained them for the married estate, hast blessed them also with fruits of the womb, and hast typified therein the sacramental union of thy dear Son, the Lord Jesus Christ, and the Church, his bride: We beseech thy groundless goodness and mercy that thou wouldst not permit this thy creation, ordinance, and blessing to be disturbed or destroyed, but graciously preserve the same; through Jesus Christ our Lord. Amen.

Text: Ulrich Leupold (ed.), *Luther's Works, 53, Liturgy and Hymns* (Philadelphia 1965), p. 115; discussed above, p. 127.

6. The Book of Common Prayer (1549)

O God whiche by thy mightie power haste made all things of naught, which also after other thinges set in order diddeste appoint that out of man (created after thine owne image and similitude) woman shoulde take her beginning: and knitting them together, diddest teache, that it should neuer be lawful to put a sonder those, whome thou by matrimonie haddest made one:

O God, which hast consecrated the state of matrimonie to such an excellent misterie, that in it is signified and represented the spiritual marriage and vnitie betwixte Christ and his church: Loke mercifully vpon these thy seruauntes, that both this manne maye loue his wyfe, according to thy woorde (as Christ did loue his spouse the churche, who gaue himselfe for it, louing and cherishinge it euen as his owne fleshe:) And also that this woman may be louing and amiable to her housebande as Rachael, wyse as Rebecca, faithful and obedient as Sara: And in al quietnes, sobrietie, and peace, bee a folower of holy and godlye matrones.

O lorde blesse them bothe, and graunt them to inherite thy euerlastinge kingdome, throughe Iesus Christ our Lorde. Amen.

Text; F. E. Brightman, *The English Rite* (London 1915), II, p. 812; discussed above, p. 138.

7. The Liturgy and Other Divine Offices of the Church (Catholic Apostolic 1847)

O Lord our God, who didst make man out of the dust of the ground in Thine own image, and out of his side didst form woman, that she should be an helpmeet unto him, and man might not be alone upon this earth: Send down Thy blessing upon these Thy servants, whom we have joined together in holy matrimony. Grant unto them purity of heart and integrity of will; that, according to Thy holy mind, marriage may be honourable in them and the bed undefiled. Unite their hearts to fear and love thee; and may they abide in mutual love one toward the other, and in Thy peace, so long as they both shall live upon the earth. Do Thou crown their life with Thy goodness, and vouchsafe unto them the abundance of such things as they shall need: through . . ..

Text: *The Liturgy and Other Divine Offices of the Church* (London 1912), p. 419; discussed above, p. 149.

8. Ordo Celebrandi Matrimonium (Rome 1969; original draft by Louis Ligier)

Holy Father, you created mankind in your own image, and made man and woman to be joined as husband and wife, in union of body and heart, and so fulfil their mission in this world. Father, to reveal the plan of your love, you made the union of husband and wife an image of the covenant between you and your people. In the fulfilment of this sacrament, the marriage of Christian man and woman is a sign of the marriage between Christ and the Church. Father, stretch out your hand, and bless N and N. Lord, grant that as they begin to live this sacrament they may share with each other the gifts of your love and become one in heart and mind as witnesses to your presence in their marriage.

Help them to create together (and give them children to be formed by the gospel and to have a place in your family).

Give your blessings to N your daughter, so that she may be a good wife (and mother), caring for the home, faithful in love for her husband, generous and kind. Give your blessings to N your son, so that he may be a faithful husband (and a good father).

Father, grant that as they come together to your table on earth, so they may one day have the joy of sharing your feast in heaven. We ask this through Christ our Lord.

Text: *The Rite of Marriage* (Dublin 1970), pp. 36f.; discussed above, p. 187.

9. The Methodist Service Book (1975: written by David Tripp)

Praise God, King of the Universe, who has created all things, and man in his own image. Praise God, who has created courtship and marriage, joy and gladness, feasting and laughter, pleasure and delight, love, brotherhood, peace and fellowship.

Praise God, who has sent Jesus Christ to save us from sin and redeem our love from selfishness, and has given us the Holy Spirit to make us one with each other and with him.

And so with all the company of heaven we join in the unending hymn of praise: Holy, Holy, Holy Lord . . ..

Text: *The Methodist Service Book* (London 1975), p. E 13; discussed above, p. 201.

10. The Alternative Service Book 1980 (drafted by Hugh and Elizabeth Montefiore)

We praise you, Father, that you have made all things, and hold all things in being. In the beginning you created the universe, and made mankind in your own likeness: because it was not good for them to be alone, you created them male and female; and in marriage you join man and woman as one flesh, teaching us that what you have united may never be divided.

We praise you that you have made this holy mystery a symbol of the marriage of Christ with his Church, and an image of your eternal covenant with your people. And we pray for your blessing on this man and this woman, who come before you as partners and heirs together of your promises. Grant that this man may love his wife as Christ loves his bride the Church, giving himself for it and cherishing it as his own flesh; and grant that this woman may love her husband and follow the example of those holy women whose praises are sung in the Scriptures. Strengthen them with your grace that they may be witnesses of Christ to others; let them live to see their children's children, and bring them at last to fullness of life with your saints in the kingdom of heaven; through Jesus Christ our Lord.

Text: *The Alternative Service Book 1980*, p. 299; discussed above, p. 191.

Notes

1. Strong accent on creation and covenant; *after the meal.*
2. Extended collect, with hints of themes in 1, but exclusively bridal; *before communion.*
3. More related to 1 than 2; God 'joins' the couple; *before crowning.*
4. Hints of 3, and the curious epithet, *'protoplastus'*; Visigothic structure; *between 2 and communion.*
5. A new composition, didactic in style, biblical in tone; *after sacred reading.*
6. New, but based on 2; aggressively mutual; during *intercessory* part of rite, ideally before Communion starts.
7. New, but based on 2, 3, and 6; *in same position as 6.*
8. New, but similar structure to 1 and 3, still with slight accent on bride, as 2; the roles of the partners are still seen in a traditional way; *same position as 2.*
9. New, but based on 1; *at the end of the rite.*
10. New, but based on 6 and 1; *similar position to 6.*

2 The Sarum and Byzantine Rites: Structure and Main Sources

(a) *The medieval Sarum Rite*

	Sources	
At the door	Bury, 12th cent	
Address	Sarum, 14th?	Cr
Consent: 'Vis habere...'	From 11th: cf. Rouen, 13th	Cr
Vow: 'I take the'	Sarum, 14th? (Anglo-Sax. vern. orig.)	Cr
Blessing of ring:		
'creator et conservator'	Bury, 12th; Bayeux, 12th	Cr
'benedic domine'	Robert, 11th	Cr
Ring-giving: 'with this rynge'	Bury, 12th	Cr
Short blessing: 'benedicti sitis'	Ely, 12th	
Psalmic verses: 'manda deus'	Darley, 11th	
'Raguel' prayer: 'ds Abraham...ipse vos'	Vich, 11th; Robert, 11th	
Short blessing: 'benedicat vos deus'	Short version in Egbert, 8th	
Psalm 127—*proc. into church, altar*	Bury, 12th	Cr
Six short blessings:		
'benedicat vos dnus'	British Manuals only, 14th	
'ds Abraham . . . benedic'	Vich, 11th; Robert, 11th	Cr
'respice de coelis . . . et benedic'	Robert 11th	Cr
'respice, dne, propitius'	Lyre, 12th; Ely, 12th	
'omnipotens sempiterne'	Bury, Lyre, Ely, 12th	Cr
'benedicat vos ds omnipotens'	Lyre, 12th; Ely, 12th	
Mass of the Trinity:		
Trinity prayers	Bayeux, 12th (orig. Alcuin)	
Nuptial mass prayers	Gr. Sac., 6th	
Epistle: 1 Cor 6.15–20	Monte-Cassino, 7th	Cr
Gospel: Mt. 19.3–6	*Codex aureus, c.* 800	Cr
After Sanctus, prostrate, pall	*LO*, Vich, 11th	
Before Pax, nuptial blessing:	(trad. Roman?)	
'proptiare, dne'	Gr. Sac., 6th	Cr
'ds q potestate'	Gr. Sac., 6th (sing. ending)	Cr
After post-communion:		
bl of bread: 'benedic . . . panem'	Bury, 12th	
Blessing of bedchamber:		
'benedic dne thalamum'	Bury, Lyre, 12th (cf. Durham, 9th)	
'benedic dne hoc cubiculum'	Vich, 11th	
'benedicat deus corpora'	Irish, 12th	
'manus dni sit super'	Irish, 12th	
benedicat vos pater'	Durham, 9th	

'Cr' indicates material adapted by Cranmer.
Material in italics in the left-hand column is in the vernacular.
See pp. 79ff for full discussion of the rite, and antecedents.
See pp. 134ff for full discussion of Cranmer's use of traditional material.

(b) The Byzantine marriage service
(Barberini 336 and other supposed early elements in italics)

1. Betrothal

Short question on willingness to marry (*at door*)	Sinaiticus 973 (1153)
Candles (*procession to head of nave*)	Patmos 105 (13th century)
Opening blessing	14th century
Litany, with special biddings	Sinaiticus 957 (9th–10th c)
Prayer: 'Eternal God'	Barberini 336 (8th century)
Prayer: 'Lord our God'	Barberini 336 (8th century)
Ring-giving, with short formula	Sinaiticus 958 (10th century)
Prayer: 'Lord our God, who accompanied Abraham'—long blessing of betrothal	Sinaiticus 973 (1153)

2. Marriage (follows immediately)

Ps 127	Grottaferrata G b VII (10th c)
(questions and consent—Russian form only)	(17th century)
Opening blessing	14th century
Litany, with special biddings	Barberini 336 (8th century)
1st marriage prayer: 'Holy God, who made mankind'	Barberini 336 (8th century)
Another marriage prayer: 'Undefiled God'	Grottaferrata G b VII (10th c)
Another marriage prayer: 'Blessed are you, Lord'	Patmos 715 (15th century)
Crowning, and formula	Patmos 105 (13th c) + later
Prokeimenon and *Ephesians 5.20–33*	Basil of Caesarea?
Alleluia and *John 2.1–11*	Gregory of Nazianzus
Litany (short—no special biddings)	Grottaferrata G b VII (10th c)
2nd marriage prayer: 'Lord our God, who in the economy'	Barberini 336 (8th century)
Litany (short—no special biddings)	14th century onwards
3rd marriage prayer: blessing of common cup	Barberini 336 (8th century)
Troparion	Mt Athos 1468/Patmos 104 (13th c)
Walk in a circle	Mt Athos 1475
Taking off of crowns and prayer	15th/16th century: earlier?
Short blessing	Mt Athos (13th century)
Final blessing	Sinaiticus 962 (11th/12th c)

For early sources see pp. 21ff.
For discussion of texts see pp. 97ff.

Select Bibliography

a. Liturgical studies

BASILIUS BINDER, *Geschichte des feierlichen Ehesegens.* Abtei Metten 1938.

CABROL LECLERQ, *Dictionnaire d'Archéologie Chrétienne et Liturgie*, X, ii (Paris 1932), coll. 1843–1981.

P.-M. GY, 'Le nouveau rituel romain du mariage', *Maison-Dieu* 98 (1969), pp. 7–31. The other articles in this issue are also apposite. Gy's article has been popularized into English by Vincent Ryan, 'The Roman Rite of Marriage', *Liturgical Review* 3.2 (1973), pp. 1–8.

PIERRE JOUNEL, 'La liturgie romaine du mariage. Étapes de son élaboration', *Maison-Dieu* 50 (1957), pp. 30–57; a pre-Vatican II study, setting Trent in a wider perspective, in a thorough manner.

W. LÜDKTE, 'Ordines ad facienda sponsalia', *Festschrift R. Haupt* (Kiel 1922), pp. 95–128.

J. B. MOLIN and P. MUTEMBE, *Le rituel du mariage en France du XIIè au XVIè siècle.* Paris 1974.

A. RAES, *Le Mariage dans les Eglises d'Orient.* Chevetogne 1958.

K. RITZER, *Formen, Riten und religiöses Brauchtum der Eheschliessung in den christlichen Kirchen des ersten Jahrtausends*, Münster 1962: French translation (used here): *Le Mariage dans les Eglises chrétiennes du Ier au XIè siècle.* Paris 1962.

b. Texts: appendices in Binder, Molin/Mutembe, Raes, Ritzer (above), and the following:

W. G. HENDERSON (ed.), *The York Manual* (Durham 1875), for text of York and other Manuals, as well as Appendix V, 'Ordines ad faciendum sponsalia'.

ENZO LODI, *Enchiridion euchologium fontium liturgicum.* Rome 1979.

E. MARTÈNE, *De Antiquae Ecclesiae Ritibus* II (Antwerp 1763), Cap. IX, Art. V, Ordines I–XVI (pp. 127–44); but these need to be used in conjunction with A. G. Martimort's study, *La Documentation Liturgique de Dom Edmond Martène.* Vatican City 1978.

c. Other useful studies

I. H. DALMAIS, *Liturgies d'Orient* (2nd edn., Paris 1980), pp. 153–62; English translation of 1st edn: *The Eastern Liturgies* (London 1960), pp. 116–24.

J. G. DAVIES (ed.), *A Dictionary of Liturgy and Worship* (London 1972), articles under 'Matrimony'.

W. K. LOWTHER CLARKE (ed.), *Liturgy and Worship* (London 1932), pp. 458–71.

M. RIGHETTI, *Manuale di storia liturgia* IV (Milan 1959), pp. 455–72.

Index

Appendix

The appearance of a U.S. edition soon after the original British one affords the welcome opportunity to make the following additions and corrections:

1. Clement of Alexandria (p. 15) mentions the use of the ring with symbolism which seems to refer to fidelity and to sharing domestic matters (*Pédagógiae* 3. 11); this in part corroborates the evidence of Tertullian.

2. Luther's *Traubüchlein* (p. 128) did *not* come to Denmark with Bugenhagen, but had appeared in editions at Viborg and Malmö in 1530 which have since been lost. However, a Danish *Handbog* (dated 1535) has recently been identified in Århus; it contains a rite which seems to be mid-way between Luther's and that of Palladius. I am indebted to Jette Holm, of Århus University, for making available to me her researches into Danish Lutheran marriage-rites; see also S.H. Poulsen (ed.), *Danske Messebøger fra Reformationstiden* (København 1959), pp. 93–98.

3. Wesley's rite (p. 158) is *not* the first to abbreviate the BCP; he follows Theophilus Lindsey (= 'Dunkirk Book'—*q.v.* in Index) in omitting the psalm though not in the other omissions which Lindsey had proposed in 1774; see G.J. Cuming, *A History of Anglican Liturgy* (Macmillan, 1982), pp. 137, 139; see also Theophilus Lindsey, *The Book of Common Prayer Reformed according to the Plan of the late Dr. Samuel Clarke* (London 1774), pp. 72–78, esp. p. 77 (NB *second* edition of that year).

4. American Episcopal Methodists (p. 158) made further reductions to Wesley's form; the 'three reasons' disappear (as Lindsey); the *Kyries* and the *preces* (before and after the Lord's Prayer respectively) also disappear; as does the prayer for child-bearing; see *The Doctrines and Discipline of the Methodist Episcopal Church in America* (Philadelphia, 1792), pp. 240–243. I am indebted to Dr. Kenneth Rowe of the Drew University Library for this.

5. Orchard (p. 166) was *not* involved in the 1929 Free Church BCP; this was the work of J.M. Lloyd Thomas together with a group of associates.

6. The Odense Missal (p. 227 n.8), apart from using the singular ending in the nuptial blessing (unlike Notmark which has plural), contains a freak phrase in the 'Raguel' prayer referring to the 'kiss of love' (*osculo dilectionis*) which is repeated in another book identified with Odense by Knud Ottosen; I have not seen this elsewhere (*Missale Ottoniense*, fo. 32–38).

7. The early American Episcopal rite (p. 235, n. 28) is described in its evolution by Marion Hatchett, *The Making of the First American Book of Common Prayer* (Seabury, 1982), p. 49 (1785 proposals at Boston Convention); p. 56 (1785 Philadelphia Convention); p. 82 (1786 proposals for radical abbreviation—see p. 177, n. 28); and pp. 125f. (1790 text agreed at 1789 Convention). There appears to have been little adverse reaction to this truncated rite, as it was often shortened by local clergy.

There is much more to be gleaned from further medieval and post-medieval researches. In the former category, groups like the Scandinavian *Nordisk Kollokvium for Latinsk Liturgiforskning* encourage the study of texts and fragments. The writer remembers meeting the indefatigable Père J.-B. Molin in Paris, in August 1981 at the end of his work on this book; Molin had recently unearthed an *Ordo* 'quite different from anything else' and hoped to have it published; so the work continues.

K.S.